"*I have known Max since the late 80s. He was quite self-assured and he gained my deepest respect when I learned that he had survived concentration camps Auschwitz, Mauthausen, Melk and Ebensee. A little more than a year later he emigrated to the U.S.A. and established himself in San Francisco and became an architect. He helped us obtain one of the tunnels that he, and his fellow prisoners, had dug into the mountains, so that we could establish a museum within that tunnel and visitors could see, for themselves, what the prisoner had to endure.*

When I heard Max speak during the annual memorial lectures he, of all the other speakers, was more censorious than the others and pointed out that the Ebensee citizens stood on the sidelines while hundreds of his fellow prisoners died daily in the camp."

Dr. Wolfgang Quatember
Chief Curator
Memorial Museum, Ebensee, Austria

"*As a member of the Board of Directors of the Austrian Camp Community Mauthausen, it is my distinct pleasure to thank you for your interest and input you have shown to those who were born after world War II and thereby assisted the local people in towns where concentration camps had existed in getting a better understanding of what democracy is all about. In countless presentations in our schools, Gymnasia and Universities you, as an eyewitness, have reported about the National-Socialistic System you were forced to live under and the torture you had to endure and the murder of your parents and sister in the gas chambers of KZ's Auschwitz and Sobibor.*

You successfully organized constant pilgrimages from the U.S.A. to us in Austria and brought us the Veterans of the U.S. Army who had been the liberators of the many victims and who also helped to eliminate the former 'Ostmark' (Austria) and the German and the Austrian Nazis.

This book, with its many facets, is a testament about your courage and the successful life you have led since your arrival in San Francisco."

Helmut Edelmayr
Upper State Representative.
A very long time friend.

Tacoma, WA, Oct. 21st, 2011

To Lisa, may the sun continue to shine on your path through life. Good luck!

AUSCHWITZ, AUSCHWITZ...
I CANNOT FORGET YOU

As Long As I Remain Alive

(From a prisoner's song)

Social
Thinking

Think Social Publishing, Inc., San Jose, California

www.socialthinking.com

In loving memory of my parents, Elias and Rozetta Rodrigues Garcia, my sister, Sippora and my wife Pat

AUSCHWITZ, AUSCHWITZ...
I CANNOT FORGET YOU

As Long As I Remain Alive

(From a prisoner's song)

Max Rodrigues Garcia

as told to

Priscilla Alden Thwaits Garcia

Social
Thinking

Think Social Publishing, Inc., San Jose, California

ISBN 13: 978-0-9792922-7-9
ISBN 10: 0-9792922-7-1

Library of Congress Control Number:
2008910990

Published by
Think Social Publishing, Inc.
3550 Stevens Creek Blvd., Suite 200
San Jose, CA 95117
Tel: (408) 557-8595 ext. 303
Fax: (408) 557-8594
www.socialthinking.com

Cover design and layout by Elizabeth A. Blacker
rowantreegraphics@comcast.net

This book is printed and bound in California by Medius Printing.

To learn more about Max R. Garcia, please visit his website:
www.auschwitzmaxgarcia.com

Contents

Preface

This book, *Auschwitz, Auschwitz...I Cannot Forget You*, was originally published in 1979, under the title *As Long as I Remain Alive*, written by my late wife, Priscilla Thwaits Garcia. After that date she and I continued our research and travel, expanding our knowledge to such an extent that we realized we must make a second edition. Not long after we began our revisions and additions she was diagnosed with cancer, and our collaboration diminished as chemotherapy and radiation sapped her strength. Our family's concerns understandably centered on her health and comfort as she succumbed to this assault. But during those years she directed my revisions as long as she could, and I took over the project as a kind of therapy after her death in 2002, extending each of her original chapters, and adding two chapters of my own at the end.

It is my hope you'll find it interesting reading.

Max R. Garcia

Original Preface

Like the ancient Mariner, Max has often tried to buttonhole a friend and make him listen to some small part of the story of what happened to him, a Dutch Sephardic Jew, as a result of Nazi policy in World War II. Whenever he is asked, he talks to classroom students about his experiences in Nazi concentration camps. Many listeners are taken aback or are a little embarrassed. Few invite him to elaborate. The subject does not qualify as polite conversation. Most of us Americans have not concerned ourselves with the implications of the Holocaust. On several occasions, however, Max has met and talked with fellow concentration camp survivors, and their conversations have lasted for hours – grim, soul-searching exchanges. No one seems to question that the survivors should carry this burden.

In 1975, Max and I sat down to begin taping sessions of his

recollections. We wanted our children to have an honest account, when they were mature enough to read it, of what happened to Max's family, and to him. We wanted them to know how a man could become as cunning as his tormentors in order to survive his planned death at Nazi hands as well as years of persecution and degradation as a Jew. We wanted them to understand the confusion of a young man trying to apply his camp survival education in a peacetime world that could not use it. We wanted them to know about terror so great that their father chose to hide from his Jewish heritage for many years. We wanted them to understand how their father gradually came to realize his individual work in American society, how he came to renew his commitment to Judaism, and what he then went through to carry out his lifetime dream of becoming a practicing architect. Yet we wanted to convey that coming to terms with the Holocaust has been, and will continue to be a lifetime effort.

The emerging manuscript appeared to have much to say to many people, not just our family. Though Max took no notes as a young man, he proved to have an excellent memory of events and experiences that educated him. After the dictating, we did hours of backup research. We read many sources and learned a great deal more than Max had known as a participant in one significant phase of modern Western history. However, this account relates only Max's personal recollections. Except as Max and his family saw and were affected by events, we have not attempted to interpret the history of the German occupation of Holland, or of the concentration camp system, or of the American occupation following Germany's defeat.

Much has been said about the Holocaust, and yet enough will never be said. Perhaps Max's account will motivate readers to seek out other accounts or scholarly studies. Max mentions in the last chapter that there are other human conflagrations that have devastated people and to this day are gobbling up thousands of lives in various countries in the world. Few free people are interested. But we must recognize these events as a terrible part of our human history.

Priscilla Alden Garcia
San Francisco, California 1979

Acknowledgments

We want to thank Max Knight, recently retired principal editor of the University of California press, for his patient guidance and advice throughout various stages of the manuscript. He was our mentor in story development and knowledgeable editor of our European historical material.

Max and Priscilla Garcia

It is unusual for a person credited in an acknowledgment to respond. Yet there seems to be no other place in this book to draw attention to the extraordinary devotion and empathy of a wife who spent years in patiently encouraging her husband to record this story.

Max Knight 1979

Our mom, Priscilla Alden Thwaits Garcia or "Pat" as she was known, was the inspiration and guiding light for our dad, Max, as he continued to recover from his experience with the Holocaust throughout their married life. Sadly, mom passed away in June of 2002.

The plan to update mom's original writings was agreed to by her before her death. While our dad has many talents, writing does not come easily to him. Thanks to the persistent dedication of mom's sister and brother-in-law, Dr.'s Helen and Robert Buttel, retired English professors, the updated writings in this latest edition have been edited lovingly by them. While this project was at times stressful, we know mom would have been very pleased with how painstakingly Helen and Bob maintained the original integrity of her book given the additions of our father's writings. We, the children of Max and Pat; David, Tania and Michelle want Helen and Bob to know how much we appreciated their time, patience and persistence in helping with the telling of this compelling history.

David Garcia, Tania Garcia Fowler and Michelle Garcia Winner

Part 1

1945

Max R. Garcia, wearing a Dutch Flag patch, as aide to First Battalion, 319th Infantry Regiment of the 80th Infantry Division, U.S. Army, 1945.

3 65. The 3rd Squadron moved into the zone at 0605 on this date [May 6, 1945] and immediately advanced south reporting no enemy resistance of any kind. Here again PW's surrendered in droves and occupied much of the area. At 100 A [sic] Troop forward elements entered the town of Ebensee and reported that a concentration camp was located in that town. Further investigation proved that the conditions in the camp were deplorable. As many as 300 were dying every day from starvation and unattended diseases. They lived in filth and stench [and] were at a stage where eating their own dead was the sane thing to do. The camp compared easily with Buchenwald or Ordhruf [Ohrdruf]. Immediate action was taken by the Group Commander, who examined the camp and requested food and medical attention for the indescribable scene. While food and medics were in route, the men of the 3rd Squadron did whatever possible to ease the situation. They took estimates of the sick and dying and decided what would be needed to treat them, feed that [sic] and evaluate them. The information they compiled and the preliminary work that they did was a great help toward the final rehabilitation of the prisoners."[1]

Crowding the fence and listening intently, we heard them on the road below. An unfamiliar rumbling that we had not heard before. We saw dust rising from the valley. The rumbling, squeaking sound of their climb up our road grew louder with their approach; then two enormous tanks lumbered into view around the bend of the road, followed by a curious, small, open vehicle. On our side of the fence, we prisoners surged toward the locked main gate as the tanks and auxiliary vehicles slowly pulled to a halt just outside.

---

1   *After Action Report, 3rd Cavalry Group, Mechanized, 9 August 1944 to May 1945.* P. 90. Max Garcia's later research established that the time was 1000, not 100, and it was B troop rather than A, as quoted above.

Soldiers in unfamiliar uniforms peered in frank amazement from the tops of their tanks at a mass of shrunken, ghastly scarecrows in filthy, striped rags, a reeking mass with head shaved except for a center stripe. The soldiers stared at us and we stared at them.

Two old *Volkswehr* stood trembling and silent but still at their posts outside the gate. Too old to serve in the German Army, these men did service as home guardsmen in their village of *Ebensee*. Suddenly a soldier leaned down from the nearest tank, yanked the rifle out of the hands of the *Volkswehr* at the right side of the gate, broke it over the gun turret, and hung it over the gate to our camp. That thrilling crack still resounds in my memory.

The day, I was to learn later, was the 6th of May 1945, a Sunday. It was midday.

The silence of the first shock of our encounter now broken, the gates somehow were opened, and we drew back to allow the roaring tanks and their small escort to roll slowly into the barren *Appellplatz*. Prisoners swarmed around as the engines idled. The soldiers in and on the tanks seemed afraid. They looked as if they did not care to come down among us. They may have been fresh from the latest battles, but we appeared to be too much for them. These hungry eyes. These sunken faces and skeletal bodies. These stinking sub-humans. Us!

Some of us tried to climb onto the tanks but were politely rebuffed with hand gestures. Standing among the crowd of prisoners around the tanks, I watched a soldier in the first tank take out a pack of Lucky Strikes and light a cigarette. Now these were American cigarettes, I knew, for I had seen just such cigarettes in Holland and even advertised in English-language papers and magazines my father had brought me, insisting that I learn some English. So these were American Forces!

"It's been a long time since I had a Lucky Strike," I yelled up over the din to the soldier. He looked down in surprise, singling me out. "You speak English?" In my daring I answered,   "Yes." "Well, come on up here."

He reached down to give me a hand up onto the tank. Once there, I was given that Lucky and the soldier lit it for me. I took a long pull, inhaling deeply. The sea of faces on the Appellplatz reeled. I had become accustomed to smoking brown wrapping paper but my first drag of that American cigarette made the world spin all around me and made me dizzy. I braced myself, then switched my smoking method to an occasional cautious puff. Meanwhile the soldier was pelting me with questions. Trying to signal him to slow down, I struggled to understand and to answer with single words or gestures. What was my name? Where was I from? What was I doing here? How many prisoners were in this camp? What were they doing here? Where did they come from? I had very few knowledgeable answers, but we worked hard at exchanging information with my few words of English and many hand signs. The American spoke no other languages. For my part, I asked if the war was over, and, more or less what was going on. The Nazis, I learned, had not yet officially surrendered but surrender was expected at any moment. A report of Hitler's death had been confirmed.

The soldier radioed to his headquarters that our camp had been opened and that a prisoner who spoke a little English had been found. My soldier friend, I noted, was a sergeant, and apparently in command of the small tank force liberating the camp. I set about trying to persuade him to come down and take a look around. He was hesitant but he and the sergeant of the second tank, as his companion, were eventually coaxed down from the tank to take a walking tour of the camp with me as their guide. I talked in my English and they in theirs, and as we walked we were accompanied by a mass of prisoners. The prisoners applauded and crowded around to touch and pat the soldiers; a sacred moment for them, probably a frightening one for the soldiers. Even I was slapped on the back by my fellow prisoners. A moment of high honor for me.

I took them first to tour the kitchen where the cooks offered the soldiers some soup as a hospitable gesture. Looking into the proffered bowls, they tried to refuse. Oh, you cannot refuse their offering. They will be insulted, I managed to convey with frantic words and gestures. And so they each accepted a bowl, tasted a spoonful, complimented the cooks and offered me their portions. I made short work of those two windfall bowls of watery mush, knowing the cooks could do nothing about my supreme feat of *Organisierung*, which was what we prisoners called the art of scrounging whatever we could for personal survival. The cooks and I showed them the extent of our small food stores, aging soup staples, coarse bread, and such.

We toured the barracks, the streets of the camp, the hospital jammed with the seriously ill, the crematorium which had stood cold since the flight of the *Schutzstaffel (SS)* a couple of days earlier. The Americans looked at the sea of emaciated prisoners, noted the appalling conditions under which they were clinging to existence, and from time to time as they walked, they had to step gingerly among torn-up parts of bodies lying around the campgrounds. These combat veterans returned to their tanks looking almost sick from what they had seen.

While we were gone, the radio had reported back to tell the sergeant that transportation was on the way to take the English-speaking one to headquarters in the town below. A little while later a small, open vehicle arrived – like the one that followed the tanks into the camp – and I was driven out of the gates and down the road. A "jeep," the driver instructed me when I asked, and I squirreled away my new word. On the lower road, as houses came into view, I noticed white flags, sheets really, hanging from many windows. There was not a swastika in sight as we entered the town.

We pulled up at an inn that had been commandeered earlier in the day as company headquarters for "F" Company, 3rd Cavalry Reconnaissance Squadron (Mechanized). It was late afternoon. I was invited to sit in the outdoor *Biergarten* of the inn, and from there I watched a house across the street being forcibly vacated by the Americans. Three people were leaving with their small parcels of belongings. Later I heard that the house had belonged to an Austrian doctor, an avowed Nazi, and his family.

No one else came out of the houses of the village and nobody seemed even to peer from their windows. I turned my attention to two enormous tanks unattended on the street outside the inn. Sherman tanks, I would soon be instructed, the same as the ones that liberated us. I stared in awe at the size of these machines; and as I did so, another jeep arrived with four more former prisoners. The five of us were escorted to the house across the street that the Americans had just "liberated." We were assigned the second floor as our quarters.

Addressing me in English, a soldier directed me to tell my new roommates that we were to clean ourselves up in the bathroom and help ourselves to any suitable clothes we could find in the closets. Several soldiers staggered in under the weight of five huge cartons, which, I was told, were food rations for each of us to eat as we saw fit. We could hardly believe the size of the cartons, and no sooner had the door closed behind us than each of us tackled his carton with frenetic intensity. We were baffled because we could not open them; tight metal straps held them fast. We searched the house for a hammer, a screwdriver, or cutters, and finally did manage to find some tools. Taking turns, helping each other, expending a great deal of sweat and effort--for we were very weak--we pried the boxes open and rifled in amazement through the contents. Each carton contained 10 army regulation meals for field use, plus candy bars, cigarettes, soap, and so on. We sat on the floor and started opening cans. We ate a bite of this, a bite of that, then opened more cans, anxious to taste each new offering. We ate candy, lit cigarettes, and fondled the smooth soap, almost eating that as well. The floor was strewn with our food. Yet each of us was so protective of his own rations that we lunged at one another threateningly as one tried to taste from another's allotment, even though we all had the same rations. But as we filled up, we began to bargain and trade with one another over food preferences.

At long last we were sated and could turn our attention to the pleasures of a hot bath, though once again, not without haggling. We haggled over turns, over time in the bathtub, over supply of hot water.

"You've used enough hot water."

"I've hardly had time to soak compared with you. Let me bathe."

"I'm next after he's finished. Wait your turn!"

My turn came. I took up my wonderful soap and filled the

bathtub with hot water. I scrubbed, soaked, and scrubbed again, but soon discovered, as each of us did, that there was no scrubbing off in one bathing session the ingrained dirt of years in the camps. My bath water turned black, and when I crawled out to try the luxury of drying myself with a bath towel, I found I was still dirty. The evidence came off on the towel. I was to find that it would take me about two weeks of daily bathing to rid myself of the grime that had penetrated the pores of my skin.

For the first time in years I looked at myself in a full-length mirror. Long accustomed to the emaciated appearance of my fellow prisoners, I was still surprised to see myself skin over bones, a walking anatomy lesson. My cheeks were fallen in. My eyes had receded into my head. My skull was crudely shaven except for that stripe. I probably weighed 85 pounds, an adult male, five-feet-and-a-half-tall, almost 21-years-old.

We rummaged through the closets and tried on clothing. Everything hung like sacks from our bodies. We looked comical but had not quite relearned the knack of laughing at ourselves. We made do, tied or belted ourselves in the middle, and flapped about like dressed-up birds.

Our stomachs full, our bodies partially cleaner and dressed in fresh clothing, we turned to one another for the first time as interested human beings. Who were we? One was a former high-ranking official of a Hungarian government. Another was of some former prominence no longer recalled. Two were mere boys, Jewish, the younger one no more than 10 or 11 years in age. I was a Sephardic Jew, a former diamond polisher from Amsterdam, Holland, who could speak a little English.

Everything had happened so fast since the tanks rode into camp that I had had little time to reflect about what we had just been through. I was free, that I knew. I no longer had to go into those damn tunnels and, presumably, our meals would improve as well. Would I be going back to camp after the officers had interviewed me?

Many thoughts went through my mind but they meant nothing to me on that first day of no longer being a prisoner. I knew; however, that I had to adjust to the food that had been so generously given us all and to the luxury of the baths each of us had just taken.

We did not have much small talk to exchange. We were very tired. We have overeaten. We headed for the beds and couches. I was tense. As of this very day I am no longer in camp and am slowly becoming aware of it. No more regimentation. What am I supposed to do? What about tomorrow? How will I get by? Freedom is a worrisome state. I lie in a comfortable bed with a pillow and blankets, no longer scratching and pinching lice. I mull things over uneasily. Sleep finally comes.

In the morning we returned to our food packages, our new toys, and then to the bathtub for another good scrub. By mid-morning a couple of soldiers walked up our stairs.

"Which one of you speaks English?" one asked.

"I do."

"You're needed over at headquarters. Can you come with us now?"

I followed them back across the street to the inn. There the Americans needed help in interrogating a German, and I found myself concentrating on the effort of translating from German into English. In spite of my limited ability, I made some sense with the translations, apparently because I was asked to wait in order to be introduced to the officers. Once more I sat in the *Biergarten*; and while I waited, a number of soldiers gathered around to stare at me.

I stared at them too. Big boys they were, and very young looking conquerors. Eventually, we looked away from one another, and I turned my attention to my surroundings. The *Biergarten* was a pleasant place, as romantic as a scene in an Austrian operetta. Soldiers sat at wooden tables in a flower-filled patio garden. Vine-covered trellises surrounded us. I was aware that I sat among my liberators as a free man in the village of *Ebensee*, that only yesterday I was locked in the concentration camp in the hills above. I looked down the short main street of the village to a clear, blue, long lake, the end of which disappeared from sight among sharply rising green mountains.

In my mind's eye I saw again the forced march of hundreds of us ragged prisoners many weeks before as we struggled along the lakeside road and through the main street of this village, over the bridge that crosses the river, and up that final hellish mountain road to the camp above, where we were thrown among thousands more gaunt prisoners who looked worse than we did. To shouted orders we assembled for the inevitable count on the camp's Roll Call Square. Oh, we were so tired, and very, very thirsty, beyond hunger almost. We thought we were at the end of our endurance. Yet, inwardly we were triumphant. For months all of us had known that the end of the war was near, that we were being force-marched to interior work sites where our labor was desperately needed for Germany's failing war machine. We had pulled and dragged our weaker comrades along, determined that they not meet Nazi bullets with the end so near. Yet, quite a few were shot while on the forced march. For all of us who had been shoved out of the barges at *Linz*, and had walked some 75 kilometers to *Ebensee*, this was our great triumph over the Nazis, that so many of us had survived this death march (though bitterly enough, many were to die during the harsh last weeks of our imprisonment in *Ebensee*).

Until this moment I had not known that *Ebensee* was a pretty Austrian village, that the lake was refreshing to look upon, that the mountains were beautiful.

Anxiety filled me as a soldier stepped out to call me inside the inn. I was introduced to the officers in charge, a captain who was the company commander, and his lieutenants. They too were young, some perhaps younger than I. They explained to me that Germany had formally surrendered early that morning, that they were now assigned to remain in *Ebensee* and administer the camp and help govern the area. They had been disturbed to discover that the territory they had captured, and now controlled, included the concentration camp they had opened the day before, freeing about 18,000 prisoners, for whom their small tank unit had no food or medical supplies. They asked me to serve with them as their interpreter in exchange for their care, since none of them spoke German. They needed information about the nature of the problems and of the prison population. They needed a go-between to communicate with prisoners.

This small contingent of the American military did indeed have a problem on their hands because most liberated prisoners were too weak or sick to walk away from the prison, and needed a great deal of help. Then there was the reality that most of them, like myself, were Jews who had no place to go if they did walk away. In the countries Germany overran, Jewish families had been systematically consigned to death camps, if not murdered on the spot, and their properties confiscated. On a smaller scale, other "inferior" peoples and individual enemies of the state had been thrown into these camps as well, to be exterminated or to work until they rotted. We homeless survivors of the camps were called "displaced persons," "D.P.s," and at war's end all was confusion about what to do with us.

I jumped at the chance to stay on with my liberators as their interpreter. I was free all right, but freer than I had ever wanted to be, like a rudderless boat. Amsterdam had been my home, but how could it be home now? My sister and parents had been taken ahead of me, as were most of my relatives, friends, and neighbors. I was well aware that most of the Jews rounded up and sent to the camps had died there. Who would be left to hold out their arms to me in my old neighborhood? My dread was too great to want to find out.

I would be pleased to stay and serve as their interpreter, I told the American tank commander; but I had been so embarrassed by the many curious stares in my direction that in the next breath I asked him if the Americans could provide me with clothes that fit.

A call went out at once to some of the smaller soldiers in the outfit for any pants, shirts, underwear, socks, and shoes they could spare for my use. Within an hour I found myself transformed into a GI, which my clothing suppliers taught me was their term for themselves as common American servicemen. General Issue! A starving prisoner on Sunday, a regular GI on Monday, except for that damned stripe down my head, which a mirror appraisal of my new self seemed to emphasize. I walked across the street to the barbershop below the house in which I was billeted.

"Trim my hair down evenly." I ordered in German. Seeing my head, the barber knew very well I was a former prisoner, though dressed as a GI, but he said nothing and I paid him nothing when he finished with his work.

With my help the officers interviewed my billet companions about what they had been through and where their homes were. Concerned about our starved bodies, they made arrangements for us to start taking three meals a day with the troops. We ate sumptuously, as if each meal were to be our last, and almost immediately the sudden switch to a rich and plentiful diet had a disastrous effect upon the five of us. We developed severe and chronic diarrhea. The officers then gave us permission to obtain food from the kitchen any time we felt hungry, but the diarrhea persisted. It took weeks for my intestines to be able to adjust to the new diet and for my body to function normally again.

Meanwhile, except to sleep, my home became the headquarters inn and particularly the pleasant *Biergarten* where I sat at my interviewing duties much of the day. Daily my English started to get better as I became better acquainted with my American liberators. I accumulated new words like a sponge. I understood more. I expressed myself in more detail. In a few weeks I began to think in English as well as in German, and I took satisfaction in becoming more valuable in my work with each passing day.

The officers and men wanted to know all I could tell them about the camp in the hills above. They needed the information officially in order to obtain policy directives from higher up and to expedite the services of the United Nations Relief and Rehabilitation Administration (UNRRA), which had already been established to aid liberated populations in war-devastated areas. They were also personally curious about the unspeakable secrets of the Nazi regime that prisoners like ourselves were able to reveal: brutal torture, starvation, slave labor under unimaginable conditions. That was the good news – some of us were still alive! Death for millions of men, women, and children for racist and political reasons. That was the bad news. Some of the soldiers told of things they witnessed or stories they had heard about appalling discoveries coming to light every day. We were numb with shock and could hardly comprehend the reality of the news we were exchanging with one another.

I told the soldiers about the forced death-march of hundreds of us from *Linz* to *Ebensee*, that I had come there after stops in concentration camps *Melk* and *Mauthausen*, that I had been in one of the last transports out of concentration camp *Auschwitz* as the Russians closed in. That also had been a death-march in the heart of winter. I told the Americans about our daily lives as prisoners in the *Ebensee* camp.

Concentration Camp Ebensee was laid out on a wide plateau in the mountains, whether natural or cut by man I did not know. One fence-surrounded ledge overlooked the valley and from there we could see the river and the road below that led to *Ebensee* village to the right and the town of *Bad Ischl* to the left. The concentration camp was entirely surrounded by a high voltage electrically wired fence, which began and ended at a high arched gate at the main entrance.

Streets of wooden prison barracks stood to one side of Roll Call Square, referred to in German as the *Appellplatz*, and the prison fence defined the limits of the square on the other side. An outside road ran alongside the fence, on the other side of which stood the barracks of our *SS* and *Luftwaffe* guards. Each of the prison barracks held about a thousand prisoners, who slept in narrow rows of bunks stacked one on top of another four tiers high. Within the fence and behind our barracks was the hospital and crematorium, both of which were always busy. The camp kitchen was also within the prison compound, recessed in an area beside the main gate and to the left of it.

Every morning we were awakened around 4:00 or 4:30 AM, and lined up to receive a cup of hot liquid which tasted strange, but which was called tea. At least the brew was hot for it was the extent of our breakfast. We turned out on the *Appellplatz* for the morning Roll Call, then were sent out the gates on our daily march down the road passing the *SS* and *Luftwaffe* barracks on our way to the work site. Our march was actually the slow shuffling of spent men, and we stumbled in our wooden clogs over cobblestones and rough places. When we reached the valley we turned up another mountain road, climbing laboriously upward until we reached an opening, which was part of a tunnel complex. It held a factory of some sort all of which was dug into the side of the mountain. This underground factory was a beehive of busy German workers and technicians.

What they were producing there, we prisoners were not invited to understand nor were we in good enough physical shape to take much interest. We fetched and carried, stooped and lifted, hauled and pushed, did anything we were told as well as we were able. I did not care what was going on there. I concentrated on being able to make it down the mountain road and then up the torturous hill again to camp at the end of the day, where I could receive my hunk of bread and lie down. Down that hill, up that hill, day after day, we stumbled, and always the *SS* and the *Kapos* controlled us with their truncheons, shouting, *"Los! Los! Mach schnell! Mach schnell!"* Their rubber truncheons hit our backs regularly, but could not hasten us. With time we could no longer feel them, nor could we any longer hear the shouts of our tormentors.

The road grew steeper as we grew weaker. My memory of what the days were like is hazy. Like the others, I was severely affected by malnutrition. Without food the memory fades and awareness very much lessens. The will is reduced. In addition to the cup of "morning tea," we received a bowl of thin soup at midday on the work site, then in the evening a hunk of bread with a piece of margarine. In the factory we sometimes begged food from the Austrians we worked under; mostly we were ignored. At night sleep on a hard and lumpy bunk was our only luxury. We lately-arrived *Ebensee* prisoners slept two to a bunk, and some unfortunates, who arrived even later, slept three to a bunk. To recall our sleep time as a luxury is to recall the depth of our misery.

I wanted the Americans to know about the exaltation in the camp when they liberated us. I wanted them to understand what it meant to me who had come through so much for so long. I told them of how the camp had been swept by rumors that the *SS* were going to machine-gun us because the war was near an end, and how we whispered at night about how we might be able to resist. Those of us who were able and still had a will to survive began to gather up club-like objects and to sharpen tools secretly with which we could either attack or defend ourselves. We did not know how many hours, or days, or weeks stretched before us until liberation, but survival became all-important.

The Saturday before our liberation all prisoners who were still able to get up and walk were ordered to the *Appellplatz*, as was common, but this time when we got to the *Appellplatz* the *SS* camp commander was waiting for us and with him was nearly his entire staff. In addition, the entire area from the main gate and the nearby area was secured by *SS* guards who stood there holding machine guns pointed in our direction.

This time we did not have to stand block by block as was the custom for Roll Call but we could stand around as we pleased. This was very unusual. The *SS* camp commander addressed us in German and told us that the American troops were coming towards *Ebensee* and that he and his staff had decided to fight them and in order for us not to be in the ensuing crossfire he wanted us to go into one of the designated tunnels so we would not be harmed.

No sooner had he finished talking when all those who understood German started to shout "No." A table was brought forward and placed in front of the *SS* camp commander and his staff and a senior prisoner from one of the Slavic countries, who had performed interpreting duties for the *SS* Administration, now climbed onto the table and began to translate the speech we had just listened to. Each time when he finished his translation in one of the Slavic languages the answer came back in even louder "No's" until the entire assembled prisoner complement were shouting their "No's" in their own languages. The *SS* camp commander appeared to be dumbfounded and could not believe his ears. One could also see the same befuddlement and wariness in the members of his staff and soon thereafter all the *SS* who had been inside the fenced area left. That day we did not go to work.

The following morning we awoke to realize that, by God, no bells had sounded to arouse us. The feeble lights were not on. The usual cries of *"Aufstehen! Aufstehen!" "Los! Los!" "Heraus! Heraus!"* were not heard. No one called us out for the morning count, or lined us up to go to work. There was no hot tea. An oppressive silence hung over the camp. Our routine was upset. Fear crept into our barracks. What was next for us?

Slowly, noise arose in the camp. The sound grew. There was excitement outside. We rushed out to join people running around the streets between the barracks, shouting the unbelievable news:

"They've gone! They've gone! The *SS* have left. They've sneaked off in the night, the cowards!"

"We have the camp to ourselves except for a couple of old *Volkswehr* at the gate!"

We were slow to believe it. We thought it could not be true. We rushed to the fence, the fence that overlooked the road and the Nazi barracks. And right! They were gone. No smoke came from the chimneys of their housing. Their wagons were gone. Some discovered that the electricity in the fence had been turned off, and we pushed against it, cheering. But the fence was strong and we were weak. Two old *Volkswehr* with rifles on their shoulders stood guard outside the gate, two old men to guard thousands of us. They bargained with us, asking us not to try to attack them because they were only obeying orders and acting as our caretakers until our liberators arrived. They also told us that their rifles held no bullets. For our part we were all too weak and apprehensive to think of doing anything other than agreeing with the old men that we would await liberation.

But we could have used some hot tea. No food was being prepared from whatever small stores had been left us. Camp organization had shut down. Still we rejoiced that we did not have to go down that damned hill anymore. We did not have to enter those tunnels anymore to labor within the mountain.

Almost immediately the *Blockältesten* and the *Kapos* issued orders to the kitchen for the serving of meals. Already severely underfed, we now were further rationed because the camp leaders realized they should stretch our stores as much as possible, not knowing when liberation would come. Many among us were so close to death that they did not care any more. The leaders passed orders that those who gave up caring for their own health would be punished by their fellow prisoners. The only work we had to do now was to clean our barracks and to take care of the sick. There was no saving those who were on their way out, but keeping life in those who could be saved became very important. Tensions built up, and yet at the same time there was mood of jubilation in the camp. We've done it! We're out of it! We cannot afford to die now! (And still, some persisted in dying.)

Yet we were underfed, starving. Nursed grievances flared and suddenly deadly revenge parties raged through the camp. Some of the prisoners were singled out for attack. These were men who had reputations as tough *Kapos*, unfeeling *Blockältesten*, informers. Weak prisoners managed to attack and kill those men; they literally tore their bodies apart. Now we accustomed ourselves to detouring around a head, a leg, a limbless torso – pieces of human flesh and bones lying around the grounds of our camp. Incredible vengeance had had its day. But for many of us who had lived with death in the camps, this scene was not surprising. How cool we were: "He had it coming, the son-of-a-bitch!"

There was a miraculous happening too, and unforgettable.

Flags began to appear on the fence overlooking the valley. One by one they began to appear along the fence until there were quite a few of them. Great flags, not miniatures. I had not been aware of my fellow prisoners making or stealing these flags, nor did I know from what they could have been made, who had made them or who could have hidden them. But they appeared: the French flag, the Polish flag, the Dutch flag, the Hungarian flag, the Belgian flag, and there were many others. I pictured how it must have looked from the valley road, a ribbon of festive flags on the shelf of our mountain. I was light-headed, delighted with the flags, already feeling free. I was fairly bursting with hope and good will. We did not have to work anymore or live in fear of anyone or even have to take our caps off to anyone. The old guards at the gate were dress-ups.

We waited. It may have been quite a while, a day and a half, perhaps, since the *SS* and *Luftwaffe* guards had disappeared during the night from Saturday to Sunday, when a shout arose in the early morning hours from the watchers at the fence: "There they are! There they are!"

Everyone rushed to look. Fighting for a place at the fence myself, I saw trucks moving eastward, toward *Ebensee* village. That was significant. If they were traveling from west to east, they were not retreating; they were coming in. The morning flew by in anticipation. Gradually, we heard a rumbling on the road we used to walk up and down on every morning and evening. It was a noise I had not heard before. Like damned up water suddenly rushing loose, the prisoners flowed towards the fence near the road to watch and listen to the sound growing louder.

I tried to describe to the Americans about the miracle of how it felt from inside our gate and to see the rifle of the *Volkswehr* being broken over the gun barrel of the first tank and then placed over the light fixture that hung over the main gate of our camp.

II

During the first days of liberation, the Americans got busy on their radio, transmitting and receiving messages about supplies that were desperately needed. For our small unit, of which I was now a part, these days brought enormous problems, most of them pertaining to my erstwhile fellow prisoners. I would wake unbelieving my good luck to be no longer among these sorry men, no longer hungry, not having to learn what it was like to be homeless and rootless. My liberating tank outfit had given me a home, food, companionship, and a job engaging my mind instead of physical labor. I had clean, warm clothing, a daily bath, and a real bed to sleep in under wool blankets. I did not look down the road or think about tomorrow. I clung to my rescuers.

The prisoners continued to live in the squalid camp above, waiting, trying to gather strength, and looking forward to the arrival of UNRRA relief. Left to their own devices, they cooperated to maintain the camp themselves. The American company commander made a trip up to the camp to assess the situation. Bodies were accumulating at a hazardous rate. Food rations gradually improved but nutrition was still far from adequate, and many prisoners continued to fail and die. Over 300 people were dying every day. Down in the village the Americans confronted the villagers, with me along as interpreter, about permitting such an inhuman camp to operate in their midst.

"Oh, we had no idea what was going on up there," they protested. "We were not consulted. We did not see it. How could we know?"

"That's a lot of shit," I blurted out angrily in German.

"Did we not march by the thousands through your village and up that road to the camp? How many of you showed sympathy or tried to help? Did we not work six days a week in those tunnels side by side with your fellow villagers? How many of you shared your food with us? Did you not see and smell the stench and smoke that floated down from the camp every day? What did you think was happening?"

General George S. Patton, Jr. had ordered that all *Ebensee* residents, young and old, adults and children were to march up to the camp, walk through it and help carry the bodies for burial. The villagers rebelled at this odious order, but in the end they had no choice. All of them marched reluctantly up to the concentration camp at the appointed hour, a sobering experience. As they brought down the emaciated, stinking bodies, people fainted, vomited, or cried hysterically.

The Ebenseers all felt that the Americans had imposed an unspeakable indignity upon them, but they did as told. The bodies were buried alongside the road leading to *Bad Ischl* by orders of General George S. Patton, Jr. so "that the people living in this area would always remember what had happened here."

As the prisoners grew stronger, they began to venture down the hill in increasing numbers. They promenaded up and down the short main street that extended from the nearby lakeshore to about two blocks beyond the inn. Many foraged through the village and surrounding countryside, scavenging for food, plundering whatever they could. They derided any local citizen who had the guts to come out of his house. The five of us privileged prisoners, while taking our lunch and dinner with the troops in the sunlit *Biergarten*, would experience the awkward shame of feeling the stare of our fellow prisoners on our plates as we ate. We tried not to look, but if there were men we knew, we took some food over for them to eat. Yet the company kitchen could not feed them all. The officers and GIs lavished care and attention on the few of us – we were symbolic of what they had fought for. The rest were too many and they had to wait for the establishment of the supply lines.

Acting as an interpreter between my fellow prisoners and the American authorities became my most important job. All grievances and petitions were transacted through me as I sat day after day in the *Biergarten*. Prisoners were brought in on complaints of local citizens for stealing, or for this infringement or that. The GIs were reluctant to discipline them except superficially because their sympathies lay with the prisoners. Nevertheless, some semblance of order was gradually established.

One day I was sitting in the *Biergarten* attending to my duties when a loud tumult was heard. A great crowd surged toward the *Biergarten*. The prisoners were dragging a man they had captured; he was the former *SS* camp commander of *KZ Melk*. The prisoners demanded immediate justice, preferably theirs. The officers posed questions in English, which I translated into German for the former *SS* camp commander, then back again into English. The prisoners stood outside the *Biergarten* heckling and shouting for the GIs to turn the *SS* camp commander over to them. The officers refused to do this because the captured man had to be considered a prisoner-of-war. They called Military Government for instructions and were told to escort the man to headquarters in a nearby town, but the whole street was filled with threatening prisoners, making the Americans extremely nervous. The officers decided to relieve the situation by allowing some "fun" with the *SS* camp commander. One of the GIs had an armband with a swastika on it. This he pulled up on the *SS* man's left arm and made him raise it while saluting Nazi-style, and shouting "Heil Hitler!" "Heil Hitler!" Everyone derided him loudly and mercilessly. He was made to march up and down the *Biergarten* in goose-step, still saluting and shouting "Heil Hitler!"

The GIs snapped pictures of him. Our carryings-on may have resembled a *Punch and Judy* show, but we felt a need to go through with this. Again, as their symbol, perhaps, I was invited by the GIs to take the *SS* camp commander into a back room and punch him at will. I knew damn well I was too weak, and even still afraid of him. I declined the honor. Eventually the officers ordered the captured Nazi driven off to military headquarters.

Not much more than a week passed before UNRRA personnel and supplies arrived, bringing to *KZ Ebensee* an extensive aid program. The Wednesday after the liberation a U.S. Field Hospital arrived by special orders from General Patton once he had been informed about the severe conditions in *KZ Ebensee*. This Field Hospital had been stationed in France and was instructed to fold its tents, pack up and drive day and night to get to *KZ Ebensee* as soon as possible.

For those who had waited, the time had seemed long, but the medical, feeding, and rehabilitation programs quickly transformed the concentration camp into a supervised hospital and way station. By then I had begun to gain some bodily strength. I was becoming more self-assured. With UNRRA personnel assisting the prisoners at the campsite, my interpreting duties became much lighter.

"Can you drive an automobile, Max?" a GI asked. I laughed. In Holland almost everyone rode bicycles.

"Of course, I can't drive." I've only ridden as a passenger in trucks and your jeeps once in a while."

"Well that won't do, Max. Everyone in this unit can drive every piece of equipment we've got. If you're going to stay with us, hell, you've at least got to know how to drive a jeep."

To my delight some of the GIs took me out on some mountainous Austrian roads and began to teach me to drive, a crash course in every respect. This is the steering wheel. This is the accelerator. This is the brake. This I how you clutch, shift gears, go forward or in reverse. My adventures in the jeep with my GI teachers were both hair-raising and hilarious, exhilarating and frightening. Finally, within a few days, I was allowed to take the thing out by myself. I could drive a jeep.

Next the GIs turned their attention to teaching me to shoot. Again, a necessity, they told me, if I was to stay with their combat outfit. In part, there was concern for our protection as roving bands of prisoners became bolder and a few of them menacing. Part, too, was the fun of fraternizing military style with an admiring liberated prisoner from the "old country". These American boys, most of them younger than me, enjoyed teaching me to shoot rifles, revolvers, forty-fives, and after all that, even burp guns. Heady stuff for a tough, young survivor who never held such weapons before.

One day word reached the camp that General Patton was due to come through on an inspection trip. The whole company bustled about, polishing, refurbishing, and reshaping themselves into correct military order. A grand villa, some distance away from the village, was chosen in which to install their distinguished leader. Along with the cooks, I was delegated to go out to the villa to interpret between the local help and the Americans.

At a huge victory dinner thrown in his honor, I was able to see General Patton. He was a tall man, a huge man in riding boots and breeches. He wore two conspicuous revolvers at his hips. Even without the military trappings and hardware he would have dominated the room with his high pitched voice and imposing personality. The Americans had long since briefed me on the progress of the war from the Allies' point of view, and on the bloody battles and eventual triumphs of the 3rd Army in particular. I was awed to be in the presence of General Patton. To me he was a real American hero.

However, General George S. Patton, Jr. never did inspect *KZ Ebensee.*

I had no desire or reason to return to the concentration camp on the hill until the UNRRA began to issue Identity Cards and I had to present myself in person to the UNRRA officials in order to obtain documented discharge papers. Without documentation I was in danger of being picked up for the growing D.P. camps because I had no official status with the American Army. I was allowed to drive the jeep up there myself, cocky and in American uniform, in the company of a couple of GI friends. At first the officials tried to dismiss me as a GI playing games. Abandoning my initial bravado I began to explain my circumstances in earnest. In the end, I received a small document confirming that the number on my left forearm, 139829, was that of a *KZ Auschwitz* prisoner, that I had also been held at *KZ Mauthausen*, *KZ Melk* and *KZ Ebensee*, and that I had been liberated from the latter on May 6th, 1945.

At some time during the course of service with the tank unit, I was asked by some people if I would be interested in joining a large contingent of ex-prisoners who were awaiting release to go to *Palestine* where they planned to help pioneer a new Jewish state. I told them no, thanks, that I had never been devout, that I did not wish to live in a nation composed only of Jews, that I had never lived that way before, except in camps.

My 20-year-old mind had already rejected a return to Holland to live. I could not yet deal with what had happened to my family and to me there after the occupation. I knew there was no one close to me to return to, and I saw no other reason to return. I had lived through years of degradation and dehumanization as a Jew, first in occupied Holland, then in the concentration camps. I wanted to turn from the stigma of it, start all over in a new country as an individual, not as a Jew. I was not yet ready to look to the future. I clung anxiously to the tank outfit that had adopted me, to their open friendliness and encouragement. I felt safe so long as I stayed among them.

One by one the former prisoners with whom I was housed disappeared as headquarters command took charge of their repatriation or resettlement. Not long after, I was assigned to housing with the GIs. I pulled routine duty with them and accompanied them on patrols. I was their devoted volunteer "recruit." So I was not prepared to be called to headquarters one morning and told, "Max, we're moving out. We've been ordered to *Trieste*, but, unfortunately, you're not going to be able to come along."

"Sir," said I, "this is my outfit. I can serve down there as well..."

"Max, we have been glad to have you with us, and you have served well, but we cannot take you along. We may see some action in *Trieste*, and after we get that ruckus wound up we're scheduled to go home. Why don't you go home too, Max? You've got to face going back to Holland sometime. Why not now?"

My world was coming apart, again, but there was no pleading my case. The ruckus referred to was an impasse between Marshall Tito of Yugoslavia and the Italians over the disposition of *Trieste*. The 3rd Cavalry Group, a Reconnaissance Regiment, had been ordered to *Trieste* to hold Tito in check. Even if the unit did see action, I was more frightened at the idea of being left behind, and made up my mind that I would not settle for it.

By the morning of departure I had persuaded some of the boys with whom I was close to allow me to climb into their tank and sit at the bottom. The tank convoy moved off and I was with them. We rode southward all day, pulling in for bivouac late in the afternoon. Everybody fell out to stretch and relax, including me. We were lined up for a head count, and there I was. My strategy had been to rely on their letting me stay once they saw my determination to get this far. But, alas, the first sergeant walked over to me:

"Max, what'n hell are you doing here? I've got strict orders. You can't come with us. You've got to go back, as we've told you before. I know how you feel, but it's out of our hands."

I burst into tears. I had truly looked upon this unit as my new home, my friends of whom I was a part. The boys with whom I had lived and pulled duty all stood around me and commiserated. They tried to argue with the sergeant, and when the officers saw a budding conspiracy they called me over and repeated what the sergeant had just told me. I was not a member of the U.S. Army and I could not accompany them. They advised me to return to *Ebensee*, report to the authorities, and then start back for *Amsterdam*. They assigned a lieutenant to drive me back to *Radstadt*, the nearest seat of Military Government. He was to explain to authorities there who I was, where I came from, and where I was to go. That evening he drove me to *Radstadt*. As ordered, he explained my circumstances to the authorities there. My papers were scrutinized, and I was assigned a bunk for the night. In the morning I was driven back to the highway and permitted to hitchhike toward *Ebensee*.

Two GIs in a jeep picked me up, assuming I was one of them. I did not deny it. When they heard my accent and also my faulty answers to their questions about the States, they became suspicious and wanted to see my dog tags. I had none to show them, of course, but I showed them my papers and tried to explain my story. The doubt in their minds had not been erased when we arrived at a roadblock on the north side of the river at the village of *Aich-Assach*. The GIs were waved on but I was detained because I was in American uniform, but without dog tags. My accent, uniform, and story made me highly suspect, it seemed.

I was ushered to a bench alongside the outside wall of the Command Post (CP) building to await questioning. An officer came out and listened to my story. He was patient. Another officer joined him in questioning me. They gave me a cigarette. As we talked, some Austrians approached the American officers and began to talk to them in German. Not understanding a word that was said, the officers called over a member of their Intelligence and Reconnaissance (I&R) unit. This soldier struggled to understand and interpret their words for them but much of what the Austrians were trying to say was lost. I could not resist putting my recent training to use and clarifying the dialogue all around. The group began to turn to me for interpretation, and within short order the Austrians' problem was understood and resolved. The Austrians left, and the Americans walked back inside the CP.

After some minutes one of the officers came back outside, thanked me for my interpreting work, and introduced himself. He was Lieutenant Colonel Arthur H. Clark, commander of the First Battalion, 319th Infantry Regiment, Headquarters Company, 80th Infantry Division. He directed me to accompany him inside and to explain once again to yet other officers my background and events that had brought me to the village of *Aich-Assach*. After I had answered all their questions I was asked to leave; then, after sitting outside a while longer, I was called back inside. Colonel Clark acknowledged that after checking out my papers and noticing my concentration camp number on my left forearm, they believed my story. It was mentioned that they were currently on the alert for some former *SS Corps* members who were rumored to be hiding in the mountains hereabout, which was their reason for checking me out so carefully. They had been impressed with the help I had just given them in interpreting, and asked me, in view of my separation from "F" Company, 3rd Cavalry, because of reassignment, if I would serve in a similar capacity with Headquarters Company of the First Battalion, 319th Infantry Regiment.

Would I serve? I was elated, but at the same time a cautious thought passed through my mind.

"Sir," I said, "I would very much like to serve as your interpreter, but there is one condition you will have to agree to before I accept."

"Ohhhh?" questioned the Colonel.

"If and when you get reassigned, you must take me with you."

"Mr. Garcia, we cannot take you back to the States with us. You must get that straight."

"I know that, sir. I am asking that while the 319th is in Europe that I stay assigned to it wherever you go."

Again the officers asked me to leave so they could discuss this condition. I was amazed at my boldness but I desperately wanted to stay. Here I was summoning the nerve to make a contract with another party. If they wanted something from me, I must have something in return. Had I not just learned one more time the bitter fact that I was expendable? I was worth no more than my services, so I had to gamble that the value of my services could be transformed into some security for me. I was soon relieved by the Colonel's affirmative answer. "Okay, Mr. Garcia, we're going to try it your way, that is if you behave and do the best you can for us. We can't guarantee that we'll be able to take you with us if we are reassigned, but if you keep your end of the bargain, we promise to try."

We shook hands. I was introduced to the officer who stood next to Colonel Clark, Captain Jesse R. Miles. He, in turn, introduced me to a sergeant in charge of the I&R unit to which I was to be assigned. Scheduled into the routines of my new platoon, I now wore the 80th Division patch on my left sleeve and the blue braid on my infantryman's cap. In addition to regular hours of rotating duty at the command post, I was sent for whenever the Americans and Austrians needed an interpreter.

I was housed with the I&R men in a nearby farmhouse, and took my meals with the troops. A little scrip money from the Soldiers Fund was given me to buy cigarettes and a few necessities at the Post Exchange (PX). The men exchanged news from their hometowns and their girlfriends, but mostly they talked about baseball and baseball players, a summertime subject that seemed to bring all Americans closer together. I learned the names of major league teams and their star players, and tried to talk about baseball too.

Awakening one morning with a headache and fever, I went on sick call. The doctor sent me for an examination to the nearest field hospital, which was in a town some distance away. I was examined, given rest and medication, and then discharged within a few days. The doctors had questioned me as they read my record, since I had no military documentation, but in the end they discharged me as routinely as any GI, with no strings attached. I hitchhiked rides by military ambulances back to *Aich-Assach*, by way of *Gmunden*, and was congratulated by Captain Miles upon my return. He had not expected to see his interpreter again as he had assumed I would be identified in the hospital as a D.P. and sent off to a D.P. Center for processing.

I went back to duty. Our village, *Aich-Assach*, was nestled in breathtaking Alpine country, but this was very high terrain for a lowlander. I developed headaches that intensified with my growing anxiety over rumors that the 319th was about to be reassigned. I asked Captain Miles directly who confirmed that the 319th was getting ready to move to *Bavaria*. Most troops would be going by train. A few would travel by truck with the supplies.

"Remember our deal, Captain, about bringing me along. Am I on your list to move?"

"Max, I'm too busy to think about that right now. Let's take it up later."

He never did. Moving day came. Most of the men were loaded onto trucks and sent to the train station. I was also packed up like everyone else, but without orders. This time I had a whole duffel bag full of personal belongings, and was sitting on it, hoping for orders, when Captain Miles drove up in a jeep.

"C'mon, Max, let's go."

I hopped in fast, throwing my duffel bag in the back seat.

"You're taking me with you, Captain?"

"That's our deal, isn't it, Max? When we can control it, you can come along with us. We're going to lead the convoy and Colonel Clark wanted you to ride with me in case we need your interpreting help along the way."

I sank into the rear seat, next to my duffel bag, relieved and grateful, for they had not let me down. As the point vehicle of a large convoy of trucks and staff cars, we drove north through *Salzburg*, then west into *Bavaria* and to our destination, *Bad Worishofen*. We were still in mountain country, but no longer as high as in *Aich-Assach*. The headaches let up.

Our convoy arrived on a tree-lined street of the prosperous-looking resort town of *Bad Worishofen*. The Americans knew that the place had served as a resort for Nazi officers during the war, and so it had been little altered through those years. The town presented itself, therefore, as an ideal rest station for battle-weary American occupying forces.

The 319th set about immediately to alter the town's satisfied appearance. I was ordered to enter all houses on the left side of the pretty street on which we had chosen to stop, and to demand that they be vacated within two hours. I took my assignment with enthusiasm.

"Attention, occupants!" I would say, "You must clear your home for the use of the American occupying forces immediately. You have two hours in which to gather your personal belongings and get out. You must leave all furniture, beds, bed clothing, and kitchen utensils..."

"How can you do this?" they asked. "It is illegal!"

"You must allow us to see the *Burgermeister* first."

"Go see him, but pack what you need first."

"Where is my family to go? We have no place to go."

"That's your problem, madam. I have no place to go either."

Oust them I did, and within the time suggested to me. The problems of resettlement were left to the families. Some of us from I&R were assigned that afternoon to a comfortable two-story house at the end of the street.

There was little of importance for us to do now, and the company was permitted to relax in *Bad Worishofen*. Time slowed down. We tossed baseballs back and forth. Military vehicles parked everywhere. GIs in great numbers roamed the streets and through luxury hotels where they were currently billeted. Though the windows we looked at the elegant interiors of stores that had once flourished but now were closed. We gathered evenings in beer halls and listened to American dance music on records provided by the U.S.O.

I imitated the Americans and allowed the townspeople to mistake me for one of the occupying Americans. Headquarters eventually got wind of my deception and took me to task for it, ordering me, from then on, to wear an identifying Dutch flag insignia. I looked around town to find someone who could stitch a flag patch for me in a neat and interesting way, and was directed to a nun in a local convent, who consented to sew me a handsome Dutch flag. I, in turn, sewed the patch carefully, and with budding pride, on the pocket of my shirt where not too many years ago there had been a yellow star with the word *"Jood"* on it.

My buddies and the officers of our unit, a few at a time, began to try to get through to me the importance of planning a future for myself beyond the 319th. Though they were familiar with my history, they urged me to go home and try to find some surviving relatives. I am sure they could see my loneliness in my desperation to cling to them. They wanted to help and to see me on my feet before they left, reminding me that I would be left behind when they were sent home within the next few months.

The officers gave me a leave of absence and permission to hitchhike home. I agreed to return to *Amsterdam*, longing to return yet profoundly reluctant to arrive there. I was too aware of what I would find. From the time I was 15 years old, (I became 16 in June, 1940) when Nazi Germany had invaded Holland in May 1940, I had learned what it was to be isolated as a Jew, first from our fellow townspeople, then gradually from each other as the Nazis hounded and hunted us like criminals, thinning our numbers at will. I knew that almost everyone in my large family of relatives had been picked up before my hiding place was discovered, that my sister was gone, my parents were gone. I knew about the sealed freight cars in which we all had been shipped off, and about the death camps at the end of the ride.

Yet, here I was, alive, and asked by new friends to go home and resume my life. Guilt and dread and fear engulfed me, but I reached out for the hope the boys spoke of. The Americans longed to go home. Rips and tears would be mended at home. Home was home. The recorded hit songs of the mid-forties sang to us about the joys that awaited us at home. Everyone wants to go home.

I hitchhiked home. It was before the atomic bomb fell on *Hiroshima*, sometime in early August 1945, for I was in *Amsterdam* on V-J Day, August 15th. I spent about a week in *Amsterdam*. What I did there comes back in puffs of remembrance, like my last hitched ride into town on the back of a Dutchman's motorcycle. He picked me up some distance outside of town and tore with me over gravel roads on the most frightening ride of my life. I could feel the rear wheel skipping beneath us, and held on with an iron grip. After all I had gotten through, I thought, what a way for me to go. The streets of *Amsterdam* were a welcome sight.

I walked the streets where I used to live. I walked through the old Jewish area on the other side of the *Amstel River*. It was a jumble of torn-up housing where blocks and blocks of ancient buildings had housed generations of families. I walked up and down the *Amstellaan* and some of our neighborhood canals. I went downtown. The "*Mokummers*," as Amsterdammers called themselves, bustled around me, everyone speaking Dutch. Because Holland had been liberated by the Canadian Army, Canadian soldiers swarmed through the streets, mingling with the Dutch. On V-J Day the cafes on the *Rembrandtsplein* and the *Kalverstraat* overflowed with townspeople and Canadians who where celebrating in a subdued mood the A-bomb-hastened victory over Japan that brought an end to World War II. Some Canadians invited me to have a drink with them, and I drank with my country's liberators, an uneasy stranger in my own town.

There is much that my mind refuses to recall. I do not remember where I slept. I do not remember visiting the Boas family who had hidden me during the Nazi occupation until someone had reported my hiding place. Yet I have pictures of the wedding of one of their sons, Lou, immediately after the war, and I have my architecture books I had left with the Boas family when I was forced to flee. There is an added architectural volume inscribed to me by Lou and his wife, Rita.

Some of my wanderings I do remember. I walked again into my old neighborhood and down *Graaf Florisstraat* where I had last lived. I approached the building my family had occupied, and looked over the tenants' names posted by their doorbells. An unknown name was posted for our apartment, and, in fact, there was not one familiar name among the listed tenants.

I crossed the street to the walk-up apartments opposite ours. Sure enough, one familiar name was posted still. It belonged to a gentile family who had begun a friendship with my parents when my father sold them some cheese on the black market of wartime *Amsterdam*. Papa had told me when he had last visited me in my hiding place that he was planning to leave our personal papers and valuables with this family. I rang the bell and was let in.

The couple registered shock and surprise when I identified myself then hugged me and cried. Old griefs were remembered. I asked about my family and other neighborhood Jews we knew in common. They told me they had not heard again from any one of them. The woman brought out a shoebox that she placed in my lap. My tears fell in splotches on the familiar old papers, the wedding and birth certificates and other records. My mother and father at various stages and ages looked out from photographs. My sister, Sienie, and I were recorded in careful poses from birth to teenage. The smiling faces of my relatives looked at me once more, even my whole grammar school class under *Mevrouw van der Roest*. There was my mother's silver-etched needle case, my father's brown leather cigar case and cigar bone holder, my Bar Mitzvah watch that had been my grandfather's gift to me. My father's diamond stickpin and my mother's diamond ring were not there. I asked about these items and was told they had never been included in the box. Maybe, after all, my father changed his mind about leaving such valuables behind. I did not need them. I had my family's records and photographs. From that time on, I toted them with me everywhere, looking at them only at times when I needed to remind myself that once I had belonged to a firmly rooted family. I thanked the couple with genuine gratitude for keeping my family's records through the occupation.

I walked to the house of an *Amsterdam* police officer with whom my father had worked closely in the black market during the occupation, and to whom I knew my father had entrusted a valuable stamp collection. He was shocked to see me, and, at first, denied that he had ever been given my father's stamps. We talked at some length and, at last, he capitulated, admitting that he had once held the stamps in his possession, but explaining that the reduced circumstances of his own family's lives had forced him to sell them. He told me how the occupied Dutch had been starved and bled white to feed the German war machine as the war progressed. He sold the stamps, he told me, after the Jews had all been rounded up and sent off, and after talk had gone around that all of them had been put to death. I asked him why the old buildings of the old Jewish section of *Amsterdam* had been gutted. He told me that during the severe winter of 1944-45, just passed, these empty buildings had been torn apart for their wood by townspeople who had no other fuel to heat their frigid homes.

I had seen my neighborhood and my town, but just as I had feared, there was no one there to greet me with joy and to encourage me to begin again. I thought of my confident American friends and the new kind of life they had shown me. My mind no longer wavered. I did not want to stay in Holland. I decided to return immediately to my unit in *Bad Worishofen*. I hitchhiked to *Maastricht*, a rest area for GIs, a town located on the train line into Germany. The Dutch border was controlled by the Allies to prevent the passage of war criminals and various other unauthorized refugees. Only Allied military personnel could cross these borders unchallenged. I had been given a military pass into Holland, but no return pass. American M.P.'s controlled the *Maastricht* railroad station, which was the last border train stop before entering Germany. Dutch police patrolled the station as well. I noticed these cops eyeing my Dutch flag insignia on my American uniform. Quickly, I approached the American M.P.'s for help, explaining that I was a Dutchman assigned as an interpreter to the 319th Infantry Regiment in *Bad Worishofen*, that I had hitchhiked home for a week, had lost my pass, and wanted to return. The M.P.'s helped me board the train without being questioned by the Dutch cops. The train puffed off to *Cologne*. The kilometers clicked by and I was grateful for the distance that was lengthening between me and my homeland, glad to be fleeing before someone could grab me and make me stay.

From the train I took to the roads again until I was back on our Company street. My ears and eyes were greeted with the familiar thwack and thump of a baseball being hurled from glove to glove.

"My God!" Will you look who's back?"

"Max! You ain't ever goin' t'leave us. What happened?"

"Well, I just can't stand it without you guys. Besides, no one is left for me to go home to."

Somebody got on the squawk-box with the news that Max was back. The street began to fill up with my American GI friends.

Elie Rodrigues Garcia (Max's father), as a young man, left; Elie's sister Jaantje, middle; his brother Maurits, right. Date of photo unknown.

PART 2

A Dutch Jewish Family of Diamond Workers

1924-1937

Dismissal time at Graaf Florisschool Primary School found Appie Klaverstijn, Robbie Bleekrode, and me dashing for the school yard to play soccer or kickball with our schoolmates. At the dinner hour we walked home together, for we lived in apartments on the same block. During our free time at home we played together on a brick-paved island, interspersed with trees, in the middle of *Saffierstraat*, on which our apartments fronted. Sometimes we trotted down to the *Amstel River*, a block away, to watch boat club members racing their shells of all sizes. In icy winters we skated on that same *Amstel* or on the canals. We strapped on our wooden skates and joined our friends on the ice, lunging forward with long strides, hands clasped behind our backs.

Appie, Robbie, and I had been born in *Amsterdam* within a day of each other in 1924, on June 27th, June 28th, and June 29th. We went through most of the primary school years together and grew to know each other like brothers. (My parents named me Meijer at birth after my deceased grandfather, Meijer Veerman, but I was always called Max.) Ours was a working class neighborhood of people employed, for the most part, in the diamond industry. We were mostly Jews. There were a few gentiles and mixed marriages, such as Appie Klaverstijn's parents, and, like Appie's father, there were those among our parents who did not work in the diamond industry.

My father was a diamond polisher, and highly skilled. My grandfather, too, had spent a lifetime in the diamond industry, until his retirement. But during my lifetime my grandfather lived in *Antwerp* where he had moved after retirement to work as a shamus in a small Sephardic Synagogue there. He had also remarried since the early death of my grandmother, whom I had never known. It was evidence of my father's skill that he remained employed in the industry during the early 30's when the depression deepened and most of our neighbors were laid off.

Elias Rodrigues Garcia, my father, was a handsome man and

well proportioned. There was a good-natured set to his face and a twinkle in his eye that advertised a mischievous, bold, but cheerful disposition. No matter how bad times became, Papa would strive to make the best of the situation and show an optimistic face to his family and the world. My father could be deprived of just about everything and still take a forward-looking point of view. He tried to find matters to laugh about when others were merely depressed at the ever-worsening problems of our lives. As a family, we warmed ourselves at the hearth of his good humor.

My father was also a political man, an ardent Social Democrat, and an active member of his labor union. For him the fight for "social democracy" was a crusade of the workingman to introduce social reforms by democratic means. He and others of the movement were opposed to radical socialism, or worse, communism. These latter movements, they believed, spelled violence and repressive government. Social Democrats held that social reforms must stem from reason and gain acceptance gradually by democratic processes. They wanted public ownership of community service industries and basic heavy industries. Their socialism did not extend to the small businessman or farmer.

Papa looked with alarm at the rapid expansion of fascism in Italy and Nazi-Germany. He was incensed by rumors of purges and liquidations resulting from the Russian Communist system that emerged from their bloody revolution and civil war. Over the years his convictions strengthened that these systems should be opposed. I was taught that the fascists, believing in privilege for the few, state regimentation for the many, and the communists, believing in complete state control to create equal pay and goods for all, took off in opposite directions but traveled in a circle to meet at the same point. That point meant forceful compliance or death for the average man.

Pretty and amply made Rozetta Veerman Rodrigues Garcia, my mother, was easygoing and very much under the strong influence of my father. Still, she voiced her anxieties more than my father, about us children, about the times; and she had her own close family to fall back on for reassurance. Mother was the youngest daughter in

Rozetta Veerman (Max's mother), posing at *Zandvoort* when a young woman. Date of photo unknown.

a family of eight Veerman offspring, all of whom were married and lived in *Amsterdam*. To my young eyes, her strengths were those of a devoted homemaker, wife, and mother. If a cake was needed for a special occasion among our large family of relatives, my mother was usually asked to bake it. That is, she put the ingredients together in her kitchen, a process my sister and I loved to watch, before taking the batter out to the baker for baking. Our kitchen had no ovens, no iceboxes, not even hot water, yet my mother cooked well. Her sisters often dropped by for recipes, and it was readily acknowledged that hers were the outstanding dishes at any family gathering. She made a particularly delicious boterkoek from a family recipe that I try to duplicate every year to this very day. When sewing had to be done by anyone in the family, mother's advice was also sought. She sewed for all of us, and in lean years did "piece work" at home and in sewing ateliers. There was much about my mother I did not know because as soon as I was old enough to walk to school by myself I was out of the apartment and playing in the streets. The occupations of my mother and sister hardly interested me.

On a trip back to *Amsterdam* a great many years later, my wife and I visited at length with the senior Klaverstijns. Mrs. Klaverstijn reminded us that she and my mother had worked in the same sewing atelier on the *Jodenbreestraat*, recuperated in the hospital together when Appie and I were born, and were close friends as young women. She remembered my mother's ready intelligence and how willingly she took on new duties with my father's changes in fortune. I was aware that both of my parents had a passion for opera and operetta, but I had not known that my mother went with her friends almost every week to enjoy the operettas at the Rembrandt Theatre. Mrs. Klaverstijn recalled that the "girls" were particularly fond of one singing star, Else Grassan, and that at one point they gathered their courage and sent her a note that they would like to meet with her. The singer acknowledged the note and set a date to receive them. My mother and her friends chipped in to buy an elegant box of chocolates, only to suffer great disappointment at the interview because the singer stood chatting with them for only a few minutes, accepted their gift of chocolates, but did not offer as much as a cup of tea.

Mrs. Klaverstijn also told us of my mother's infatuation with elegant clothes and expensive hats, a taste she was hardly ever in a position to indulge. "One day she told the girls at the atelier she had seen an, oh, so wonderful little hat in the window of van Sweden, a hat shop in the *Utrechtschestraat*. Oh! Like a poem! But so sorry she had not enough money yet; so she had to wait and save money, for she should have it! Well, one of her friends, Saar Slager, was a poet and that day the girls sang in an operetta melody the following song:

> *Het mooiste dat Rozetje op aarde kan verlangen,*
> *Is 't hoedje dat ze in het van Sweeden fenster ziet hangen,*
> *Maar daar Rozetje nu dat hoedje nog niet kan betalen,*
> *Kan zij dat hoedje bij van Sweeden nog niet halen!*

> *The most beautiful thing on earth that Rozetje could desire,*
> *Is a small hat she saw displayed in the window at van*
>   *Sweeden,*
> *But because Rozetje cannot pay for that little hat,*
> *She cannot pick up that hat at van Sweeden!*

My sister, Sippora, whom we called Sienie, was said to have our grandmother's Garcia good looks. By teenage she was well on her way to becoming a beautiful young woman. Though we shared a bedroom, until she was picked up by the Nazis at the age of 16, I noticed little about her except that she liked sweets too well. About one-and-a-half years younger than I, and a girl, I gave her little of my attention as we grew up together.

Our family orbited mainly within the circle of my mother's family, the Veermans, all of whom lived within easy distances. Though my Portuguese-Sephardic-descended family's relatives also lived near us in *Amsterdam*, my mother, Rozetje, as she was called, steered our relationship towards her own close family. My father, called Elie, was even looked upon as a bit crazy by the Veermans, and his craziness was blamed on his Portuguese-Sephardic descent.

It made no difference that Papa's family had been Mokummers since the early 17th century when they came to Holland after a long settlement in South America. As a result of the Spanish Inquisition of 1492 the Garcia family had fled from Spain, first to Portugal, and then were forced to flee again and eventually settled in South America. After a sojourn of almost a century in South America, they migrated to *Amsterdam* via the Eastern Seaboard of the British Colonies and England. The Veermans were Ashkenazi Jews who had lived in *Amsterdam* for probably a little less than a century after fleeing Polish or German pogroms; but to the Veermans the Garcias were somewhat eccentric outsiders.

My earliest boyhood memory is of being taken to visit my grandmother Veerman on the *Jodenbreestraat*. She lived in the house of one of her sons, my Oom Philip Veerman, and his wife, Tante Rebecca. I visited my ancient grandmother in her sleeping cupboard off the kitchen. My age was four or five. During that time I looked forward every day to attending a Montessori kindergarten school in our neighborhood near the *van Woustraat*.

We lived in a fourth floor walk-up apartment consisting of a living room, two bedrooms, a kitchen, a clothes closet, a water closet (a toilet), and a dumbwaiter for hauling up our groceries and packages from the ground floor. Just as one took cake batter and bread dough out to be baked by a commercial baker, so one went once a week to the neighborhood bathhouse on *Smaragdstraat* to take a shower. The bathhouse was at the other end of the street on which the private rowing club was located, and behind the bathhouse were two primary schools, one of them mine, the Graaf Florisschool.

One of the luxuries in our apartment was a radio-like box that could be tuned in to any of four stations by paying a monthly fee. My parents kept our radio tuned only to VARA, the Social Democrat station, about which my father was dogmatic. Mother tuned in to her programs of music when she was able to listen during the day. Both parents would listen in the evenings to political talks, operas, operettas and light music. I listened to very little of this until my teenage years when I began to enjoy the operas and operettas to which my parents were devoted. I remember switching the station to try out some American jazz one Saturday only to have my father insist I switch it back again to a familiar opera.

Papa encouraged me from an early age to establish some independence from the watchful eyes of my mother. I played in ever-widening circles, coming to know the streets of our neighborhood very well. As a very young boy my world extended from *Saffierstraat* to *van Woustraat* to the *Amstel River* to the *Josef Israels Kade* (canal) to the *Tolstraat*, where my father worked in the Asscher Diamond Factory.

On Saturdays we boarded the No. 8 streetcar to the *Jodenbreestraat* to visit the families of one of mother's two brothers and several sisters who lived on and around that street. We children

Rozetta Veerman Rodrigues Garcia (my mother), Elie Rodrigues Garcia (my father), and Tante Duifje (my mother's sister). This photo was taken in May 1940. before the war came to Holland, and before the German invasion.

looked forward to these visits and to being indulged with refreshments and an occasional stuiver by our relatives. Our streetcar rode on tracks straight down the center of the *Jodenbreestraat*, nosing with clanging bell through walkers and shoppers who spilled from the sidewalk onto the narrow street. We passed vendors' carts catering to knots of shoppers looking for bargains in groceries, clothing, and housewares. Horse and bicycle carts wove slowly behind and in front of the streetcar. A car or truck was only rarely seen. Friends stopped to visit in the shade of awning-covered shops, causing walkers to detour into the streets and slow traffic further.

We headed first for a visit with mother's brother, Oom Philip Veerman and Tante Rebecca, his wife, a warm and colorful woman, who had no children of their own. Oom Philip, a dapper dresser, owned a fairly prosperous poultry store, which both husband and wife helped maintain. When we called at their shop I romped with their German shepherd dog "Egon," and sucked out some of the broken eggs.

After a brief visit we walked next door and climbed a dark, steep, stairway to the second floor apartment of mother's closest sister, Tante Griet, and her husband, Oom Meijer Rubens. Oom Meijer was a traveling salesman dealing in picture frames and lampshades. Their one son, Hans, was five years older than me, too old for me to know him well.

Across the street, we called on another sister of my mother, Tante Duif, married to Oom Salomon Melkman, and their three children, Floortje, Anneke and Hartog (Broertje). The Melkmans, too, managed a prospering poultry business and, in the early days of these visits, lived upstairs from their shop. Duifje and Salomon were cheerful, hardworking people. Their daughters, Floortje and Anneke, were vivacious, and Floortje, the oldest, was always well dressed and considered one of the prettiest girls in the Veerman tribe. The girls were six and five years older than I, but Broertje was my age and my closest cousin. While our parents visited, Broertje and I often played together in the streets or went to the movie theatre, the Top Hat, dutifully taking my younger sister with us.

One block over and down an alley was the *Waterlooplein* where

Max Rodrigues Garcia and his sister, Sipporah. December 1930.

the apartment of Oom Michel and mother's sister, Tante Klaartje Cohen de Lara, was located. Their four boys, Appie, Meijer, David and Philip were also older than I, but the younger boys, David and Flip (as we called Philip), were often good company even though they were closer to Floortje's age than mine.

Oom Michel was my wealthiest uncle, a dealer in the feathers of geese, swans, ducks and chickens, and in all kind of pelts, such as rabbits, hares, cats, and moles. His oldest son, Appie, worked as an accountant-manager of his father's business after completing his studies in accountancy. Meijer, the second son, also a young adult (named, like me, after our grandfather Meijer Veerman), was studying to become a rabbi when I was a boy. In the fateful year 1939, he was to know the honor of being appointed the assistant rabbi of the Portuguese-Sephardic Synagogue, of which our families were members.

Oom Michel owned some warehouses along one of the waterways in the Jewish section of *Amsterdam* which were filled with feathers and pelts, and at times he hired me, a youngster, to work with my cousins David and Flip, doing odd jobs. Often we stood at the side of the waterway before great mounds of pelts that we were required to flail, one by one, on the inner skin side in order to soften them up and clean them. As we worked we watched the working boats and barges as they slipped by us, exchanging quips and cracks with some of the families aboard them. Our noses were accustomed to the ripe odors of the garbage scow tethered nearby. I was at home in my uncle's warehouse and liked being paid to work there, but the pelts had to be handled carefully and we took our work seriously. I was quite in awe of Oom Michel, not because he had money but because he had a huge belly that he carried before him with dignity. He was a short man and so rotund others had to tie his shoes.

There were other relatives on my mother's side with whom our relations were more distant. I hardly knew my mother's oldest sister, Rebecca, or her husband, Oom Gerrit Reens. Occasionally we visited another older sister, Tante Jetje, and Oom Folia Hester. They had four children: two boys and two girls. Their oldest son, Meijer, was nearly my father's age and he left in the early thirties for

South Africa. Nico, their youngest son about six years older than I, chatted easily with me when our families visited. Just before the Nazi-Germany invasion of Holland he passed some examinations that earned him a coveted queen's scholarship for medical school, but the Nazi occupation happened soon afterwards, and so Nico was not destined to start his higher schooling or even to live much longer. Their youngest girl was named Annie but I do not recall the name of their oldest daughter. Abraham, mother's oldest brother, was in some way mentally deficient, and had to be taken care of, along with his wife and children, by all of the Veerman relatives.

My father's family was smaller and, as I have mentioned, not so close to us as mother's family. The men of his family had always been diamond polishers. Grandfather Judah Rodrigues Garcia, and grandfather's brother, had polished diamonds. My father, Elie, and his brother, Maurits, were both diamond polishers. Maurits and his wife had three children, two boys and a girl, and lived in the neighborhood of the Heksters. However, we barely knew them because my mother did not care for the company of Maurits' wife. I do not remember her name or the names of their children since we hardly saw them. Father also had a sister, Jaantje, who did not marry a diamond polisher. Her husband, Oom Aaron Delden, in partnership with his father and uncles, owned several shops specializing in bicycles, bicycle parts, electrical supplies and equipment. The Deldens had two boys, both younger then Sienie, and again I cannot recall their names. They lived on the fringe of the Jewish section of *Amsterdam* and stayed in close touch with my father though our families did not often exchange visits.

We Garcias belonged to the venerable Portuguese-Sephardic Synagogue, the interior of which P. Fouquet, Jr. etched so carefully in the 17th century, recording for us comfortable proof that the interior did not change as did the congregations and their clothing styles. As a family, however, we were hardly devout, and rarely attended services on Saturday before setting forth to visit one or another of our relatives. Sometimes, but rarely, we attended services on the High Holy Days and on special occasions such as Bar Mitzvahs and weddings. Oom Michel Cohen de Lara and his son, Meijer – who would one day become the rabbi there – are remembered particularly among our family as devout members of the Portuguese-Sephardic Synagogue.

My father had one ritual to which he looked forward every week: to join some of his fellow diamond workers for a Saturday morning game of whist and a good cigar at a restaurant on the *Rembrandtsplein*. It was the custom of our family to meet downtown, after Papa's game of whist, and from there go visit our relatives on the *Jodenbreestraat*.

One Saturday when I was six or seven years old, mother dressed me up, as usual, in my best clothes, then sent me out to play as she and Sienie dressed. We were planning to take the streetcar to meet Papa on the *Jodenbreestraat* after he finished his game. Outside I saw some of my friends running about in an apartment building under construction around the corner, and I ran to join them. We followed one another through the open framing and up and down the ramps. We began to dare one another to jump out of the second story window frames and into some piles of sand beneath. In no time we were all jumping waist-deep into the sand heaps that contained a chalky substance that whitened our clothes and our skins. When my mother saw the scene she was furious. She took me home to wash and redress me, scolding angrily, handling me roughly. We were late meeting my father, and I cringed as mother began to relate to him what I had done. I feared my father's anger, which could be swift and explosive. But instead of turning on me in anger, he laughed, throwing back his head. "Oh, Rozetje," he said, "don't be upset. Now I know I have a real boy!"

I liked school, putting in my first five years with the same classmates and the same teacher, Mevrouw van der Roest. These were my happiest years for I had close friends and a teacher who was both familiar and devoted. Mevrouw van der Roest grew to know her students extremely well, and we felt comfortable with her. A gentile, originally from the Province of Zeeland, she taught a class of about 30 children, half of them Jewish, shaping us into a receptive but disciplined group of students. She learned our strengths and our weaknesses, and helped us where we needed it most. She filled

1933 classroom photo: At lower left, Appie Klaverstyn (in glasses) sits beside Max R. Garcia, grinning and in dark tie, white shirt. Close friend, Robbie Bleekrode sits directly behind Max in striped sleeveless pullover. Teacher, Mevrouw van der Roest, in white-collared dress, stands among children near wall.

us with the excitement of learning and the desire to learn more. I remember at one point recovering from an illness that kept me out of school for more than a week. When I returned to class Mevrouw van der Roest took me home with her after school, fortified me with milk and cookies, and then tutored me two hours a day until I caught up with my classmates.

We learned to swim in a new swimming complex called the Miranda Baths at the end of the *Rijnstraat*. As a swimmer I started late and did not feel at home in the water. We had to pass some ability tests at the Miranda Baths, the worst of which, for me, was the backstroke. Invariably I sank, and came up sputtering for air. I felt sure I was going to drown, but I finally passed the test when I realized my friends were finishing up the course and leaving me behind.

Skating on ice was more my sport. I very much remember when I received my first tie-on ice skates on Sinterklaas. I must have been eight. In Holland, everyone celebrated Sinterklaas, on 5 December, a day practically set aside for children. Christmas for the gentiles was a religious holiday of major significance. Chanukah for the Jews was a minor religious holiday. Sinterklaas was awaited with excitement by all children. Within our apartment building tension would build as the day neared. We sang traditional songs on Sinterklaas Eve and placed our stockings, each containing a crisp carrot for the horse of Sinterklaas on the floor next to our coal-fired stove in the living room. Sinterklaas was the children's affectionate term for Saint Nicholas. After what seemed like hours, Sinterklaas arrived, in the company of "Zwarte Piet" who would read to us, awe-stricken children, from the record book he held in his hands. Zwarte Piet told Sinterklaas about the bad deeds we had done during the year just gone by all of which had been faithfully catalogued. We cried and promised never to do such things ever again. We were always forgiven, and then we all sang again as Sinterklaas handed out candy and would strew candies on the floor that we dove for. Games were played and winners and losers alike received small gifts. The next morning we would find our gifts next to our socks and the crisp carrot was gone. That is how one year I received wooden skates and

Sippora and Max Rodrigues Garcia in a studio portrait. August 7, 1935.

began learning to negotiate the *Amstel* and the city's canals.

Some years later I skated with my friends to the outlying villages of *Ouderkerk* and *Diemen*. We took lunch and some small change in order to buy hot soup and hot cocoa on the way. The bitter winter winds pushed us along or held us back when we reversed our direction. The delicious smelling steam from soup and cocoa stalls along the ice enticed us as we exerted ourselves. We stopped on occasion to warm ourselves inside and out before steaming-hot cauldrons on pot-bellied stoves.

Amsterdam, then a city of about 750,000, had a Jewish population that was probably close to 100,000. Of this population only a few thousand were Orthodox Jews. We Jews chose to live near one another, but we were not forced to live so. Almost no one in the days before the occupation made an issue of the Jewish community. We were accepted as fellow Mokummers, and all of us townspeople got along on the basis of interests we held in common. Business transactions, the hobbies of housewives, the activities of school children led to many friendships between Jews and gentiles. A few Yiddish words made their way into the vernacular, like "smeris" or "shamus" for "policeman." *Amsterdam's* Jews came and went about town at will. By the time I was 11, I was making my way around most of Amsterdam on my bicycle. Gradually I felt at ease in any part of the city I cared to explore.

My friends and I were great fans of American movies. The Saturday afternoon movies on the *Ceintuurbaan* became a way of life for us during the long afternoons when our parents did not go visiting family. We jumped eagerly into new worlds with such romantic, if differing, fare as the films of Shirley Temple, Charlie Chaplin, Boris Karloff, Tom Mix, Laurel and Hardy, and Rin Tin Tin. The movies played in English with subtitles, enabling me to learn a few words and phrases. We were profoundly impressed with the apparent wealth of American city people, each with his own car and elaborately furnished home, smart clothes changing with every scene. We were awestruck by the adventures waiting in the western hills for anyone foolish enough to leave the cities. In adolescence I fell under the spell of Fred Astaire and Ginger Rogers, I followed them worshipfully as they glided about opulent sets in tails and satins. In my mind I joined them, dancing off gracefully with a beautiful partner of my own.

I was growing old enough also to begin to understand some of the conversations of my parents with relatives and friends. I gradually learned that my father, regardless of his general good humor, had never really liked being a diamond polisher, and resented the fact that his own father had insisted that he stay in the family trade. There were bad feelings between father and son. My *Antwerp* grandfather was a devout Portuguese-Sephardic Jew, but religion sat more lightly on my father's shoulders. When Papa was a very young man he had gone to England and, finding it to his liking, returned to ask grandfather's permission to move there and try his hand in business. Grandfather told him he had to stay home and learn the family trade of diamond polishing first, that he could not drift around without a trade. Father learned the trade, beginning to earn money as his skills increased, and beginning to take interest in some local girls as his money increased. Within a couple of years he married my mother, and the dream of starting a new life in England was dead. I think he cherished the hope that I might make it in his place, and so he encouraged my independence and my easy facility for languages. He brought me English-language newspapers and insisted that I learn some English.

As the depression deepened and more and more jobs were lost in the community, Papa hit upon an idea for going into a new business. My father was basically a frustrated entrepreneur who dearly loved business. He went to see Oom Philip Veerman, his brother-in-law and poultry store owner, to ask his cooperation in allowing Papa to open up a branchlike poultry store in our own neighborhood. It would be supplied by Oom Philip and staffed by my father and mother for a percentage of the profits of Oom Philip. Oom Philip agreed to try it, and so my father rented a garage, built a counter, some racks, and a storage shed in the back. There was even a kerosene heating lamp and an icebox. Located on the *Diamantstraat*, around the corner from the *Saffierstraat*, the store opened up for afternoon business only, the time of day when people were in the habit of going out to make their purchases for the evening meal. Mother tended the store. Papa continued working at the diamond factory where layoffs were occurring with increasing frequency. Because a two-hour lunch was customary everywhere, even in the schools, we all gathered at the store for a noon meal together. Mother had our lunch ready when we arrived, and father cut up chickens while he ate.

I was taught to help clean, cut up, and wrap chickens, then deliver them. It was a fascinating process. The chickens were slaughtered in a basement room under Oom Philip's store on the *Jodenbreestraat*. Access to the basement was by covered cellar steps to the left of the shop's front door. Live chickens delivered in crates were slid down a wooden chute placed over the steps. Oom Philip's employees would pull out the chickens, one by one, slit their throats and throw them hard against the bloodstained wall in order to stun them before they died. The plucking was done by expert hands, a chore of little more than five minutes per chicken. I was trained to help with all processes over the protests of my mother, who did not appreciate my bringing home chicken lice. Each time I worked in Oom Philip's cellar she sent me to the bathhouse while she washed my work clothes. Oom Philip occasionally rewarded me for helping with a gift of a cracked egg from which I would enthusiastically suck out the raw contents. During lunch and after school I helped in our store. I delivered chickens on my bicycle to waiting housewives, who placed them in their veranda coolers or started their cooking immediately.

On cold days I found my mother tending the shop red-nosed, bundled in sweaters, long underwear, and scarves. Most of the orders were standard each week. Sometimes neighbors would run into mother on the street and tell her what they wanted. She took and filled orders conscientiously.

"Hey, Rozetje! I want you to put by a two-pound chicken for me for Friday afternoon."

"How are you, Rozetje! Will you please have Max deliver a half dozen eggs to me by five this afternoon?"

Oom Salomon Melkman had a poultry shop diagonally across the street from Oom Philip's main store, and both, incidentally, were within a few doors of Rembrandt's historic house. Now Oom

Salomon saw how our branch store with Oom Philip was flourishing; he decided to open an extra store of his own about a block and a half away. Needless to say, the new store caused a bitter rift within the family. My father deeply resented Salomon's new store because he himself had formulated the idea and was succeeding with it. Now neither store had enough business. By now, too, my father's fears had been realized, and he had been laid off at the diamond factory. Just as we became solely dependent on the poultry store, our customers were growing poorer by the day. They could no longer afford to buy whole chickens, and began to order only a half or a quarter of a chicken at a time. They had purchased only two or three eggs a week. At least we had some food along with our tiny income even though we ate mostly chicken. It is a wonder that I still like chicken, but I do.

My father insisted that I read the works of Pieter Jelles Troelstra, the founder of our Dutch Social Democratic Labor Party and of *Het Volk*, the socialist newspaper to which we subscribed. Considered the father of social democracy in Holland, Troelstra had left a good legacy of reform legislation by the time he died in 1930. At the turn of the century he had represented the party in parliament, and had devoted himself to influencing social legislation from then on.

I joined the Social Democratic Youth Movement, which took girls as well as boys into its ranks, and attended their meetings and rallies in the blue shirt and red neckerchief that made up our uniform. Our activities were not much different from a co-educational scout troop, minus merit badges.

Economic conditions became precarious. My sister and I went about in hand-me-down clothing. We walked with my parents in an enormous national strike march near the *Vondel Park*. During the elections my father busied himself with the campaigns of the Social Democrats. One night he came home splattered with blood, and told my mother about fights in the streets with the Communists.

"Why is it any of your business?" mother screamed. "Let them alone, Elie! Stay out of it. Do you want to be killed?"

"If we don't stop them, who will?" Papa shouted back.

My father left on a trip to Belgium – the year was 1935 – and when he returned he announced we were moving to *Antwerp* where he had landed a job at a Belgian diamond plant.

We moved at night, along with a family named Prins, who lived across the street from us on the *Saffierstraat*, in a rented truck driven by a hired driver. Papa had already rented a very modest apartment for us in *Antwerp*, and the following day we unpacked in unfamiliar surroundings. Overnight my friends were gone and my life changed completely. I was 11 years old, a difficult time to lose the familiar surroundings of my brief lifetime. But there was no question that we had to start again. My sister and I easily learned Flemish, a dialect of Dutch, and we finished up the last few months of the school year, for me the sixth grade. In the fall I started classes at the Meerdere Uitgebreid Lager Onderwijs (MULO), or middle school, equivalent to the American junior high school. I reached the school, which was on the opposite side of town, by means of a long streetcar trip. The MULO was a school for boys, offering a rigid educational program. Few memories of the place stay with me except that it was the first school I attended that required my submitting to the services of a school dentist. For the first time in my life I was examined by a dentist and, as a result, put through some excruciating hours of tooth filling and an extraction. Dentists suddenly headed my list of people to avoid. The MULO took me efficiently through a standard curriculum including some fluency in French, which was a necessity in bilingual Belgium.

During the summers that followed we took brief vacations to Holland. Months became years and I came to know *Antwerp* well. My father prospered in his work. We were able to move to a larger, modern apartment, complete with hot water, bathroom with shower, and even a telephone. Our neighborhood was made up almost exclusively of Dutch migrant diamond workers. Wages were generally lower in *Antwerp* than they had once been in *Amsterdam*, but the industry was still in full operation.

I have mentioned that my grandfather Judah Rodrigues Garcia lived in retirement in *Antwerp* with his second wife and performed duties as a shamus in a small Sephardic Synagogue there. But Papa and grandfather still did not heal the rift between them, and we did not live near one another. Nevertheless, when I began studying for my Bar Mitzvah, near the age of 13, I was sent for training to my grandfather. There was little joy in the process. He was strict, and I was not attracted by my grandfather's orthodoxy.

There was not much joy in the actual ceremony either. The Bar Mitzvah was held in an impersonal walk-up temple in a converted office building rather than our ancient Portuguese-Sephardic Synagogue in *Amsterdam* where my father's Bar Mitzvah had been celebrated as well as those of other male relatives and ancestors. Our family was pleased to entertain Tante Griet, Tante Rebecca, and Tante Duif, who had traveled by bus to *Antwerp* to attend the ceremony, but none of us were happy to be so far from home for this momentous occasion.

1937-1939

In Belgium and Holland schooling was not mandatory after the age of 13. In my family it had long been a necessary practice to drop out of school and go to work at the legal age. I took it for granted, then, that following my Bar Mitzvah and the finishing up of my spring semester at the MULO in 1937, I would accompany my father to the factory and begin apprenticing as a diamond polisher. The knowledge of my father's own dissatisfaction with his trade made me reluctant to follow in his footsteps, yet I saw no alternative to my fate.

But here I was back in *Antwerp*, and my father introduced me at the factory. I was greeted warmly as the son of Elie Garcia. The teacher assigned for my apprenticing was a goliath, over six feet tall and big in the shoulders. We sat opposite each other at his workbench. During the ensuing months he revealed to me gradually the slow, tedious steps of the polishing process. I was allowed to progress in these steps according to my mastery of each previous step. The work was dust producing as well as monotonous. Eventually I adjusted, learned, and progressed. I discovered I had a good three-dimensional sense and could quickly perceive the facets of a diamond.

My basic allowance money of a few Belgian francs began to grow with my skill. I took home ever-larger amounts to my mother, who gave me in return an allowance for my weekly needs.

At the age of fourteen-and-a-half, I cracked a very large stone. I gave it to my teacher who exploded and called me a variety of depressing names. My own anger boiled up. I turned abruptly and walked silently to my locker, changed clothes, and headed for the door.

"Where the hell do you think you're going, Max? I haven't dismissed you yet."

"I don't care whether you dismiss me or not. I'm quitting," I answered. "I don't want to be a diamond polisher."

"And what do you think you're going to do with yourself if you can't make it as a diamond polisher?"

"I'm going to be an architect!" I shot back foolishly.

"Aha! You hear that? You hear that, everybody?" he shouted about the room. "Max Garcia is going to become an architect. And where is your father going to find the money to send you to the university? Where do you get these hare-brained ideas?"

I turned back to the door and walked out.

"How come you are home so early, Max? Are you sick?" my mother asked, advancing anxiously to search my face. When I explained what happened she started to cry.

"Oh, what's to become of you, Max? What's your father going to say? Architect? Architect? What's this all about?" She continued to quiz me through her tears until Papa walked in.

The word, it seemed, had spread like a flame through the factory rooms that Max Garcia had cracked a stone and had quit, that he had further boasted that he was going to become an architect. At least my father was prepared for what he would find when he arrived home.

"Rozetje, I've heard," he told my mother as she began to explain my disaster. "Look, Max, this is a serious matter. Tell me now, what is this? Everyone is telling me about your quitting and about wanting to become an architect." I told him about my realization on our last trip to *Amsterdam* that I would like to study to become an architect.

"Papa," I pleaded, "I know it is not possible at this time for me to go to the university, but it is my dream to be able to try one day. One thing I am sure of, I don't want to be a diamond polisher."

My father looked at me for a long time, and asked me if I understood I would have to work long and hard to be able to earn the money for school, assuming that I could study enough to pass the entrance examinations. After dinner, my polishing teacher, who lived in the neighborhood, came over to talk to my father about me. I was soon called into the living room and my teacher apologized for his outburst. He confessed that a hairline crack had been visible in the stone when he gave it to me and that he should have brought it to my attention. He realized he had expected too much of me to assume that I would notice it and polish it accordingly so that the crack would not show. He apologized for that too, and I accepted his apology.

"Come on back with us, Max," my teacher offered. "You have been doing a reliable job, and if you continue you should be due for a raise."

"No," I replied, "I meant what I said this afternoon. I do not want to try diamond polishing again, and I do not want to return to the factory."

There was a silence before my father spoke. "If Max does not want to continue with diamond polishing, I will not make him. Let him see what else he can do with himself."

That was that. I did not return to the factory except to pick up my belongings.

The streets became a lonely place as I drifted about jobless, hating to return home to face my worried mother. I did not fail to appreciate *Antwerp's* age-blackened buildings and the handsome contemporary apartments of my own neighborhood as well. I learned my way around the districts and neighborhoods of *Antwerp* almost as well as I knew my way around *Amsterdam*.

Within a couple of weeks I found temporary work with a butcher, helping to make sausages. I stuffed intestine casings with a mixture of raw meat, peppers, and spices, preparing them to send out to the smokehouse, a job I enjoyed learning. When we had made a generous supply of sausages the butcher no longer needed me, and I approached my father for permission to take a vacation trip home to *Amsterdam* on my bicycle, a distance of about 150 kilometers. I was often homesick for the town of my birth, and longed for a chance to visit relatives and childhood friends. Such a bicycle trip by a boy my age was unheard of, and my mother began to make a great fuss. Papa, however, turned the idea over in his mind for a while, and then agreed to let me go.

Mother wrote in furious resignation to Tante Griet, Tante Rebecca and Tante Duif to expect me by bicycle because of the foolhardy plot of the mad father and the mad son. Mother's sisters wrote or telephoned back agreeing with mother's objection to this dangerous trip. Nevertheless my parents managed to set a date for my relatives to expect me in *Amsterdam*, and I left on schedule early one morning with a small packet of food and a few changes of clothes. I was a little uneasy at first as I pedaled along the bicycle path beside the main highway, but I kept a good pace and stopped only once when I had to fix a flat tire – a routine affair. As I recognized the outskirts of *Amsterdam* my exhilaration grew; and entering the town in the early evening, I rode proudly and directly to Tante Duif's house.

I stayed for about two weeks, wandering happily about my hometown, visiting friends and relatives, accepting without question their generous hospitality in keeping and feeding me. I was allowed to return to *Antwerp* on my bicycle with none of the family hysteria that accompanied my initial trip. My father, my mother, and my sister were a welcome sight when I arrived home. Yet my trip had been an exciting adventure that greatly boosted my self-confidence. My father was proud of me for having undertaken it, I could tell. My mother began to understand that she was no longer to look upon me as a helpless boy. Her boy was reaching for manhood. I worked at odd jobs until the late spring of 1939 when my father decided that we should return to Holland.

In 1936, Germany had remilitarized the Rhineland, a territory taken from the defeated Germans by French and Belgian forces in World War I, and administered under terms of the Versailles Peace

Treaty. The Rhineland territory was fully restored to Germany by 1930 with the stipulation that the Germans maintain no fortifications or military equipment within the area. The Rhineland was of considerable importance to Germany because of its coal resources and iron and steel mills in both Ruhr and Saar districts, as well as rich agricultural and vine-growing regions. Belgium touched on an eastern border of industrial sections of the Rhineland, and when Hitler moved in troops, Belgian newspapers screamed the bad news. In 1938, there was the "Anschluss," as Hitler quickly annexed Austria, and that move in turn set up the partial isolation of Czechoslovakia. The Sudetenland was also taken in 1938. Czechoslovakia capitulated in 1939. Memel, at Germany's northeast border, was retaken in 1939. Hungary, Rumania, and the Balkans were left independent but vulnerable from both east and west.

My parents and their friends were outraged that the governmental strategists of England and France seemed to be burying their heads in the sand rather than trying to check the drift of Germany's reawakened militarism. My father came to realize that the situation would continue to deteriorate unchecked, that war was imminent, and that he had better begin protecting his family as best he could. Remembering the strategies of World War I, Papa believed that the Germans would probably repeat their invasion of Belgium in order to get to France without trying to penetrate the Maginot Line. Holland, he figured, might just be safe again and left as neutral territory. No matter what happed we would surely be better off in our own country as Dutch citizens.

My father returned to *Amsterdam*, obtained a diamond polishing job back at the Asscher plant, and rented an apartment for us on the *Graaf Florisstraat*. The three of us then followed by bus, and our family was divided up and placed around with relatives until our furniture could be shipped and our apartment set up. I stayed with Tante Duif because her son Broertje and I were friends. On the night before my fifteenth birthday in late June, the telephone rang for me. It was my father calling to tell me that on my birthday he was going to let me accompany the driver of a rented truck to *Antwerp* to oversee the moving of our possessions to the *Graaf Florisstraat*.

He told me he considered me a man now, and he even gave me his permission to smoke.

Graaf Florisstraat was on the other side of the *Amstel*, directly opposite the *Saffierstraat* where I had grown up. The people living on the *Graaf Florisstraat* were blue-collar workers and traveled on their bicycles wherever they needed to go. The apartment houses all had four floors and very steep stairs, as was the custom in *Amsterdam*. Each apartment consisted of a living room, one bedroom and a smaller room, a kitchen without hot water or a refrigerator and a toilet: no bathroom. Once a week one went to the local bathhouse. We learned to adjust rather quickly and Sienie got herself a job in an atelier where they made clothes and other items.

The driver and I traveled by truck back over the road to Antwerp, and once there I directed him to our apartment. We tackled each room, packing boxes, loading furniture, working like field horses in order to return the truck next day to *Amsterdam*. Back on the *Graaf Florisstraat*, the work was even harder, as every box and piece of furniture had to be unloaded, and then hoisted by pulley through a third-story window. Within two days our family was reunited in our furnished apartment. I was proud to have been called on and been able to help so responsibly.

By July I had hired out as a stevedore at a dockside warehouse. I recall one strange duck there who sent me out every day to the baker for a cream puff for his lunch. It was not long before I traded in my laboring job for a chance to work at a travel agency where I hoped I could eventually put my drawing ability to some use and try my hand at advertising layout. I did routine paste-up jobs there, envelope stuffing, and typical backroom work, but the atmosphere was pleasant, and associating, even peripherally, with world travel seemed glamorous.

Our work came to a standstill on Friday, September 1st, 1939, when word swept into our office that Germany had attacked Poland. For the next few days everyone was in a state of suspended motion. Listening to and passing on radio reports was about all that was being accomplished. I was required to work on Sundays and it was on Sunday, September 3rd, that England and France declared war on Germany. We closed up and ran out into the streets to join a milling crowd that grew even larger. The travel business withered almost overnight and, once again, I was out of a job.

1939 – 1942

We stayed close to our radio for news reports and poured over our newspaper, *Het Volk*, for detailed bulletins. Direct reports from England and France reached us through short-wave radios of our wealthier friends and relatives. Oom Aaron Delden, whose wife was father's sister, Jaantje, and who now owned several electrical stores, put speakers up outside his radio shop on the Vijzelstraat. I would stop by to stand with great knots of listeners to hear the latest direct news bulletins.

Following the attack on Poland, protest rallies sprang up one after another all over town. The Dutch Nazi party, which had been swelling in numbers and activity in recent years, was now openly attacked by the left and communist elements. Everyone we knew was in a state of nerves, recalling the severe shortages and disruptions of World War I, and wondering how soon we would be in for the same fate, or worse. Did we face conquest and occupation? What then? We drew even closer to our relatives, getting together with them whenever time could be found. Among the adults there was speculation about what might be in store for Dutch Jews in the event of occupation. We were aware of the large number of German Jewish refugees among us already and of the reasons for their flight from Germany. At this time my father was 43 years old, my mother 44, my sister almost 13, and I, 15.

Poland fell within a very few weeks, after which all fronts became ominously quiet. The loudest noises to be heard were the propaganda broadsides between the opposing nations. We tried to concentrate on our daily lives. Oom Aaron gave me a job in one of his electrical stores. I performed miscellaneous stockroom chores and often acted as a messenger-carrier between stores located on the

Haarlemmer Dijk, the *van Peckstraat*, and the *Plantage Midden-laan*. The *Plantage Middenlaan* was a beautiful wide street, lined with trees, a major artery leading to and from the Jewish section to the eastern part of town, and I liked working there. Tante Klaartje and Oom Michel lived on a side street, *Plantage Parklaan*, near Oom Aaron's shop, and I sometimes stopped by to see them and to accept refreshments. When my parents heard about these workday visits, however, they put a stop to them with a stern lecture. I was not to take up my relatives' time or look forward to refreshments from them on weekdays. I was reminded that they had four sons of their own to look after.

During the winter the Nazi-German war machine was quiet. Only the war of nerves was loud, fed by rumor and propaganda. As the months passed, our tensions built up because we expected a spring offensive. The Dutch army reserves were activated. Holland prepared for her own defense, initiating plans for breaking dikes and flooding southern portions of the country from the *Zuider Zee* all the way to *Zeeland* in order to create a wide moat against the enemy's onslaught. The Dutch Nazis were watched and catalogued as a 5th – column organization, though political freedom in Holland continued to guarantee them unrestricted movement. The German government broadcasts promised to honor Dutch sovereignty, and vehemently denied rumors of German intentions to invade.

On the evening of May 10th, 1940, however, with strong pro-testations that Holland had betrayed her neutrality the Nazi-German Army invaded us. Unknown to us then, Denmark, Belgium, and Luxembourg were invaded at the same time. The Nazi-German armies moved swiftly into Holland just as they did into our neighboring small countries. The dreaded spring offensive was upon us. The dikes were broken as planned, and whole areas inundated but German planes full of paratroopers and equipment flew over the flooded areas, confounding Dutch defenses. Work came to a stand-still. Reserves were ordered into action overnight. The Dutch Army set up defensive positions.

Nazi-German paratroopers in civilian clothing dropping behind our moat became a formidable threat. They linked up with undercover Dutch fascists who were still at large, and seized key locks and water control points. On the third day of the war the Nazis issued an ultimatum that Holland surrender immediately or *Rotterdam* would be severely bombed. The ultimatum was ignored and *Rotterdam* was severely bombed. Holland surrendered soon thereafter to protect her other cities from similar devastation. The conquest of our country took only five days. Queen Wilhelmina, with members of the Dutch government, fled to England and set up a government in exile.

During those few days of war, my father had walked the neighborhood as an air raid warden while my mother draped windows and waited anxiously for him with my sister and me. During the day we began to encounter Dutch Army roadblocks which were set up throughout the city to catch Nazi-German paratrooper infiltrators. Whoever walked the streets was challenged to pronounce clearly various words that only Dutch born people could properly enunciate, such as "*Scheveningen*," "*Schravenhage*," or "*schelvis.*" Anyone whose pronunciation was faulty was detained for further questioning. The German Jews who were living in exile among us quickly learned to stay in their homes rather than risk being picked up as German spies.

Five days later we were a conquered people. I watched the Nazi-German troops march through *Amsterdam*, entering from the direction of *Utrecht* and coming down the *Amstellaan* a few blocks away from where we lived. Though my mother had begged me to stay home, I could not resist running into the street and crossing the bridge to watch. Dutch fascists and Nazi-German sympathizers came back into the streets in black uniforms. As the troops passed by they sent up their right arms: "Heil Hitler! Heil Hitler!" This proved to be premature in our just-conquered city because these same sympathizers were badly beaten that night when the parading was over, and the next morning numerous bodies in black uniforms were found in the canals. Gradually the occupying forces became organized, and such acts of defiance were dared by fewer and fewer townspeople once stringent punishments were administered as the price of disobedience. Proclamations were issued to the effect that

Dutch civil authorities would remain in control, that people were to continue as usual with their work. Everyone went back to work but no element of our lives went "back to normal." Nazi-German troops and trucks were all over town. A system of registration was begun, followed immediately by food rationing.

Our Social Democratic Party newspaper, *Het Volk*, was forced to cease publication and our political radio station, VARA, was silenced. Dutch citizens were forbidden, on pain of severe punishment, to listen to unauthorized broadcasts. Radio Free Holland and Radio Free England, which were broadcast from England, were expressly forbidden. Rules multiplied and were strictly enforced. Dutch Nazis were elevated to official positions, including Burgermeester, operating as front men for the occupying forces. The Jews were not yet treated much differently from the rest of the occupied population except for having to endure a well-nurtured campaign of anti-Semitism.

By the latter part of 1940, however, Jews were beginning to experience cruel discrimination. Jews in civil and government jobs, college professors and schoolteachers were being dismissed. In February 1941 the dockworkers initiated a strike which they tried to widen throughout the city in protest of a street round-up of some Jewish men in the Jewish section of *Amsterdam*. They had been picked up at random as hostages, beaten, and sent off to *KZ Mauthausen*, a concentration camp in Austria, in retaliation for some Nazi-provoked violence the previous day. The workers' strike was a protest in the name of the Dutch people against the Nazi treatment of Dutch Jews. The strike seemed a wonderful victory to us Jews; however, this victory was short-lived because the Nazis threatened to pick up hundreds more Jews if the strike continued. It ended in two days, and was publicized in the press as Jew-incited. More repressive measures followed.

Dutch industry changed considerably. Much of it, including the diamond industry, was forced to re-gear toward industrial production for the German war effort. My father's work became an essential wartime industry, which was fortunate because Jews in unessential work were being deprived of their jobs, or businesses, in ever-increasing numbers. As his factory re-geared production, Papa called me to his side one evening and told me to come back to work in the diamond factory. As your father and a Jew, he advised me, now is a time to seek safety, not dreams.

Once again I accompanied my father to work, and actually it was a relief to do so. Our own neighborhood was on the other side of the *Amstel*, and this required our taking a little rowboat ferry to and from work at the old Asscher factory on the *Tolstraat*. I worked on another floor from that of my father and, again, under a teacher. Picking up quickly on my earlier training, I moved swiftly in my apprenticeship. My small earnings began to increase. My father and I enjoyed taking the ferry home for two-hour lunches with my mother and sister.

Times were anxious. There was now a curfew for Jews. Our prospects looked gloomier by the day, but I did not forget my personal dream. I had bought a few architectural books, and since the curfew confined us to our homes at night, I poured for hours over the texts. There was a volume on the history of architecture, and there were handbooks of technical details then being used in Holland.

I nurtured some secret daydreams, however, about a private ambition that had sprung to life on one of our recent vacation trips to Holland. During a summer vacation trip, in 1941, by myself, to the middle of Holland I had met an attractive and sophisticated young lady from southern Holland of about my age. In a matter of moments she had turned my mind upside down when she began to tell me of her plans to become a licensed pharmacist. A pharmacist! And she…a girl! She asked me what I planned to do with my life. I was taken by surprise but knew I could not tell this girl with whom I was rapidly becoming infatuated that I had never thought about my life as my own to control. I cast about quickly in my mind and remembered my talent for sketching, for which Mevrouw van der Roest used to take me to task as a sign of daydreaming, and I also remembered what I had told my diamond polishing teacher in *Antwerp* a few years earlier. At the same time I had a sudden insight into how much I loved returning to *Amsterdam* and looking about at her buildings, old and new, many of them bearing cornerstone inscriptions to the effect that they were erected by the design of Architect So-and-So in such-and-such a year. I confessed to her that I hoped to become an architect and watched her beam approvingly as if I had not made a perfectly outlandish statement. Such was the moment of my first dawning thoughts on directing myself to a profession I so greatly respected. I began to look at buildings with increasing awareness, noticing with satisfaction that sedate contemporary buildings could live in interesting harmony with medieval neighbors.

During some of my free daytime hours, I roamed the streets studying details of various buildings, old and new, that had been mentioned in my texts. I took a new proud interest in the Asscher Factory where we worked when I read of its design by the distinguished Dutch architect, Dr. H.P. Berlage, and studied, first hand, the features mentioned in my book. The new brick apartment housing on *Saffierstraat*, the similar modern housing in which we had lived in *Antwerp*, the Miranda Baths swimming complex: these projects took on significance as I realized that they were part of the new social planning being evolved by architects of my own time. My father's Social Democratic Party had raised the funds for some of this housing. I delighted in noting the unending variety of brick design work in these structures. From afar, blocks of apartments looked uniform, orderly. On closer inspection each brick complex had its own motif, its own song to sing.

When my sister, Sienie, reached the age of 14 in November 1940, she too was removed from school and put to work. Sienie became a seamstress in a small sewing atelier, or workshop, within the Jewish section on the other side of Professor *Tulpplein*. Her shop made uniforms and other clothing for the Nazi-German Army.

Inflation ballooned and rationing tightened. An active black market sprang up in foods and goods no longer available to the Dutch population. My father jumped into this market as into an exciting new adventure. He enlisted some *Amsterdam* police officers as contacts, who, in turn were in touch with other black marketers and the underground. He began to buy and sell coffee, cheeses, and the like, eventually doing very well for himself. Dad and his accomplices knew that they must not be caught, and so they stuck with known contacts.

He worked out a trade in black-market cheeses with a farmer he knew down the *Amstel River*. In this enterprise I was invited to lend a hand. We rode our bicycles after work, and on weekends, down the *Amstel River* to the farm where we each picked up a couple of great wheels of uncured cheese and concealed them in our saddle bags for the ride back to town. Once back home we carried the cheeses up the three floors to our flat where we placed them on boards in the closets. Every day the cheeses were turned over until they were completely cured. My father sold them whole or in part to those who could afford to buy. He delivered his orders by bicycle, usually to the wealthier sections of town. Looking back, I have to laugh at our black-marketing caper. The whole apartment reeked of cheese. All of our apparently trustworthy neighbors could not help but know about it. The bicycle trips down the *Amstel* with my father were like holidays. Sometimes we made a family outing of our cheese expeditions when my mother and sister accompanied us by bicycle on weekends and brought back extra cheeses.

My mother could now afford to buy cocoa, real coffee, and a few other rarely available delicacies because of my father's enterprise. There was little else to buy besides basic necessities, so my father began to spend the extra guilders he was earning to buy stamp collections. He reasoned that they were good investments and easy to conceal. A good number of months later when the pogroms against the Jews began in earnest, father turned these collections over to one of his police officer associates for safekeeping. He also instructed me as to exactly where they were.

It was not until the spring of 1942 that we Jews were ordered to wear the yellow star patch inscribed *"Jood"* on our outer clothing. From this indignity there was no appeal. When we first appeared in public, marked as ordered, we were heartened that a number of our non-Jewish, working class neighbors donned the star in sympathy. But this protest, too, was swiftly put to an end as these protestors were threatened with having to register as Jews or be imprisoned for misrepresenting their identities.

With stars duly affixed to our chests, we were then easily

subjected to curfews and, for many of us, an unaccustomed ghettoizing. No Jew was allowed on the streets after dark. Jews could shop the stores only at certain hours of the day. Restaurants, movie houses, theaters, and concert halls were forbidden to Jews. All Jewish creative works from books to music were banned to the general public while the Jews were permitted to partake only of Jewish culture. Jews could no longer be treated in non-Jewish hospitals or buy medications from a non-Jewish pharmacy. Our separation from the rest of the population of *Amsterdam* became almost total. We now had to travel quite a distance to the Jewish section for prescription drugs. We associated now only with Jews, fearing for their sakes and ours to visit openly with one-time gentile friends.

A legitimate Jewish theater sprang up on the *Plantage Middenlaan*. This was not a Yiddish theater but a true Dutch Jewish theater, organic and spontaneous, interpreting our experiences. The theater featured some distinguished talent, and was popular with all of us. We attended the Jewish symphony as well, and listened to a limited repertoire of music composed only by Jews but played with inspiration by a fine orchestra, many of whose members were former Concertgebouw players. I was particularly impressed by my introduction to the Jazz innovations of "Rhapsody in Blue," composed by an American Jew, George Gershwin. It is ironic to reflect that this period awakened the sensitivities of us working-class children to the wealth and variety of Jewish cultural life. The movie houses, once an entertainment mainstay, but now closed to us, were replaced by far more rewarding entertainment alternatives.

1942-1943

Shortly after her sixteenth birthday in November 1942 – my sister, Sienie, was still working as a seamstress alongside the new, young wife of my cousin, Hans Rubens, at the uniform atelier in the Jewish section of town. As did my father and I and other working Jews, Sienie carried with her at all times her cherished work permit,

Sippora (Sienie) Rodrigues Garcia taken on her 16th birthday in Amsterdam, The Netherlands, on November 24th, 1942.

which allowed Jews engaged in essential work to pass on the streets. One evening, however, Sienie did not return home from work at the usual time and mother was just beginning to get alarmed when friends rushed in to tell her that Sienie and Hans Rubens' wife had been picked up with other Jewish workers in a street raid in that area. My father and I walked in our front door to find mother in hysterics.

Mother managed to tell us the story of what she had heard, but she could not believe that Sienie, with her work permit, had been picked up. My parents reasoned that the incident had been a terrible mistake. Leaving me to calm mother, Papa ran to the police station to try to get Sienie back. Papa pleaded for hours with a whole bureaucracy of authorities, but to no avail. He learned that the Nazis had raised the drawbridges over the canals surrounding the Jewish section and had picked up Sienie's group near their atelier on a canal on the other side of the Diamond Exchange.

At home my mother screamed and screamed, and tried to throw herself out of the window. My father became very worried, knowing he could no longer leave her alone. He enlisted neighbors and aunts to take turns looking after mother while we continued to go to work. Mother's mind gradually deteriorated after the disappearance of Sienie, and my father no longer laughed or joked. The mood at home was very depressing and one could assume the same thing was true all over *Amsterdam* where similar situations had suddenly happened. Experience was to teach us that this was one of the early calculated raids in which Jews were rounded up at random on the streets, permits or not. Families were torn apart and were afraid to start strong resistive measures for fear of retaliation against their captured members. It was not long before many families we knew had lost someone dear to this diabolical game of psychological roulette. No word of my sister's fate ever did come back to us.

Not knowing what next was in store for any of us Jews, we grimly continued to go to work. Many an evening Papa and I raced our bicycles as usual down the *Amstel* on our cheese-smuggling expeditions in order to make it back home by curfew hour. We felt very close on those rides. In spite of mother's condition Papa tried to stay rational. He was intent upon making, and saving, as much money as possible against the growing uncertainties of our future. In spite of great risks, he continued to deliver black-market cheese. Daily we faced unknowable hazards, and our lives became miserably anxious. Though we lived outside the Jewish section of town, we were registered along with other Jewish neighbors, and our neighborhood began to feel the terror of unexpected raids. Having learned over the months about the Nazi's strange passion for official documents, my father obtained a stamped document from a doctor certifying that I was a chronic sufferer of migraine headaches. Indeed, I had suffered from severe headaches occasionally for many years. In my ninth year my mother had taken me to a doctor who had diagnosed the headaches as migraines.

Papa tacked the doctor's certificate to the door to my bedroom, and told me to be ready to take to my bed at a moment's notice with a feigned migraine attack. When the Nazi's were heard on our street and we knew the inevitable raid was about to descend on us, Papa had me drink a few slugs of Jenever from a bottle he had bought in order to bring on a headache. I then lay down on my narrow bed in the darkened room I had shared until recently with my sister. I heard the approach of boots through our halls and my father's voice talking with the raiders. Then Papa was calling attention to the document affixed to my door. The door swung open and I heard everyone troop in to look at me as I lay on the bed with eyes closed. It is hard for me to believe today that they walked out again and left me to my headache which, by then, was very real and persisted for several days afterwards.

My parents were shaken by my narrow escape and began to look into ways to place me in hiding. Mother became more alert and encouraged father to find a place for me to go. After many weeks of maneuvers, my father managed to secure a hiding place for me though the underground. A network of underground workers served as a conduit to families willing to hide Jews. It was understood that Jewish families would pay the costs of boarding those to be hidden. False documents and ration cards also had to be paid for. I do not know how much it cost my parents to secure a family to take me in and to have the necessary papers forged, but they used much of our black-market savings to pay what was asked. In January 1943, I dropped out of sight at work and in my neighborhood.

I went to an apartment house, as instructed, where a family took me into their third floor flat. It was the Jaap Boas family. They were a middle-aged couple with two sons slightly older than me and they also had a daughter, also older than me, who was married and no longer lived at home. The head of this family was Jewish and had to wear a star but his wife was a gentile. Their children had been raised as Christians and did not have to register as Jews.[2] My father had known my new guardian as a fellow diamond-polisher and as a former socialist colleague. In addition, he was a past chess master of Holland.

My new home was in *Amsterdam-East*, the *Indische Buurt*, a gentile working class neighborhood. Living with the Boas family, I was a voluntary prisoner, not permitted to leave the apartment or even go near the windows, nor was I allowed to wear shoes. For a boy who had once roamed the streets of *Amsterdam* with total independence, this self-enforced restriction to quarters was extremely difficult. Actually, very few Mokummers were on the streets any longer without good reason, and definitely not if their families harbored a Jewish member. Thus, all of us found ourselves restricted to the apartment, and we entertained one another with games, read, or listened to the box-on-the-wall, the radio. The former chess master taught me the rudiments of chess, which I had never played before, then some of the intricacies of strategy as my game developed.

I was hidden before my father finished his negotiations to obtain my false identity papers. The process took a number of months. When the papers arrived, Mrs. Boas accompanied me out of the apartment and into the neighborhood for the first time since I moved in with her family. She took me to a photographer who was considered trustworthy to take my identity picture. Once my papers were in order, members of the Boas family began to drill me relentlessly about my new identity. What's your name? Where were you born? What's

2   In Holland, Jews of mixed marriages and their offspring were often spared if they claimed to be converts. They were apparently spared because of official confusion and disagreement about what should be done about them.

your father's age? Your mother's maiden name? Where do you live? What's your birthday? Every day at odd moments someone would pop a question at me, and my responses had to be automatic, I did not forget the answers, even though I have forgotten them now.

I had brought with me my architectural and technical books. To help me in the study of these, my father had also enrolled me in a correspondence course in architectural drawing. I worked for long periods on course assignments, and then mailed them off, using the name of one of the sons. My father sneaked up to see me on occasion, a trip of great personal risk since he had to remove his star and hope he would not be challenged for an inspection of his papers. With both children gone, mother's mental condition had continued to worsen, and father could not disguise his own depression in telling me this and other news. Mother sent heart-breaking messages of love. I missed them both very much, and wept with my father as we talked. Many members of our extended family had already been picked up. Papa went over with me exactly where our few valuables were hidden.

Late in June my father and mother had come to see me to help me celebrate my nineteenth birthday. In order to do so they had to remove their stars from their outer garments at great risk to themselves, as I have stated before, but now with my mother's deteriorating mental condition the jeopardy to themselves and to the Boas family had increased tremendously. The Boas family allowed them to come and visit but they never stayed long. I received a few gifts and to this day I do not remember what they were. I did not know, then, that I would never see them again.

One nightmarish day the news was brought to me that my parents had been picked up in a neighborhood sweep. The news was not unexpected. Many other relatives and friends had been picked up. The disappearance of Jews had become routine. But my father's and mother's disappearance was almost more than I could cope with. I tried to bear my grief silently. The Boas family understood and tried to comfort me. My grief was a great block within me. Tears did not come, except sometimes in the night when my inner numbness gave way to despairing wailing.

The Boas family and I continued to study, read, and play chess. I was not to realize until many years later that my parents had given me far more than their love and their savings trying to insure that I, at least, could be spared. I was to be reborn many times on the strength of their parenting. My mother had been attentive and affectionate. She had kept me firmly rooted and busy in our family and community. My father encouraged my independence and my abilities. He had been pleased to have me learn my way around the city. He had approved my bicycle trip from *Antwerp* to *Amsterdam* and back. He had assigned me the task of moving the family furniture from one city to another. He had allowed me to try to change my status as a diamond polisher.

Every time I recall having yelled, "It's been a long time since I had a Lucky Strike," to a liberating American tank sergeant, I thank my father for teaching me to think on my feet and for insisting I learn English. That yelled phrase changed the course of my life.

Again, I thank my father for sharing with me his gift of humor. The ability to laugh, even in desperate situations, is as good for life as food and drink. To cry is to feel worse. I know. I have wept copious tears and suffered great headaches and great depressions. To laugh is to feel better. I prefer laughter. I make an effort to laugh.

July – August 1943

Night air raids on Germany had begun by the summer of 1943. The Allies, on one occasion in early June, apparently plotted their course to Germany by way of *Amsterdam-East* where some key German war plants were located. These plants were bombed one night in June by Allied planes. When the air raid sirens sounded the "all-clear" practically our whole neighborhood ran out of their apartments to watch great fires leaping in the air where only hours before the plants had stood. I joined the milling crowd before the Germans arrived to chase us all back into our apartments.

In late July, early evening, after dinner, one of the sons of the Boas family thought he heard cars stop in front of our building and taking a peek through the curtains he practically shouted:

"The Gestapo is below!"

"Max, get to the roof! Hurry!"

I ran up the steps to the roof, tore across it, and hid behind a raised skylight on the far side of the roof. Sure enough, the Gestapo was looking for me. They searched the apartment thoroughly but could find no trace of me since I could and did wear the clothes of the sons. Two Gestapo agents finally came up the stairs to the roof. I saw the strong beams of their flashlights illuminating every detail along the roofline, including my skylight. But the agents did not cross the roof. They retreated back down the stairs. I remained crouched behind the skylight in the still night air, hardly daring to breathe, for what seemed a very long time. Finally, I was called back down and told that I would have to leave the apartment at once because somebody must have betrayed my presence. A few things had been packed for me, including some money. We parted with feelings that could be seen in one another's eyes but could hardly be expressed in words. Only a couple of weeks had gone by since I had seen my parents when they came by to help me celebrate my birthday and they were gone, picked up, and now I was being hunted down.

I was on the street before I could collect my thoughts. The Boas family had given me an address of a safe house where I was to go at once. I realized, when they gave me the address, that it was in my very old neighborhood, the *Topaasstraat*, and I hurried there not once being challenged while on the streets. When I rang the door bell in a prescribed manner I recognized the person at once and he recognized me. He asked about my parents whom he had known before we moved to *Antwerp*. My father and he had worked together during election campaigns. I remained in that place for a few days while the underground was trying to find me another hiding location. Alas, to no avail.

I told the people with whom I was staying that my cousin, Hans Rubens, had shown me where his parents, Tante Griet and Oom Meijer, kept the key to their apartment on the van Woustraat. I knew that they had been picked up long since. Following a strong hunch that their key would still be there, I made my way cautiously through the night streets the considerable distance to their apartment. Just as

I had hoped, the key was in its hiding place. I opened the door and walked in. The place was deserted but eerily as it must have been on the day my relatives had hurriedly left it. I took up residence, helping myself to supplies and using the place as my own, risking trips outside only for needed food. On the streets I carried with me my false identity card. My days alone at the apartment stretched into seeming weeks, but, in truth, I had lost track of time. The nights within the apartment came early, with the falling of outside light, for I did not dare put on interior lights.

I began to make elaborate plans to escape by bicycle to Belgium, then through France to Switzerland, using my assumed identity. Papa had told me that my bicycle had been entrusted to friends on the *Graaf Florisstraat*. I went to see them about it and to ask access to my parents' apartment. Our apartment had been sealed, they told me so no access was possible without breaking the seal, but they also assured me my bicycle would be ready whenever I needed it. I returned then to the Rubens apartment and dawdled further over my plans for escape. I did not want to admit to myself how truly hopeless I felt about that trip. I was spared further efforts to ready my plans, get supplies and to work up the courage to push off when the doorbell rang one early afternoon. At first I did not answer it, but when the ringing persisted, I opened the door.

"You're Max Garcia," stated one of the two Dutchmen in civilian clothes.

"No, I'm so and so," I replied, using my assumed name.

"No, you're Max Garcia. What are you doing here?"

"You can see I'm living here. Here are my papers if you want to see them."

"You are under arrest, Max Garcia. Come with us."

They marched me off without ceremony, taking me by car to a police station where I underwent my first interrogation and received my first beating at the hands of these Dutch Gestapo agents. I was then taken to the Jewish Theater on the *Plantage Middenlaan*. The theater had been transformed into a collection place for Jews who were, I was told, to be sent to Westerbork, a transit camp in northeastern Holland, near *Groningen*.

There I was interrogated again but this time by Dutch Nazis. At first I maintained that my false identity was my correct one. They insisted that they had proof that I was Max Rodrigues Garcia, Sephardic Jew, and the son of Elias and Rozette Rodrigues Garcia. I capitulated. Yes, I was Max Rodrigues Garcia. Where had I been keeping myself all this time, they wanted to know. I told them I had moved from place to place. They wanted more specifics and I made up a few places where I might have hidden. Where had I obtained my false identity papers, they wanted to know. I told them that I got papers through the underground, made up a rendezvous place, but maintained I knew no names. They worked at trapping me into changing answers but I stuck to my story even though I got my second beating from them there. They released me then and threw me into the theater-auditorium-turned-prison, which was filled with Jews.

The seats had been removed. I tried to stake out a small place for myself on the crowded floor. I spent a number of weeks there. We could hardly clean ourselves, and we reeked, being unwashed. Water was in short supply. We were fed regularly, but the meals were unappetizing. Little did I know that there would soon come a day when I would remember those meals as generous and good.

We who were held prisoner in the auditorium remained in that place for maybe a couple of weeks after which we were carted off in trucks and taken to Transit Camp *Westerbork*. Upon arrival there some hours later I was placed in a Punishment Barrack which was another "holding barrack" for people, like myself, who had gone into hiding and been caught.

To think that it had been a little more than a month ago that I had turned 19; now here it was well into August 1943 and it would be soon, I imagined, that I would go on a transport to – where? To think that my parents had been here not too long ago and before them it had been Sienie. Where were they now, I wondered.

It was either the 22nd or 23rd of August 1943 when I was removed from the Punishment Barrack and taken to the loading place where I and many others were pushed into boxcars that were then sealed. The boxcar I was in was loaded with men, women and children. A single can for relieving ourselves stood in a corner of the boxcar, the only amenity conceded, and that a mockery, it turned out, as the days went by. We carried with us rations of food and water that each of us had been given for the trip. We were also allowed to bring whatever other supplies and valuables we had with us when we were arrested. I had only the clothes I was wearing.

Daylight through slats in the siding of the boxcar was our only light. The train rolled along, then pulled to a halt from time to time, and would stand for hours. Sometimes bombs would fall nearby. Behavior broke down among our wretched numbers. Some panicked and became hysterical. Some cried. Some behaved like animals one to another. Some went into shock and withdrew completely while others copulated. We had our own specially provided hell in those boxcars, which moved, then stopped, then moved again, but the doors were never opened. After an unremembered number of days and nights the train must have come to its destination because now we had been standing still for a number of hours. Through the slats we could see it was still dark outside. Suddenly there was a great deal of noise and movement outside and the door of our boxcar was yanked open.

Blinking at the piercing bright lights and barely able to move our joints, we were hustled out of the cars by *SS* bullies who introduced us to the persuasive power of truncheons. "*Raus! Raus! Raus! Raus!*" they shouted as they laid into our backs with their clubs. During this frantic process people were also trying to collect their belongings.

"Leave your luggage alone. Leave it here. You'll get your luggage later," they instructed.

"Men over there! Women over here!"

I also saw men in vertically striped uniforms wearing peculiarly striped caps at the railroad siding and wondered who they were and what they were doing there.

Families tried to cling together, while dogs held by *SS* guards were barking, but people were roughly pulled apart and lined up by gender. Then the *SS* separated us further, ordering some of the men from the men's line and some of the women from theirs. All the men, and the women as well, had to pass in front of some *SS* officers

79

who looked us over, and in some cases they would ask questions of an individual, after which we were divided into two groups. One group consisted of men who perhaps were, or looked, older than 35 while the group I was assigned to consisted basically of boys in their teens and men in their twenties and early thirties. Later on we heard that the women had to endure a similar selection process. A "selection" which I would personally experience several times again later on, was a process whereby people were selected to stay alive or be gassed. All this at the whim of an *SS* officer or, in some cases, *SS* non-commissioned officers.

What we did see was an organized commotion of screaming, barking, shouting of orders in German. Such chicanery was meant to totally intimidate newly-arrived people. My group was taken to a barracks and told to remove all our clothes but to keep our belts and shoes. All the rest, wedding rings, regular rings, and watches were all taken away while the clothes were to be thrown onto a heap. All our hair was shaved off. After this we were interrogated individually about our histories: name, date of birth, occupation, hometown, country, etc.

When I was asked what sort of work I had done prior to my arrest I told them I had been a carpenter. Illogical as it may seem, I remembered reading in one of my texts that the basis of architecture was carpentry. If I was to work, I thought, I might as well start learning first hand about building. A number was placed on the piece of paper that held my information and I was directed to another table where that number was tattooed on my left forearm: "139829". When all of us had gone through this procedure we were taken to the showers, actually chased through them. At the end of this we received our "new" clothes, which were old clothes of indifferent fit on which stripes had been painted. We were given two pieces of cloth that had our number stenciled on them and told to sew them on; one on the left breast (where not too long ago a yellow star had been) and one on the right trouser leg facing the outside about thigh high.

The interview was done by men in striped uniforms and the only languages spoken were Yiddish and German. All of us were

Dutch and none of us spoke or understood Yiddish although there were some among us who had a very slight understanding of German and they now became interpreters out of necessity. Some of the commands shouted to us we did not understand at all, which made our guards very agitated and angry. We were completely isolated, unwanted aliens in a hostile place. It now began to sink in that we were actually prisoners although at this time we still did not know where we were. We now also received our first meal and inasmuch as we had not yet been issued eating bowls we shared the few we had and slurped down what was called a soup. Those who had brought luggage never did see their luggage again. Before we had been packed onto the train at Transit Camp *Westerbork*, everyone had been persuaded to bring their valuables as well as their clothing and had been told to prepare for a long stay. Once the Dutch Jews had left the train, the Nazis had taken everything out of the boxcars, with the help of those men in the striped uniforms who had been at the railroad siding when we arrived.

That afternoon we were marched onto trucks and driven a few miles past crowded prisoner-of-war camps and what appeared to be big chemical factories, belching smoke. We arrived at a tent camp where we were unloaded under harsh prodding by Polish Jews who spoke only Yiddish. We were assigned to a huge tent. The dirt floor was covered with a layer of yellow straw. That night, searching my mind for a few Yiddish words, I asked an old timer next to me where we were and what this place was. I learned that we had been transported to *Silesia*, a portion of southwest Poland, that we were in *Buna*, a sub-camp of Concentration Camp *Auschwitz*, places I had never heard of before. I also learned that we had been ordered to one of the fortunate lines when we were unloaded from the boxcars. Everyone else of that transport had been gassed by then.

Entrance to KZ Auschwitz - Birkenau. Photo by Lesley De Boelpaep, 123rf.com

Part 3

The Camps

KZ Buna, 1943

I labored in *KZ Buna*, a sub-camp of *KZ Auschwitz*, only a short time, perhaps a couple of weeks, helping to build a factory for I.G. Farben, a major German Chemical Company. My fellow prisoners and I were ill prepared for the harshness that was now our routine lot. Everyone who had some authority could and did beat us and badger us at their pleasure.

There were the *Kapos* who where in charge of our individual laboring groups, and *Kommandos*, who were answerable for the work output of their groups. The *Kapos* were fellow prisoners who had been around for some time, earning their position by being tough and being favored. A *Blockälteste* (Senior Block Prisoner), a similarly experienced prisoner, was in charge of either a Block or a tent, and was helped in performing his duties by favored prisoners called *Stubendienst* (Room Servers). The *Kapos* and the *Blockältesten* were often chosen from the Polish and German criminal or political groups, but there were experience-hardened Jews as well, bent on winning the daily game of survival. We ordinary prisoners were the *Haftlingen*. The *SS* guards and administrators exacted their dues in various ways from the "*Prominenten*" (Prominent Prisoners), thus sparing themselves much of the unpleasant work of the daily prison routine. This system, through which we were controlled, I learned only slowly, however, and by many bitter lessons.

We slept on straw-covered floors of huge tents. Each tent housed easily several hundred, if not thousands, of prisoners. Each morning we were awakened well before dawn and made to stand for long periods at Roll Call while our numbers and bodies were counted off in blocks, checked and rechecked. Each one of us was assigned to an *Arbeitskommando* (Work Detail), to which we then reported for yet another line-up and another Roll Call. Daily I marched off in my *Kommando*, accompanied by our *Kapos* and the *SS* Guards, to a factory, which was some distance away from our camp on the other side of the military POW camps. I worked on the second floor of the I.G. Farben plant, carrying cinder blocks back and forth. The work was heavy and was very hard on me. I had been accustomed to the robust diet of my homeland, even during the occupation, but in *KZ Buna* I was hungry all the time. We *Haftlingen* received a sweetened cup of brown liquid in the morning, sometimes called tea, other times called coffee, a bowl of so-called soup at noon at the work site, and a hunk of bread that measured about 4"x4"x2" that was doled out after the evening Roll Call. It was called "bread" but it had none of the nutrients in it that we associated with bread. It was a filler, pure and simple.

Lying on the straw of our tent at night, we Dutch Jews whispered together, exchanging shocking stories about the incredible things each of us was experiencing. We asked one another if this inhuman regimen was to represent our last days on earth. Some were already growing weak, and many were heartsick with the knowledge of loved ones having been gassed or wondering about the fate of dear ones. We tried to cheer one another with accounts of remembered family scenes but often choked back tears instead of finishing our stories. We described to one another the foods we missed most, the most memorable meals we had eaten, foods we planned to eat if we ever got away from this place.

Most of us Dutch Jews were at a loss to understand much of the German and Polish spoken by our *Blockältesten, Kapos, Stubendienst* and *SS* Guards. For this we suffered a great deal. One evening on the way back from the factory some words were hurled my way that I could not understand, and I was severely beaten by a *Kapo*. I broke down and cried. That night in my sleeping space I was still crying, utterly defeated, and too exhausted and hungry to sleep. That my father, mother and sister were gone burst fully into my mind. Remembered scenes of our lives together ran through my head and were more than I could bear. And what did I have to look forward to? These madmen were going to work me until my last ounce of strength was gone. They wanted me to die. They couldn't wait for me to die. All around me, weakened, exhausted, dying men showed me what a little more time here would bring all of us to.

As I continued to mutter and sob out my despair, I heard a voice in my ear, a Polish voice. An older prisoner, probably in his late twenties, who was a tent mate, laid a hand on my shoulder. "Hey, young one," he tried in Yiddish, then in halting French, "don't cry. That won't help."

"But I can't help it. I am afraid to die," I got across in my limited French. We began to talk to each other, switching languages, groping for words we might each understand. He asked me to tell him the story of my background, and I did as well as I could.

"That is a sad story, boy, but everyone here has a sad story. So let me ask you this: do you want to survive this camp or die sometime soon like most of these poor bastards?"

"Of course, I want to live, but how in a place like this?"

"That's what I want to tell you, boy, and listen to me well. From now on never think of where you came from or about your family and friends. Think only of today and what you must do to stay ahead of your captors. Just figure you dropped out of the sky into this awful place. You have to survive. You have to live for the future. Forget all that has passed. Toughen up. Learn their games and outsmart them."

A heavy dose of philosophy these words were for me at the age of 19, but I thought about them a great deal and resolved to try to live by his advice. I wanted to hope. Without hope, I realized, I could not last many more days.

I concentrated on learning the meaning of the German and Polish phrases and epithets barked at us constantly, and made an effort to answer in their languages. I began to withdraw from many of the evening discussions about the old days among my fellow Dutch Jews. I paid attention to how things worked, who was controlling what, and what was happening in this prison. We *Haftlingen* knew about the high voltage electrical barbed-wire fencing around the camp – a high, menacing double fence, one about 12 feet inside the other. We had seen men throw themselves against the inside fence rather than experience another day. We knew now about the gas chambers and the crematoria in the *KZ Auschwitz-Birkenau* camp complex. Instead of being gassed on our arrival as thousands were being gassed every week, we had been lucky enough to be assigned to a war factory's slave labor force until we gave up our bodies to starvation and exhaustion. We did not see the gas chambers or the trainloads of people streaming into them, but we smelled the stench of the crematoria and saw the heavy, yellow-black smoke coming out of their chimneys. The grapevine told us the rest. I saw many men give up their will to live. I swore that I would never be one of them. I would try hard to live.

At the factory we worked as flunkies to civilians, along with some British and French POWs. These were enlisted men who, according to the Geneva Convention, could be forced to work. The Convention was honored in the matter of their officers, however, who were protected from such labor. In the hope of cadging a bite to eat or a cigarette, I decided one day to try to talk to a French soldier working beside me. Hearing me, a *Kapo* put a stripe across my back with his rubber hose, and ordered me not to try to talk with the POWs. On the way back to the factory the next day, however, this same *Kapo* moved next to me and whispered:

"Hey, you! Do you like to talk with those Frenchmen? Well, now, I'll let you have one little talk today if you'll promise to get me some cigarettes."

"I'll try," I muttered in German, surprised, frightened, hopeful. I managed to cadge three cigarettes from my French work companion, which I took to the *Kapo* and was rewarded with one for myself. From then on the *Kapo* counted on me at the factory. I bummed cigarettes and small handouts of food, first with my French, then trying my English. All booty was given over to the sharp-eyed *Kapo*, who paid me always with a small share.

There were many items we did not have in *KZ Buna*. We did not have socks, handkerchiefs, underwear or shirts. Our garments consisted exclusively of a pair of very second-hand trousers and a very second-hand jacket plus a cap. We did not have a toothbrush or toothpaste, no soap, no towels and, of course, no use at all for a comb. There was no toilet paper. As stated earlier we had been allowed to keep our shoes and belt. There were no bed sheets, no pillows and we slept in our clothes.

KZ Auschwitz 1943

In the process of setting down a heavy load of cinder blocks at the factory, I crushed my left middle finger. I wrapped it up and tried to forget it but in a matter of days a painful abscess developed. I applied for and received permission to visit the first-aid station. The doctor took a look at my infection, then ordered me for treatment to the Main Camp Hospital in *KZ Auschwitz*. I was lucky for had I not still been a fairly new prisoner, still comparatively strong and well fleshed out, they would not have bothered to keep me alive. Thus, in mid- September 1943, I was transferred to the Main Camp Hospital in *KZ Auschwitz*, where I was placed in a ward of prisoners with communicable diseases. The finger was treated, I was allowed to rest, and the infection subsided. Discharged, I was not sent back to *KZ Buna* but assigned to a laboring *Kommando* with *KZ Auschwitz*. This was another typical slave laboring detail requiring us to stoop, lift, fetch, and carry.

I was assigned to an enormous brick building, called a "Block," one of similar two-story buildings on the streets, some with basement punishment cells. We slept in bunks stacked four high, two to a bunk at that time, in a forest of bunks that were reached by means of a central and several secondary corridors. The bunks were wooden, filled with wooden slats and straw, and covered with a dirty piece of blanket.

Very few Dutch Jews were transferred out of *KZ Buna* into the main camp. Along with a few Dutch Jews there was a scattering of Dutch gentiles, but in my Block none were nearby. I was surrounded mostly by Poles and Germans. Life in our Block was primitive. Arguments, pushing, and shoving, were routine.

"You stole the bread I was hiding," one prisoner would accuse another, all in German, of course.

"No, I did not steal your bread," the other would answer.

"I was in line first!"

"No, I was here first and you know it!"

Fighting sometimes broke out at the lunchtime soup line at the work site about one's place in the line. Cries of "Stir the soup before you serve me!" were often heard from prisoners who knew that unless the soup was stirred the solids would settle on the bottom.

At night, in the Block, no one complained that we were compelled to turn in early, but there were complaints, beatings and kicks over too much turning onto another's part, or constant snoring, coughs or other noises. Dim lights were kept on in the Block all through the night, but it was not unusual to have them flicker out from time to time. We knew then that some desperate prisoner had gone from his Block and had run into the high voltage electric fence that surrounded the camp, thereby shorting out the electrical system. In the morning we would see the charred remains of a former prisoner still hanging in the high voltage electric fence. It was not until all the *Arbeitskommandos* had marched off to work that the electricity was turned off and a special detail was sent to the fence to scrape off the remains which were then sent to the crematorium.

In the early days of my stay in *KZ Auschwitz*, after I had been released from the hospital, and before I was assigned to a permanent *Arbeitskommando*, I served in a detail that cleaned the twelve-foot corridor between the high voltage electric fences each morning after the electricity had been turned off. Followed by gun-toting *SS* guards, we picked up litter that had blown into that area. I managed to hide in my clothing a few usable scraps of paper and cloth.

After I was admitted to the main concentration camp, the makeshift garments I had been issued in *KZ Buna* were replaced by a gray-and-blue-striped uniform. For my feet I had my still serviceable leather shoes, and I still had my belt to hold up my trousers. We had lightweight uniforms for summer, heavier ones for winter, all of it striped – our sole possession – except for a baked-enamel, burgundy-colored bowl, which went everywhere with us and usually hung from our belts; we also had received a spoon. As part of our uniforms we also wore a matching striped cap. The cap was required daytime wear, and it had to be removed whenever an *SS* guard walked by. As a new prisoner I was sickened to witness the stomping and kicking senseless of a prisoner who had forgotten to remove his cap when an *SS* guard walked by. My head was again shaved and a two-inch-wide and about half-an-inch-high stripe of hair was left standing in the center, from my forehead to the rear of my skull. The entire concentration camp complement wore that haircut, except for some elite (*Prominenten*) criminal and political prisoners who had been in the camps for so many years that they were permitted to cut their hair in the style of the *SS* guards. Many months later our center stripe cut was reversed. The hair was then allowed to grow out about a half-inch over our skulls, and a two-inch-wide stripe was mowed down the center.

My uniform bore an insignia patch, a red and yellow Star of David identifying me as a Jew. As I remember, the red triangle of the star was up, the yellow down. My prison number, the same one tattooed on my forearm, was stenciled to the right of the Star of David. It was worn on the upper left side of the striped jacket and on the right trouser leg. The prisoners displayed a variety of insignia patches. Except for the Jews, these were in the form of triangles: Green for professional criminals (mostly German), Red for politicals (enemies of the State of many nationalities), Purple for Jehovah's Witnesses. There were Black triangles, Pink triangles and some other colors, all having a different designation.

On a typical *KZ Auschwitz* day, as at *KZ Buna*, we were awakened at 4:30 A.M. with loud cries of *"Aufstehen! Aufstehen!"* as the lights in all the Blocks were turned on. We lined up at the latrines, then the water tap to splash ice-cold water over our faces (there was no hot water) before heading into the early morning frigid air and lining up again for our daily ration of tea. At least it was hot and sweetened; I drank mine with a piece of bread, which I had learned to save from the bread ration I had received the previous early evening. Sometimes, there was a little margarine or a thin slice of salami or ersatz cheese that we spread on the bread with our spoon, one side of which had been filed down so it could be used as a knife. At that early morning hour we were usually cold, summer or winter, and the food was inadequate to take the chill from our bodies. I had learned to divide my nightly ration of bread into three pieces. One piece I ate at night when it was doled out, then another piece in the morning with tea. At mid-morning, on the job site, when I felt faint from lack of food, I would head off into the stinking latrine to eat my third piece of bread in secret, ignoring the reeking stench and filth and the hundreds of flies that swarmed about. I chose to eat and hold onto life.

Every morning at 6:00 A.M. a bell sounded for "Roll Call" and for us to line up outside our Blocks. We found our places and started being counted off by fives. We were always grouped in units of five, blocks of 20, groups of 100. When the long chore of counting and rechecking was completed, we were permitted to return to our Blocks for a half-hour, supposedly to clean them. What we were doing mainly, those of us who had the strength, was attempting to clean ourselves. Our bodies were crawling with lice, and we worked frantically to keep their numbers down. We would take extra time to wash ourselves at the ice-cold water tap, take our clothes off to shake them out then sit, like monkeys, picking lice from our bodies and out of the seams of our jackets and trousers. As I have mentioned we wore the same clothes all the time. Our work clothes by day were our extra blanket at night. Our prison stripes were never washed. When we washed our bodies, we used whatever pieces of cloth we could find for toweling and then hid those pieces away somewhere so we did not have to go out with wet clothing. We were very vigilant in our search for any scraps of paper or cloth, even leaves, not only to wrap around our feet or wear under our jackets for warmth, but to use for cleaning ourselves after bowel movements. We jealously guarded and washed scraps of material that could serve as toweling.

The bell would sound again and we would break for the area in front of the main kitchen where the prisoners lined up each day with their *Arbeitskommandos*. The process of the marching out of the *Arbeitskommandos* was not unlike the assembling of a civic parade. Curious as it may seem, the *SS* provided a marching band, composed of recruited prisoners, to tootle us out of the main gate each morning. The band *Kommando* assembled along with the rest of us, and, when we were all present and accounted for, struck up martial tunes as we began our orderly cadenced march through the formal, wrought-iron gate, each *Kommando* in its proper order and being counted once more as we passed through the main gate, always removing our caps to the order, "*Mutzen ab!*" We marched five abreast in sections of 20 each, depending on the size of the *Arbeitskommando*. Some were 500 strong. A few were composed of no more than 12 men. Each group had its *Kapo* and assistant *Kapo*. Once beyond the main gate *SS* guards fell in on either side of us and behind us. As each *Kommando* veered off in the direction of its assigned work area, prisoners dropped their military cadence; our posture slumped in favor of an exhausted shuffle toward our job sites. We worked at bending, lifting, carrying from 7:30 A.M. until noon. Our guards prodded us often to work faster, and beat any of us soundly who were caught pausing to rest. At midday, soup kettles were brought to the site and we were lined up to hold out our bowls for our daily ration of a very thin soup. This was our main meal for the day. To eat was to feel only slightly fueled. We no longer felt hunger pains but we were glassy-eyed with the effort of forcing our ebbing energy. Half an hour later we crawled back to work and labored until 4:30 P.M. when the clean-up process began. By 5:00 P.M. we were straggling back to camp in rough formation, our strength utterly used up.

The process of return was a little less demanding than the morning routine in that we could enter the camp in the order of our arrival. At the main gate we were greeted once more with musical fanfare. After the first few days we no longer looked up as we entered the camp to read the mocking words, "*Arbeit Macht Frei*" (Work Makes You Free), spelled out in wrought-iron on the entrance side of the main gate's iron archway. If an *SS* guard became suspicious that any prisoner might be concealing something he was subjected to an *organisiert*, really a body search, outside the camp. So went our routine, six days a week. Sunday was a day off and we could rest. Food rations were cut down on Sundays, but I learned it was a good day to scavenge for needed items and to make contacts among the privileged ones in the hope of being given a job or errand that paid off in food.

The soles of my leather shoes gradually disappeared from my feet, and I was issued a pair of rough wooden clogs. Fortunately,

I knew how to keep my feet warm in clogs by wrapping them, for I had plenty of practice in Holland during the lean years. I looked about me constantly on the work site and in the camp for scraps of paper or rags with which to keep my feet warm and dry. The protection of my feet, I was learning and observing, was the key to my survival. I saw feet and ankles of many a prisoner swell up due to malnutrition, and observed that death was not far behind. I saw the wet and frozen toes of some of my fellow prisoners rot from gangrene, and again death followed naturally, or was given a helping hand. Any injury, infection, or circulation defect in the lower extremities could be fatal. Taking good care of my feet became an obsession. I guarded them as well as possible as I worked, and watched where I put them down. No matter how tired or sick I might feel, I washed and dried my feet attentively each day.

One thing we prisoners wanted very badly, after we had been introduced to it, was a clove of garlic. We were told it would increase our chances of not getting ill and it had other attributes as well. We didn't doubt those who told us about it. Personally I had never heard of or tasted garlic because my mother never used it in her cooking. We rubbed it on our bread, used it sparingly and safeguarded it on our bodies. It was like gold and one could trade a stroke of the garlic on the other fellow's piece of bread for something he offered in turn.

Once every few months the camp administration surprised us with a shower and delousing process for the whole Block at one time. The order, without fail, came in the late evening or during the night. "Hey you bastards, strip and head for the bathhouse. Move!" "*Raus! Raus!*" Ordered out a floor at a time, we started running in line through the cold night air, hastened along by lashes to our backs and legs from the rubber hoses of the *Kapos* and *SS*. At the bathhouse we were driven through a battery of scalding hot shower outlets that we tried to avoid as best we could and still do some rudimentary cleansing of ourselves with a small piece of crude soap we were given before entering this watery hell. At the end of the shower room we were halted in front of other prisoners who were armed with rough-bristled brushes which they dipped in a strong delousing solution and then applied vigorously to our heads, armpits, and crotches. On our way out from the bathhouse we were given a clean jacket and clean trousers, all this while on the run, because we were not allowed to put them on, and we dashed naked back into the now freezing night air and to our bunks. There we tried to dry ourselves, but spent the rest of the night shivering, losing the battle to regain our lost bodily warmth. Indeed, we found that as malnutrition took its toll, we were less and less able to cope with extremes of heat and cold.

The term for a dying man among the *Haftlingen* was *Muselmann*, and *Muselmanner*. These, being poor workers, were not kept around long. We grew accustomed to seeing members of the *Totenkommando* pulling open carts filled with *Muselmanner* toward the gas chambers in *Auschwitz-Birkenau*. The *Muselmanner* had been stripped of their jackets and bore their prison identity numbers in bold stenciling across their bare chests. Some moaned, some cried out for help, some kept their silence, some prayed with others as they were slowly pulled to their doom. We *Haftlingen* soon learned to look away when we heard these death carts coming.

After a number of weeks of work in my assigned put-down-pick-up detail, my prisoner number was called out during one of the evening Roll Calls. This was a dangerous matter, to have my number called out like that, and my heart began pounding with fright. I reported to the location ordered and learned, to my immense relief, that I had been reassigned to another work detail. I could hardly believe my good fortune: I was to report to the *Tischlerei Kommando* (carpentry detail). By now, however, the main cause of my happiness was that I was going inside. It was almost October, and winter would not be long in coming. The card noting my trade had evidently made its way through channels from *KZ Buna*.

I started my new job in high spirits though I had never done any work like it before. All prisoners in the *Kommando* presumably were carpenters. I watched them and did what they did in the midst of the heavy and sharp-bladed machinery of our plant: rabbeters, sanders, planers, saws. I shoved boards through a planing machine to another man who picked them up. Together we stacked them. The work was hard but at least I was doing something I found interesting. Above all, it was pleasant to be indoors as the fall wind and rain blew wildly across the camp area. In addition the *Kapos* would leave you alone and the *SS* guards were not allowed on the factory floor so the beatings I had been receiving in the former *Arbeitskommando* were no longer an issue here and the *SS* dogs could no longer lunge at me. There were no other Dutch prisoners in the *Tischlerei Kommando*.

My German and Polish were improving daily. All other languages, I had come to realize, had no value. They were useful only for social communication. They did not help a man survive. For instance, all prisoner identity numbers were called out in German and/or Polish each morning at Roll Call. Woe to the prisoner who did not comprehend an order directly addressed to him. Many of the *Kapos* were Polish and, hating the Germans, did not like to be addressed in German. The *SS* only used German. Both the Poles and the Germans were extremely anti-Semitic. I determined to learn both languages well to try to overcome some of the overwhelming odds against me as a Jew. If you could converse with your enemy, I figured, there was the possibility of getting through to him as a human being, even of getting one of those extra jobs that contributed to survival.

Eventually, I managed to do just that. I was assigned to help bring the tea to the Block early in the morning and, on Sundays, the soup. This meant I had to get up much earlier than the other prisoners and give up precious resting time on Sunday, but to get a little extra tea or soup was worth it. I would scrape out the empty wooden soup bucket with my fingers. By occasionally winning the chore of shining the shoes of *Kapos* or *Blockältesten* I could get a piece of bread. Thus I traded my extra labor for food, and developed my skills of "*organisierung*," which meant the gathering in of things by any means available for one's personal needs. It did not mean stealing from other needy prisoners.

I held my ground in the carpentry shop. If I was not an efficient worker, my defects did not stand out. None of us were efficient. The Nazis understood that if they got a fifty-percent effort from their prisoners they were doing well. The heavy output of the plant came from paid civilian employees under whom we worked. Our *Kapos* were responsible for providing a certain quota of prisoners per day and seeing that they produced a modicum of work. If too many prisoners began reporting sick, the *Kapos* would crack down and would beat any man who had reported sick when he returned to work. We had to weigh these factors, and most of us did not report to the hospital without good reason.

At the time when we were chased through the showers at the bathhouse, which happened at the end of autumn, our summer uniforms were taken away from us, as I've stated above, and now we were issued winter uniforms. We got jackets, trousers and over-coats but again, as in *Buna*, no socks, no underwear, no shirts, no handkerchiefs, no toothbrushes, no toothpaste, no soap, no towels, no washcloths and no toilet paper. Our hair was trimmed every so often by the barracks "*Friseur*" (barber), and his assistants, and they also shaved us with straightedge razors the cutting edge of which was murderously jagged.

KZ Auschwitz, 1944

By late winter, probably January or February 1944, I met a fellow Dutchman, Lex van Weren. We met while both of us were being treated in the *KZ Auschwitz* main hospital. Lex was a tall Jewish boy from *Amsterdam* who had been pulled out from the coal-mining sub-Camp of *KZ Auschwitz*, called *KZ Janina*. Working in that coal mine, standing knee deep in water, one's life expectancy was about 90 calendar days. Lex told me that he had been a virtuoso trumpet player in Holland at the tender age of 14 (Lex was five years older than I) and had begun to play professionally by the time he was in his late teens. During an evening Roll Call in *KZ Janina* his number was called out and when he reported after Roll Call he learned that one of the *Kapos*, a fellow Dutchman, had told one of the *SS* non-commissioned officers that Lex was a prominent trumpet player in Holland.

It was close to Christmas 1943, and the *SS* guards had been drinking heavily. When he reported as ordered he was given an old cornet that one of them had been able to get hold of. "Play it for us." They ordered. "Play Silent Night, Jew. Surely if you are a musician you must know it well." They told him he had two days to learn to play "Silent Night," which he was to play on Christmas Eve. The cornet leaked air and was badly dented, so he spent his first day working on it until it produced a reasonably proper sound. At the same time he had to get his lips back in control, since he hadn't played for quite a while.

But he met their challenge. Standing in front of the Christmas tree that had been placed in the center of the *Appellplatz*, he played "Silent Night" for all the *SS* men and the entire prisoner complement. In their maudlin state the *SS* guards thought his performance was wonderful. After he had played it once he was ordered to play it again and then again while the *SS* guards got soused even more. He told me he could not remember how many times he played "Silent Night" but it was well into the early morning hours of Christmas Day before they allowed him to stop.

He did not have to go back into the coal mines and now became the "Camp Musician." He was allowed to practice on the cornet and was expected to play for the *SS* whenever it suited them.

Several days into the New Year Lex was transferred to *KZ Auschwitz* Main Camp Hospital with an ailment or two he had gotten while in the mine standing in water up to his knees for about 12 hours each day. The trip to *KZ Auschwitz* was his reward. As we got to know each other in the hospital, Lex described to me his nightmare ride from *KZ Janina* to *KZ Auschwitz*. As he waited at the main gate of *KZ Janina* a truck drove up that was loaded with naked corpses, stacked like cordwood, and he was told to climb on top of them. There were so many layers of those cold, dead bodies that when he got to the top he could look out over the truck's cab onto the road ahead. Halfway to *KZ Auschwitz* the two *SS* men decided to stop for a beer at a *Bierstube*, leaving Lex to wait uneasily on top of the corpses. After the *SS* men were finished, they continued their trip to *KZ Birkenau* where the crematoria were located, dropping

Lex off at the main gate of *KZ Auschwitz* along the way. After his papers had been scrutinized he was led to the main hospital.

We were both on the second floor of the sick ward of Block 9 and one of our side windows looked onto the courtyard between Block 10 and our Block. Block 10 was the experimental Block, where all sorts of quasi-medical treatments were done on young women. Quite a few of these young women were from Holland, we had been told, and many of them had heard Lex play in Holland when all of us had still been free. When they found out that he was sick they helped to *organisier* and deliver calcium tablets to him, which he shared with me. We conversed with these young Dutch women by lip-reading. Many of them were being used by *SS* doctors for experiments in sterilization and artificial insemination. Although I had sworn that I would not get involved with fellow country men, Lex and I took a liking to each other and whenever possible we talked to each other in our native tongue. Frequently he and I would meet near the window that looked out onto the courtyard that separated our two Blocks and would, surreptitiously, look toward the women's window at the other side. Whenever we were not in danger of being observed by the *Stubenalteste* we would watch their window and try to catch the eye of one or another of the women. Inasmuch as their windows were no more than 30 feet away from our window, Lex and I began to establish signals of recognition.

On sporadic occasions *SS* doctors ordered an inspection on the ward. This was yet another "selection" routine. All ambulatory patients on the ward were directed to line up naked at the far end of the ward while at the other end an *SS* doctor and his entourage would sit behind a table and decide which of us was still worth keeping and who was not. A left or right jerk of his thumb sent each of us off either to the gas chamber or back to our bunks for further recuperation. By now, at the age of 19, I knew my captors well. When my turn came I would step briskly forward and click the barely covered bones of my heels together so that the crack could be distinctly heard. I would stand smartly at attention, muscles taut. Never mind that I was skinny and run down. Never mind that I was weak and faint and scared to death. Every one of us felt that way. Every time the *SS* doctor signaled me back to my hospital bunk I would return on unsure legs, my mouth dry, my blood racing. Climbing back into my clothes I noticed that I was trembling all over. Every nerve ending in my body was on fire and I felt giddy with triumph, a real "high," and preferred to dwell on my personal euphoria rather than the plight of my fellow ward inmates who were soon to perish. Lex and I would signal our women about our survival at the selection and they would smile and gave us victory signs. They were our rooting team, cheering us on. During the weeks of our hospitalization we went through this process at least twice. Each time I returned to my bunk, heady with personal triumph.

As for the doomed patients who had been selected to be gassed, they were kept around the ward for a day or two until orders for their transportation to the gas chambers could be effected. When the *SS* turned up to herd them into a waiting truck, we remaining patients experienced the guilty pleasure of a reduced ward population. Some of us could get a better blanket now or change to a better bunk with better straw and fewer lumps. There were also lighter clean-up duties for the rest of us as the critically ill disappeared from our ranks. An ambulatory patient like me helped with the scrubbing of the floors, general maintenance, and care of the more helpless patients. Many of us hustled to do the extra work necessary to come into the good graces of the *Stubenalteste*, who controlled our food supply. Every death on the ward meant extra rations, at least for that day. We vied with one another to be rewarded with an additional piece of bread or bowl of soup.

There was an underground song that went around among the prisoners, which started:

> *"Auschwitz, Auschwitz*
> *I cannot forget you*
> *As long as I remain alive..."*
> It ended:
> *"...and if I survive Auschwitz*
> *I will never die again..."*

We both were discharged from the hospital about the same time. I went back to the *Tischlerei Kommando* and continued in my job, while Lex was assigned to one of the "make work" *Kommandos*. It was during this period that the Nazis received their first major military setbacks on the Eastern front. The *KZ Auschwitz Band Kommando*, which consisted of professional musicians most of whom were Poles and political prisoners, communists and socialists, was ordered to be relocated to the heart of Germany. This caused a dilemma for the *SS* because there was no longer any music during the marching out in the mornings and the marching back to the camp in the afternoons.

Until then, no Jew had been allowed in the *KZ Auschwitz Band Kommando*. Now an announcement was made in all the Blocks that all those who could play any instrument should present themselves in a designated Block for an audition. Lex went. When he got to the audition room he saw the number of people already lined up to be auditioned. He walked over to the cabinet where the brass instruments were stored and took out one of the mouthpieces and went to the rear of the room all the while practicing on the mouth piece. He allowed everyone to go ahead of him. He was in no hurry. At last it was his turn. He took a trumpet out of the closet, put the mouth piece in it on which he had been practicing and played a tune. He was then asked to play another tune.

The *SS* officer in charge of the auditions asked him where he was from and when he told him that he was from Holland, the *SS* officer asked him if he had ever played on Radio Hilversum. Lex told him he had. The *SS* officer said that he had recognized his phrasing and told him he would be in the *KZ Auschwitz Band Kommando*. Soon after that, after all the musicians had been selected and started their practice sessions, the *SS* officer chose him to be the lead trumpet player. Not long after that Lex was made the conductor of the Band.

The Band played mornings and afternoons at the main gate, and occasionally for *SS* private parties or socials at night. The *Band Kommando* was soft duty. The musicians were now housed in the same Block, remained in camp all day, did a few odd jobs, and practiced most of the time. Extra rations easily came their way because music was an important luxury in such a depressing environment. My friend carried his trumpet with him wherever he went, a proud symbol of his special status. But he also kept the battered cornet from *KZ Janina*, where he originally proved his talent.

He introduced me to one or two Dutch musicians in the Band, and we all become companions. Here were some countrymen with some morale left to them. I sought them out. The humor and high spirits we encouraged in one another's company was good medicine. We discovered the balm of laughter. What a joke our predicament was! We all laughed. We understood one another. The *Blockälteste* of Block 4, Leen Sanders, was a former boxing champion from Holland. He allowed us to gather in his office-bedroom to talk and to vie with one another for favors. This also included the Dutch gentiles because in Holland equality was the custom we were used to. As *Blockälteste*, he was in charge of a Block housing somewhere between 2,000 and 3,000 inmates. A cadre of *Stubendienst*, of his choosing, helped with the many housekeeping and organizational details of the Block, including supplies and record-keeping. Sometimes some of us were recruited to do this or that extra chore. We took particular interest in the details of food distribution for that Block. If an inmate died, that day there would be an extra ration of bread to hand out as a favor for work performed. No one shed a tear or felt a pang of guilt over such bonuses.

Spring had arrived and one day my prisoner number was called out again. When I reported after the evening Roll Call to find out what this was all about, I was told that I had been transferred into the *Dachdecker Kommando* (roof repair work detail). I was not happy about that change. In *KZ Auschwitz* there existed a "complaint line," after evening Roll Call, which pertained strictly to *Kommando* matters. It was located in front of the kitchen and was run by an *SS* officer who would listen to one's complaints and make decisions on the spot.

I decided to join that line and when he came to me I told him in my best possible German that I thought I was doing an excellent job in the *Tischlerei*. I requested that my transfer into the *Dachdecker*

Kommando be nullified and I be allowed to remain in the *Tischlerei*. Request denied! Whereupon I went to the end of the line and when he came to me again I said that perhaps he had misunderstood me. Before I could say another word his fist landed solidly in my face and sent me sprawling. Some prisoners rushed up to me and dragged me away berating me for the foolish act I had just committed. They took me inside one of the Blocks, and told me I could have been shot right there for insubordination.

The next morning I reported to the *Dachdecker Kommando* with a swollen face. Most of the work we did was repairing roofs on the one-story buildings in *KZ Birkenau*. We would walk over there in the morning, climb onto the roofs, work on those roofs that needed repairs, come down for our midday soup, and return to the roofs again. The work was not hard at all; it had the additional benefit that our *SS* guards were not allowed onto the roofs and our *Kapo* was not inclined to appear there either so we were pretty much left alone. Cold winds and rains blew against our backs as we worked, but we rejoiced as the sun gained strength so that, on sunny days, we were able to shed our jackets and get the sun to warm us.

Most of the time we worked in the women's camp, but *KZ Birkenau* was also the known location of the gas chambers and the crematoria. Even from the rooftops on which we worked we were not in a position to observe operations in those death-dealing buildings. We did not know which buildings housed the gas chambers, but we certainly knew where the crematoria were located by their tall chimneys and the stench that poured forth from them. I preferred to look at the women in the courtyards below. This interest was not consciously sexual – people who are starving have little sexual appetite. I had heard that many of these women were Dutch, and I longed to communicate. Eventually I wrote a note in Dutch on a paper scrap with a pencil stub I had *organisiert*. I rolled the note into a ball and threw it down among a group of women when the eyes of the female *SS* guards were turned away. Soon word was passed back to me to look in a certain place in the latrine the next day before our *Kommando* returned to camp.

The Dutch men in *KZ Auschwitz* were very interested and wanted as much news as I could bring and pass around. As a roofer working regularly in *KZ Birkenau* I continued to function as a messenger for the Dutch women. We were playing a dangerous game, but scraps of information between the camps continued. I picked up notes at designated spots, memorized them, then destroyed them. We all became wiser but sadder. We exchanged information on who was still alive and who was dead. The survival statistics did not make comforting news. From what I can now remember and from what knowledge I had then, there were probably no more than five men from my Westerbork transport who were still alive at that time. Originally there were 121 children, 233 men, and 263 women. After the selection at the train site 188 men were admitted to the camp as were 48 women. In addition another 44 women from this transport were assigned to Block 10 for experiments by Professor *SS* Doctor Clauberg.[3] I do not know how many men and women of my transport actually survived the camps with me at the end of the war.

At our work on the rooftops one day, my fellow *Dachdeckers* and I were halted from our work by the sounding of a general alarm, the signal by the main camp, and to all sub-camps, that there had been an escape. We were called down from our roofs, our *Kommando* was lined up, and the *Kapo* took great pains in counting us carefully. We stood in our places for a long period of time until the winnowing process through all the *Arbeitskommandos* turned up the missing men. Later on we heard that the men who had been hunted had been found and executed. The block from which they came had been subjected to beatings and special brutalities for allowing their escape to occur. I did not know the details for it was not our Block, but the grapevine quickly passed the news around. I was amazed at the courage of these men who had tried to escape because the chances seemed so very small. One barbed-wire fence surrounding a camp was placed a few feet outside of another, so that to get through one fence meant only to be enclosed in a new cage. If a prisoner managed the impossible and broke through all fenced compounds or, more likely, escaped from a labor detail outside the camp gates, he would have found himself free in anti-

---

3 Danuta Czech, "Auschwitz Chronicle, 1935-1945," August 26, 1943, Page 470.

Semitic Poland where help would have been hard to find even if he happened to speak Polish.

The most vivid escape attempt in my memory, while in *KZ Auschwitz*, concerned six prisoners who were caught after a long search. Mornings and evenings, over a few days' time, we then observed the construction of three gallows, in front of the kitchen, on one side of Roll Call Square. One evening when construction had been completed we were all ordered to mass on Roll Call Square, an unusual event.

Six Polish political prisoners were marched out before us, hands tied behind their backs. They were brought to a halt before the gallows, and suddenly these brave men shouted in Polish, "Down with Hitler! Down with Germany! Long live the Allies!" The *SS* guards descended on them, yanked their trousers down, leaned them over the "box" and lashed their buttocks with truncheons, leaning into the blows, delivering 14 strokes in all to each condemned man. They hung them then, one by one, before our eyes.

I had counted the blows, I could not help it, but I had tried to avoid watching this spectacle closely. I think many of us looked down or to the right or left as much as we dared. We prisoners had become resigned to watching people die around us or throwing themselves against the high voltage electrical fence. We did not like it but we expected it at any time. Death was like a fellow prisoner who always walked with us. We were so aware of his presence that we hardly noticed him. Yet to be forced to witness the brutal lashing and hanging of some of our number, a few men who had been particularly brave, was unbearable. Death was flaunting its terrible power before our reluctant eyes. We were frightened and ashamed to serve as witnesses.

As chill spring rains whipped us while we worked atop the roofs, I developed a cold that gradually grew worse. When I could no longer report for work, I was given permission to go to the clinic. The inmate doctor who examined me told me I had pneumonia. All prisoners, incidentally, were examined and treated by doctors who were themselves prisoners, wearing their insignia and prisoner numbers on their hospital coats. He ordered that I be admitted to the hospital for treatment. Inasmuch as there were no medications to take care of this illness the only way I could be treated was for one of the prisoners/orderlies to suck the fluid out of my lung. Every other morning I had to face a wall in our ward, step back slightly, and then lean on my hands. Then the prisoner/orderly would drive a needle into my lung and suck out the fluid. This was done without the benefit of any local anesthetic. The needle had a long flat point to it and was about 1/8" in diameter (3mm). Of course, it goes without saying that the prisoner/orderly had to have a steady hand directing the needle. While there I went through another selection and was about to be discharged when they discovered I had the same problem in my other lung. This, too, was cleared up and now I was discharged from the hospital.

Because I had been in the hospital for such a lengthy stay, I had been reassigned to a new Block and also been given a new bunk assignment. That very night I was awakened by excruciating pains in my abdomen. Wave after wave of nauseating pain convulsed me and nothing I tried relieved it. I could not lie down, or sit up, or stand up without great pain. Straightening my backbone was the least bearable position so I assumed a double-over posture whether walking or lying. I felt a constant urge to move my bowels but could not do so. In the morning I was to report for reassignment to a work detail because I had been away for such a long time from the *Dachdecker Kommando*. Instead, I was compelled to report once more to the clinic. This time, I figured, my fate had caught up with me. I could hardly walk, much less work. At the clinic the doctor checked me over, then sent me back to my bunk for the day with a slip of paper and two aspirin. The slip of paper indicated that I did not have to go to work that day. My condition did not improve at all.

The next morning, Saturday, back at the clinic, the doctor told me to return to my bunk and remain there through the workday and through Sunday as well. But he thought I would be sufficiently recuperated to report for work on Monday. Again I received the required slips of paper and some aspirin. Three miserable days had gone by. Fevered, in terrible pain, I writhed on my bunk, then paced about doubled-over. Each passing hour was pure agony. On Monday morning I slowly dragged my doubled-over, old-man's body towards the clinic. It was as if I could see myself through a window, heading for my own destruction but powerless to care. This time, after the doctor examined me, he stepped to his desk and made a telephone call. "I have a 20 year-old Jew here with a 4 day-old acute appendicitis — ready to burst, herr Doktor... Yes, it is amazing... very well, sir, Goodbye." The doctor returned to my side to tell me that I was to be operated on. He wrote out orders for me to take over to the surgical unit, and before I could recover from my astonishment, I was on my way.

I walked to the surgical hospital where a staff member received my note, then assigned me a bunk in which to wait. The wait seemed long before I was escorted into an operating room and assisted onto the operating table. The inmate doctor who had examined me at the clinic entered and began directing me. He was to be my surgeon. He told me to sit forward allowing my legs to hang over the edge of the operating table then bring my legs up, bring my arms tightly around my knees and tighten up my back. I did as told. In so much pain I did not care much what was next, I felt a needle entering my back. Immediately the area froze, and, as the pain receded, I was turned around and laid out flat on the operating table. While my torso was totally frozen I was cognizant of what was happening around me and to me. My body was covered with sheets. A little screen was placed in front of my face by an orderly who stood next to me on my left side. I could see mirrored images in the shiny metal lamp hanging over the operating table. An *SS* doctor entered from the right. I could see his uniform pants, his white coat and black boots as he walked past my head.

I felt a little zip like a nail sliding across my belly. Through the metallic reflection of the lamp hanging over the operating table I could see the inmate surgeon receive some instruments and bend over my body to do his work. The *SS* doctor had not moved. My operation felt and looked very remote. Then the surgeon began to stitch the incision and, as he did so, the *SS* doctor walked wordless from the room.

Orderlies placed me on a gurney and trundled me to the

recuperation ward near the operating room, then half lifted, half tossed me into a lower bunk. Here the bunks were only two, not four, tiers high. With returning awareness I was grateful for the extra room. I lay in straw with straw dust from the other bunk above me falling freely. I began to shiver from the thawing-out process that was now beginning. I was so cold that I could manage to sleep only sporadically. My teeth clattered as my sleepless body was wracked with uncontrollable shaking. Finally, I screamed out. An orderly brought me an extra blanket. It was thin and not much help, but his considerate act helped calm me.

My body did not begin to generate warmth again until almost two days had gone by. There was no medication, but we did receive better food rations in the surgical unit. In addition to the usual daily portions, there was a bowl of breakfast gruel each morning. I was expected to care for my throbbing wound by myself; there were no nurses. Other patients gave me instructions. But the area incision did not drain properly and it quickly developed pus. After a few days of this, the inmate doctor had me walk over to another building, also part of the hospital. There, on another operating table, I was opened up once again and the abscessed wound was cleaned out and repaired. I was taken to yet another recovery ward where, once more, the bunks were the typical four high, the cases of this ward being considered less serious that those of my first post-operative ward.

The ward stank from many putrid open wounds like mine. Clean cotton and bandages were scarce. Pus ran freely from our wounds as we tried to clean and drain them ourselves. Filthy swabs and rags wound up on the floor where we would slip on them when we left the bunks to use the latrines and to wash ourselves. I gave my wound close attention, learning to clean and care for it with no aids other than water and rags which could hardly pass muster as clean.

Because of the stench of our various festering openings, the windows on the ward were kept open day and night. Those of us who had an upper bunk near a window would lie there and watch the changing skies above the high-voltage electrical barbed-wire fence not far beyond the building. It was during my stay in this ward that

I watched the beginning of the destruction of the gypsies in the compound next to our camp.

Male gypsies, female gypsies and their children, rounded up and thrown together in that compound like so many chickens in a coop, could be seen sitting about or promenading dejectedly in groups. One day I was attracted to the window by shouts and scuffling in the gypsy camp. Men and women were grappling with guards, trying to overpower them, but more rifle-bearing guards soon appeared. Shots echoed through the air and some of the gypsies fell dead. Their compound quieted down again, but not long afterwards the gypsies were all lined up and led out of the compound, not to return.

The area of my incision gradually stopped draining, and after about four weeks or so I was discharged as healed. Sensitive skin now covered a ragged wound in my right lower abdomen, and to this day the operation site looks like a butcher's battlefield. As appendicitis scars go, mine may be an eyesore, but for me it is almost a badge of honor, for I know that without it I would have been ashes by the time *KZ Auschwitz* was liberated. After that lengthy stay in the various parts of the *KZ Auschwitz* hospital, beginning with my initial pneumonia, a number of months had gone by in what must have been one of the longest consecutive hospitalizations on record for a Jewish prisoner in *KZ Auschwitz*. I was released, assigned to a new Block and ordered to report for work the next morning.

The weather was warm but summer was giving way to autumn, and just about a year had gone by since I first arrived in camp. The numbers on my fellow prisoner's arms read considerably higher than mine. The number tattooed on my arm, 139829, compared with the far higher ones on other arms, marking me as a living relic, an unusual specimen among *Haftlingen*.

Morning line-up found me standing with others at the assignment area in front of the kitchen, awaiting orders from the *Chief Kapo*, also known as the *Arbeitskapo*, a fellow prisoner in charge of assigning men to the various *Kommandos* of the camp. The *Arbeitskapo* was a highly privileged prisoner, a fact we all knew but which was emphasized by the neatness of his appearance and the excellent condition of his uniform. His prison stripes actually looked tailor-made. His shoes were leather.

"Well, where have you been?" he asked me, glancing at the number on my jacket. "In the hospital," I replied.

"There are damn few of you left with a number as low as yours," he said. I nodded, and the *Arbeitskapo* continued, "It seems to me anybody who can survive as long as you deserves a break." He wrote out a work-assignment note and handed it to me. *"Melde dich an Paketstelle"* was what I read on the piece of paper. Report to the package receiving office. Wonderful! Indoor work again. I could have used a little sunlight at that point, but when I thought of the freezing Silesian winter ahead of us, I felt lucky. I knew nothing about the operation of the *Paketstelle*, or Post Office, as we called it, even though only packages, not letters were handled there. It was but a few steps to the *Paketstelle* from the work-assignment area where I stood. I entered, reported to the *Kapo*, and looked around.

THE PAKETSTELLE KOMMANDO, 1944

The *Paketstelle* was located between Blocks 25 and 26, near the kitchen, in the far left corner of the camp, opposite the hospital buildings. It was a one-story, nondescript wood-framed building, slightly narrower than the two Blocks on either side of it. Its main entrance was at the front of the building and consisted of a pair of in-swinging double doors. There was also a rear entrance through which all the packages arrived. To the left of the main entrance was a window which provided light to the office of the guard who sat there all day.

After I had reported to the *Kapo* that morning he introduced me to the *SS* guard and each of my new co-workers, all of whom were a healthy-looking bunch of guys. They hustled about their duties with a will, and they seemed to be enjoying an easy relationship, laughing and joshing one another. An unbelievable situation for me to find myself in. I must have looked particularly pale and emaciated to these men when I started my duties as instructed, sorting packages, looking up names. My fellow workers readily accepted me, asking me about my background and how I happened still to be counted among the living after a year as one of the *Haftlingen* in this place. There were no other Jews in this *Kommando*, but the workers chuckled over my survival account, until I showed them my scars. They began slipping me a variety of foods to sample as we worked. What joy! What delicious and astounding flavors! What was this place, I wondered. Lunchtime was even better. We were not, in contrast to the rest of the camp, on a ration of coarse bread and thin soup. We were served a delicious soup, concocted from many ingredients and cooked on a gas ring in the building. We dined on salamis, cheeses, homemade breads, cakes. Clearly an assignment to the *Paketstelle* was an assignment to distribute the contents of an endless cornucopia.

Our *Kommando* was in charge of packages that arrived daily from anxious loved ones who had been notified that a relative or friend had been interned in *KZ Auschwitz*. Red Cross and other organizations and governments sent food parcels. Needless to say, many of the addressees were dead, as death was the essential business of this camp. We kept files of the names of all prisoners, living and dead, in the main and sub-camps of *KZ Auschwitz*. Packages for the living were duly distributed, and at that point the recipient learned his own game of sharing his windfall to gain favors, of knuckling under pressure from more prominent prisoners. The packages for those who had died – those endless packages for the endless dead – were ours to dispose of, a circumstance that put everyone assigned to this *Kommando* in a position of power and wealth. There was the usual hierarchy within, as with all *Kommandos*, and I was on the bottom rung. It was my duty every morning to shine the boots of our *SS* guard, and to be at the beck and call of my fellow workers at all times. But considering the quality and abundance of food I was now eating, I was satisfied with my flunky status.

Every day we worked at sorting the contents of the packages of the dead, cakes went in one bin, salamis in margarine over there, schmalz (chicken fat, or goose fat, usually from the Poles) and other perishables in jars were placed here. Cookies had yet another compartment. Many of the vegetables were taken to the kitchen once a day, some to be thrown into the daily soups for the camp. The more delectable items were always kept aside for the use of the *Kommando* workers, who, in turn, supplied the Nazi camp administrators as desired. My co-workers, I observed, walked frequently back and forth from the *Paketstelle* to their Block. It soon dawned on me that they were helping themselves to a cut of the spoils, and they did so openly, as if this practice were not only accepted but expected.

After several weeks at this work I was transferred from Block 9 to Block 16, the *Prominenten* Block. Because I served the elite I had become *prominent* myself! In my new Block I was given a private *Stube*, a tiny cubicle on the second floor. It was equipped with a single metal bunk with warm blankets, even bed sheets, a pillow and pillowcase. The cubicle also had a tiny kitchen closet that held a gas-fired cooking plate and a storage space for my stolen food. I had soap and towels. Although there was still no hot water, washing facilities were easily available, and I was clean again, no longer worried about lice. I also had underwear, socks, handkerchiefs, shirts, undershirts; in short, I had all the things I had when living in *Amsterdam* before the war. We wore leather shoes, I even had a toothbrush and toothpaste and, wonders of wonders, my own shaving gear. The cutting of our hair was still done by the Block's friseur but he at least was a professional.

That I was now admitted to the *Prominenten* Block did not fill me with pangs of guilt, not after what I had seen and had lived through. The separation of *Prominenten haftlingen* from the rest of the camp was undoubtedly necessary to keep the administrative machinery from being sabotaged. Therefore, anyone who worked among the elite was destined to share in their privileges. My feelings as a man, a Dutch national, and a Jew were suppressed except for quiet expressions of how good I felt that I was winning the battle of survival; weightier thoughts I avoided.

After my first shock of amazement, I accepted the new turn of events in my life just as I had accepted the survival tightrope I had walked each day as a prisoner. So far I had succeeded in keeping my balance. The fortunes of my camp existence could just as easily have turned the other way at the whim of anyone in authority over me. The choice before us, the camp's inmates, was always to accommodate ourselves to what was demanded of us or die. For more than a year I had been coerced by means of starvation and ill treatment. Now I was being coerced with delicious foods and personal privileges.

The food from the *Paketstelle* brought us tailored prisoner uniforms. The *KZ Auschwitz* gray and blue stripes were transformed by inmate tailors into well-fitting suits with hand-painted prisoner numbers to go on the left pocket of our jackets and the right side of the trouser leg. The newly acquired belt fitted snugly. The stripes of our new tailored uniforms were aligned at the seams and matched perfectly. Our caps were constructed just as carefully. We thought ourselves to be walking fashion plates. Because of the elegant craftsmanship of my clothing, I sometimes almost managed to forget I was still a prisoner. It had not been that long ago when I had to use my sharpened wits for an extra finger or two of soup or an extra chunk of bread.

Camp rations were never served in the *Paketstelle*. We did our own cooking within the *Paketstelle* and shared the results with our *SS* guard. He, too, was content as he did not have to lift a finger to get his daily meal or obtain nearly any service he desired. All day long he sat in the nearby office reading newspapers, listening to his radio and talking with other *SS* guards. A constant stream of visitors poured through our space: *SS* guards, *Prominenten* and Prisoner Administrators. I quickly understood why we had so many visitors each day.

As I polished his boots each morning, our *SS* guard even engaged me in small talk, an exchange unheard of in other parts of the camp. It was also very obvious to me, and others, that the German I had learned in the past year was of great help to me. During one of our morning sessions, he broached the subject of politics and started to tell me how a fellow named Anton A. Mussert, the Dutch fascist leader, was a great man who was doing many good things for the Dutch people. I was foolish enough to tell him that I did not want to hear about it, that there was no way we could have a fair discussion of the subject since I was a political prisoner, a Dutch Jew, and compelled to shine his boots. He ended his discourse there and then in polite silence, acknowledging, perhaps, that I had a point. After I had completed my daily chores for him I walked away marveling that the *SS* guard had not kicked my face in as would have happened in similar situations elsewhere in the camp. The *SS* guard had taken my reprimand with grace.

How did I stumble into the *Paketstelle*? During the months I served in the camps and for quite a few years thereafter, I spent no time at all pondering my experiences. I had lived through them, sometimes by luck, and sometimes by trying very hard to survive. I was proud that I had survived, and still am. I may have been the only Jew ever admitted into the *Paketstelle*. The others were mostly political prisoners with many years of experience in the camps. In autumn 1944, however, when I emerged from my long hospitalization and was assigned, apparently by the whim of the *Arbeitskapo*, to the *Paketstelle*, the atmosphere in the camp was changing. There was an unspoken comprehension that the war was drawing to a close and that the Third Reich had been defeated.

License to steal food was a marvelous experience for a long-starved prisoner. I helped keep our *SS* guard supplied by relaying his requests to my *Kapo*: a pound of butter, a salami, a cake of certain type. These things were set aside within the office and, when the guard went off duty, he took the food out of our office concealed in his clothes. In those days, he was probably receiving better food through *KZ Auschwitz's* supply line than he could have obtained at home. What an irony! The average prisoner was always scrambling for food. If he worked outside the main gate and managed to beg some food from a civilian he worked alongside, and he did not eat it right away, there was a good chance it would be taken away from him during a body search when returning to camp at the end of the work day. Prisoners could receive food packages through the *Paketstelle* only if the packages were specifically addressed to them. The rules of the camp were carefully maintained. Administrative personnel were strictly forbidden to help themselves to this food, but the prisoners who made up our privileged *Kommando* were not in a position to refuse Nazi requests to help them smuggle food out.

Mornings, the inmates of my new Block did not get up at the God-awful early hour with the rest of the camp for inspections and Roll Calls. We rose for work after the other *Arbeitskommandos* had marched out of the camp. Our *Blockälteste* would check us off personally every day without ever lining us up to be counted. At the *Paketstelle* we hung our jackets on nails, or coat hooks, on the wall to the right of the main entrance doors and we would start our work before our *SS* guard arrived. Every day he would line us up in the *Paketstelle* for a formal count, but absences were passed over when our *Kapo* supplied an excuse. If one of us was not present at his Roll Call then he was in camp somewhere, everyone knew, and so the *Paketstelle* was run more by "gentlemen's agreement" than camp orders.

Walking across the camp any time any day, I might be accosted by some *SS* guard who would call me by my first name. It was not long ago, I would think, that I was only a number and first names were used only among friends. Taking off my cap and coming to attention I would hear him say, "Hey, Max, how about a salami?" or a similar such request. I would promise him what he wanted within a certain period of time, then see to it that he got it, and I would instruct him under which jacket, hung on the wall, he would be able to locate it. Just as I did errands in my own self-interest for the *SS*, so did fellow prisoners do errands for me to get handouts of food. In my new Block, however, I was out of contact with prisoners outside my *Kommando*.

My body filled out rapidly. I felt well, fit, and strong. The scars of my pneumonia and abscessed appendicitis were healed and behind me. I was now well dressed by day, warm at night, I even had cigarettes. Since there were no bedtime curfews in our Block, my co-workers and I often played chess or other games for hours on end. But my mind was restless as I tried, and failed, to sort some desperate thought. I made a point of getting along, but kept those thoughts to myself, sharing no confidences.

Lex and I would see each other on occasion and I would always bring him something extraordinary. He would tell me about what he had been doing, but he never mentioned until we met again in Holland in the early 1980s what a favor he had done for me at that time: he had agreed to give his music-loving *Kapo* some trumpet lessons if he would make me a permanent member of Lex's *Kommando*. It was Lex who changed my fortunes at *Auschwitz*!

Lex and I continued to visit Block 4, where Leen Sanders was *Blockälteste*. We would sit around in his office/bedroom, and other Dutch prisoners would join us as we talked about the *Amsterdam* we once called home. Lex would talk about his various entertainment adventures as Leen and the others listened, but Leen never talked about his boxing career. I would talk of my own little exploits but my stories were really those of a young boy/man and his family while those of Lex were about a young man-about-town. Since most of the talk dealt with music, I began to recall my own part in various family entertainments that we children had staged from time to time. I used to sing popular French, German, and Dutch songs at family gatherings. I had been encouraged to believe I had a good voice, and an indulgent audience watched my imitations of Maurice Chevalier, even to the straw hat and cane, and Charles Trenet, another popular French singer. Laughing over our reminiscences, we each tried out some of our old routines on our friends.

This private audience enjoyed our presentations and an idea dawned on us. Why not try some kind of show for the inmates of the camp doing popular musical numbers, small chit-chat and jokes? It could be like a cabaret, less the refreshments and price of admission. The payoff would be in lifting spirits, not only our fellow prisoners' but ours in putting together an entertainment. Our group became excited about the idea, as did Leen, who agreed to approach the camp authorities in our behalf.

Mind you it was September 1944. Lex had a good job as the Conductor/Director of the *KZ Auschwitz Band* and through his mentor, the *SS* officer, who was a fanatical music lover, he had formed a Jazz combo consisting mostly of Dutch musicians that the *SS* officer regarded as his own and would take around to the various sub-camps to show off. He even went so far as to have special uniforms made for them in which to perform.

I also had a good job in the *Paketstelle*, was fully recovered and strong while the others, who were musicians, had good job guarantees in *KZ Auschwitz*, if that is what one can say about life in a destruction camp.

When Leen presented our request, the *SS* authorities would not hear of it. We were not to play jazz music such as Lex had suggested. That was decadent and *verboten*. What about the idea in general, we asked. Could we play for the prisoners, and if so, what? After many discussions they gave us tentative approval to plan a preview performance for the *SS* authorities. We could play some German cabaret music as well as some officially approved tunes. A comedy routine that steered clear of political satire could be tried. We were not particularly pleased with the limited repertoire we settled for, but we agreed it was better than nothing, and we were ready to do anything just to perform. Energy flowed through us as we planned our new endeavor.

The show went over beyond our wildest expectations. Of course the *SS* was a captive audience too! I was not the leader of the group, but because my German was the best among any of them I could sing a little, tell jokes, and ad-lib to the audience remarks. I became the "master of ceremonies" while others played their instruments. We played German movie tunes, slapstick, and common street jokes, French songs, and some popular tunes with jazz overtones. The *SS* men clapped and roared with laughter. After the show, they gave their approval for our doing a Sunday afternoon cabaret for the prisoners, to be held in Block 2 where there was a good size performance room.

We were elated. There was something in it for us besides the love of entertaining, and we knew it. We were callously selfish in looking forward to the favored treatment and the other little extras that would come our way because of the *SS* approval of our enterprise. The prisoners laughed and applauded the cabaret, and we genuinely enjoyed entertaining them. What surprised us even more was the fact that members of the *SS* would show up every Sunday, and the first few rows of seats were always reserved for them. The *SS*, too, laughed and clapped and appeared to enjoy themselves. Because of our initial success we were allowed to hold regular Sunday afternoon performances in Block 2. Prisoners would come and go as they pleased but most of those who came were *Prominenten* because regular prisoners had other things to do on Sundays. However, we always drew a good audience.

Since the nucleus of our cabaret group were Dutch musicians, it eventually occurred to Lex to ask permission to take our cabaret over to *KZ Birkenau* for a single Sunday afternoon to entertain the women. Again the *SS* authorities stalled and debated, but we persisted and were finally granted the permission we sought, coupled with a strict warning that there were to be no attempts at personal communication. It was the Sunday morning before Christmas 1944 when the musicians brought their instruments, and a few props, to the flat-bed wagon that we would push to *KZ Birkenau*.

In the camps, all transportation of prisoners' equipment and supplies was done by using flat-bed wagons fitted out with horse shafts and having wooden wheels, large wheels in back and smaller wheels in front. Instead of horses, prisoners manned the shafts while other prisoners pushed at the sides and the back. The musicians and players of our cabaret, steering a flat-bed wagon full of instruments and equipment, pushed and sweated our way out of the main gate of *KZ Auschwitz*, then staggered and rolled, under *SS* guards of course, the awkward three-kilometer distance to *KZ Birkenau*, across an overpass, a walk of about one hour for us.

Women jammed the barracks hall in which we performed. Some peered in through the windows. Inasmuch as so many of the performers were Dutch and inasmuch as I was the master of ceremonies, we used many Dutch songs and old Dutch comic routines. As we had hoped, we were rewarded with enthusiastic response from the Dutch women. In fact, we had accolades from the entire audience. But at the same time, notes reached our hands and stealthy whispers reached our ears through the hubbub. These cheering women bombarded us with pathetic pleas: Did we know if a husband, so and so, was still alive? Had we seen so and so? What were our names? Would we please carry this note to so and so. How could we stay in touch? Would we come back?

Midway through the performance, this underlying but unvoiced scream to us of grief and despair reached a crescendo. We did not know how to cope with these women. Silent and depressed after the show, we dragged our flat-bed wagon, loaded with our equipment, back to *KZ Auschwitz*. Darkness was upon us and we could not put into words how we felt, and we did not try. On the crest of the overpass we halted and looked back to *KZ Birkenau*. After a while Lex broke the silence and said, "That's one of the dumbest things I have ever done." The experience had been unsettling. We suddenly understood how ineffectual we were before the women's reminders of our real problems. The Dutch women had looked right through our cabaret game; in fact, had played it well themselves. But they were expecting something more from us by way of help. We had to admit to ourselves that we were no longer men with power to help them. We were less then men. We were survivors.

One day I went to the clinic next door, and looked for the doctor who had removed my burst appendix. I had suddenly realized what had been bothering me these last few months. I needed to know from this doctor why he had been ordered to operate on me, since Jewish prisoners before me had been denied surgery. He observed that he, too, had found this unusual. When he had the opportunity to ask the *Schutzstaffel* doctor about it, the *SS* doctor told him that when he had been a medical student in Germany all the medical books had black and white pictures in them, some not too clear, so when suddenly there was an opportunity to see what a real "ready-to-burst" appendix looked like he ordered me operated on. When he had seen it he walked away, not caring about me at all, but my problem had furthered his education.

Lex's rehearsal rooms were on the first floor of an administration building just inside the main gate. It also housed a bordello, served by women prisoners who were promised (but never granted) early release for their services. The *SS* guards had free access to the place, while *Prominenten*, *Lageralteste*, *Blockältesten*, and *Kapos* could earn chits as behavior awards towards visiting the bordello once a month. The bordello was not available to Jews, but we glimpsed the women occasionally as one or another appeared at a window or at the clinic.

At Christmas time 1944, the *Paketstelle Kommando* met together to decide what to give the *SS* commander of *KZ Auschwitz* as a Christmas gift. The *Kapo*, a very elite prisoner, suggested that a silver tea service would make a fine gift, and, needless to say, we all agreed. Probably the tea service was ordered by the *Kapo* and our *SS* guard, who had access to a grapevine leading outside *KZ Auschwitz*. Each of us was asked daily to put aside some of the best food delicacies that we daily processed to pay for our proposed gift. Piece by piece the silver service began to arrive in the *Paketstelle*, and with each addition word was passed around to us to bring forth so much in the foods that each of us had set aside for the purpose of paying for the ordered gift. To the best of my knowledge, except for our *SS* guard, the other *SS* men who visited us regularly for food handouts were unaware of this transaction. After the entire service had arrived, we polished the pieces in secret and packed them in a large crate. Carefully bathed and in clean uniforms, my fellow prisoners pushed the flat-bed wagon, bearing our gift. Our *SS* guard shepherded the group through the main gate and towards the nearby home of the *KZ Auschwitz* commander. The *SS* commander of *KZ Auschwitz* invited the *Kapo* of the *Paketstelle* and our *SS* guard into his home, where, reportedly, he very graciously accepted our *Kommando*'s gift of a silver tea service paid for in stolen food of camp victims.

LAST TRANSPORT FROM *KZ AUSCHWITZ* JANUARY 1945

On New Year's Eve, December 1944, the *Paketstelle* prisoners threw one last celebration before my rose-colored world as a wheeler-dealer in *KZ Auschwitz* fell apart.

The Third Reich was being routed and the overrunning of *KZ Auschwitz* by the Red Army was expected; no one knew that better than our *Kommando*, who received firsthand information from

Prominenten working in the *SS* administrative office. Quite a few evacuation transports had already left some of the outlying sub-camps during late autumn 1944; now they were leaving *KZ Auschwitz* and the camp was beginning to empty out.

Since the gas chambers in *KZ Birkenau* had been very efficient, there were very few people left except able-bodied workers. During the summer of 1944, seemingly endless large transports had been arriving filled with Hungarian and Italian Jews. These people were in very bad physical condition, as if they had been starved and maltreated for a long period somewhere else. The *SS* lost no time in causing most of them to disappear. Those who survived the gassing programs were sent to *KZ Mauthausen* after a short, unregistered stay in *KZ Auschwitz*. After that, fewer and fewer transports arrived and the gassings fell off sharply. We assumed, falsely, that the Nazis had run out of victims.

Ever since the Allied invasion of France in June 1944 we had been kept up to date with the progress on the Western Front by fellow prisoners who were doing short wave radio repair work in the *SS* technical workshop. I dare say we knew better than most Germans what the true situation was in France and the daily progress made by the Allies. The same was true, of course, with the Red Army on the Eastern Front and the offensive they had begun in 1944. All German criminal and political prisoners, except for the Jews, had been called out of ranks in late 1944, during one of the evening Roll Calls and been offered an opportunity to enlist in the *Waffen-SS* on the condition that they would serve on the Eastern Front. All criminal prisoners who would enlist were promised that their criminal records would be expunged. A number of criminal prisoners accepted. Many spit on the offer, especially the political prisoners, most of whom were Communists.

What we in the *Paketstelle* did not know was that the *SS* were beginning to look at all able-bodied men with new eyes. We were usable labor for their war plants and armaments industries, seasoned replacements for their own thinning manpower. The maintenance of a destruction camp on the scale of a *KZ Auschwitz/Birkenau* was no longer necessary or even desirable.

The prisoners working in the *Paketstelle Kommando* celebrated the coming of 1945 like everyone else facing the blank canvas of a new year. We looked forward to our liberation but there were events yet to come which we could not imagine. We ordered a huge vat of ersatz coffee, the kind we got in the morning. The prisoners who staggered over with it and brought it up the stairs to the space where the party was going to be held were paid liberally in food, the quality of which they hadn't enjoyed in a long time. Similarly we obtained a tankard of schnapps from the City of *Auschwitz*, again paying our providers with valuable food items. Schnapps was dubious stuff, we all knew, for there was no way of knowing what kind of alcohol and other flavorings had been dumped into it. But who cared? All of us were hankering for a good drunk.

The coffee and the schnapps were mixed together, then passed around in cups filled to the rim. Our choicest edibles, which we had all saved for this occasion, were also passed around and eaten in great quantities. I could hardly swallow a mouthful of the beverage that had been concocted, never having developed a taste for coffee, much less alcohol. Nevertheless, I made what I thought was a good show of it, and stuck to eating as my personal means of over-indulgence. The schnapps did have the effect of loosening tongues and inhibitions, including mine. If all the *Paketstelle* prisoners were going to open up and say what they wanted, so was I, and I looked forward to the free-for-all.

Conversations zeroed in on the question foremost in our minds: What would our fate be here in *KZ Auschwitz* as Germany fell to defeat? Each of us had his own theory. One of us pointed out that we all knew that the Red Army was damn close and that all prisoners had been ordered evacuated. But, he wondered, would our *Kommando* leave too?

Another did not think so because we all were *Prominenten* and would be needed to help run the camp. He thought we would be kept as long as possible along with the *Lageralteste, Blockältesten, Kapos*, and doctors.

Another: We should start thinking of defending ourselves. They may decide to kill us.

Another: I don't think it is going to come to that. The *SS* will abandon the camp and leave us here as a welcoming committee for the Red Army. We'll be all right. We're prisoners, aren't we?

So went our nervous conjecture. Events, however, continued to run their course in spite of the independent thoughts we might have. Transports of prisoners were marched out of the camp until, just as some of us had figured, we of the *Paketstelle Kommando* were among the few *Kommandos* left in *KZ Auschwitz.*

By the middle of January 1945, *KZ Auschwitz* was almost deserted. Our daily routines fell apart. We continued our work in a half-hearted manner, but devoted much of our time to helping ourselves to the food we processed, beginning to stockpile it against an uncertain future. There were few prisoners left, but food packages addressed to great numbers of the dead or evacuated prisoners poured into camp from agencies and governments. We still did not know what the *SS* had in store for us, and tension mounted day by day. The *KZ Auschwitz Band Kommando* was also still in camp and, off and on, Lex and I would discuss the situation at hand. Excitement swelled as we began to hear the sound of distant artillery fire, then heard it grow louder with each passing day. Evenings brought more drinking bouts, more speculation, but less reliable news as our information grapevine withered.

On a Sunday morning in mid-January, all of us still in *KZ Auschwitz*, except those in the hospital, the doctors and medical orderlies, were abruptly ordered out onto the *Appellplatz.* There were several hundred of us. We were told to get our belongings together immediately and to be ready to march out of *KZ Auschwitz* by 1300 hours.

We scrambled to our Blocks to gather our clothing and our food. We each had put aside so much food and so many articles of clothing and housekeeping items we had purchased with our wealth of food that we were now faced with quick and painful decisions about what to take along and what to leave behind. Then we chose partners for the manning of the flat-bed wagons. After putting siding around the flat-bed wagons we stacked them high with our food. We had rucksacks and other carrying gear for our belongings.

These we filled and strapped to our backs. As we were called into a rough formation and told to start marching, we must have been a ludicrous sight. In tailor-made prison garb, wearing haircuts of one center stripe, we strong prisoners sweated with the effort of pushing and guiding our food-laden wagons out onto unfenced snowy roads. Armed *SS* guards in their green uniforms accompanied us, taking the shoulders of the road as we took the middle. Some of the prisoners pushed the guards' wagons, which were lighter by far than those of our *Kommando.*

At first we made nervous jokes, facing the unknown. So far, they had not shot us, but where the hell were we going? For hours we staggered along a deserted snow-covered road through brown and snow-flecked fields. The loaded wagons were all but breaking our backs. We ate continuously as we marched, but seemed hardly to put a dent in our supplies.

The *SS* guards had noticeably poorer and fewer rations than we. Soon we began to throw cans in their direction. We knew that with their hands full carrying their guns they would have difficulty opening and eating from the cans as they marched. I giggled over their predicament. The *SS* guards seemed to have become the prisoners of the prisoners as we left *KZ Auschwitz*, dependent as they were on us for food.

Our relationship to our *SS* guards as we left *KZ Auschwitz* was, indeed, a strange one. Since the concentration camp system had called for utilizing prisoners for all labor, the *Paketstelle Kommando* controlled incoming food gifts until the day we left *KZ Auschwitz.* The *SS* guards who marched out with us carried only the meager rations issued them. Access to our better food depended on the good will of the *Paketstelle* prisoners. Our *SS* guards, with their guns, walked on either side of our column but they made no effort to shoot us or overpower us for our supplies. For them the writing was on the wall. The Red Army was not far behind. Our *SS* guards hurried us along. They seemed intent on delivering us to an ordered destination while there was still time. If the Red Army caught up with us, the *SS* guards could do worse than surrender some well-fed prisoners pulling wagons of food. However it came out for the *SS* guards, we prisoners hoped the Red Army would overtake us.

I cannot remember whether we marched for one or two days or more, or where, if at all, we slept. In time our strength began to give out and our food-laden wagons seemed to grow heavier with every hour that went by even as we continued eating from them. The longer we struggled with our wagons, pushing them though the snow-covered roads during this fiendishly cold Silesian weather (Europe had one of the coldest winters on record during 1944/1945) the less we could bear that burden. Finally we walked away from it. The *SS* guards scampered all over our wagons and took what they could while the rest remained on the wagons, a chance bonus for passers-by.

Our march ended in *Gleiwitz*, at a railroad siding yard. There we slumped to catch our breath while watching freight cars being switched into position on the tracks before us. I had not seen Lex since we left *KZ Auschwitz* and looking about I could not find him here among all this mass of people who had been brought here from all over *Silesia*. We were given permission to bring with us everything we could carry. Burdened with packets of food and the clothes we wore – the other clothes we had tossed away very early during the march – we pushed our way among a crowd of prisoners and were led into unroofed coal cars. In this herding process most comrades were separated. I was pushed into a coal car among strangers. We sat jammed together, barely being able to move. I was warmly dressed wearing a shirt, underwear, a tailor-made jacket, trousers and overcoat of heavy winter cloth. I also wore socks and shoes. Even so the January weather was bitter cold. The closeness of the bodies around me was not unwelcome.

The train moved off to begin its slow roll across the bleak countryside. The track joints underneath us clicked a lazy rhythm. After a while I stood up to look around and spotted the *SS* guards in a car ahead of ours with machine guns, their muzzles resting on the top of the side walls of the car. We ate. We talked a little, mostly speculating, as usual, about where we were headed. Day turned into night as we rolled. Dawn broke on haggard, sleepless prisoners. Snow kept falling, swirling around us overhead, and creating a thin blanket inside the car that would grow thicker when we stopped. And the train squealed to a stop often, sometimes for hours. In time all conversation ceased altogether. The cold was so intense that each of us had to concentrate all his energy on trying to stay warm and awake. Time and again our train, filled with prisoners, was pulled onto a siding so that a troop or supply train could get through. We were cleared for another stretch of track only when no other train was expected.

Snow continued to fall on our exposed bodies. Our clothes were wet, frozen in places, and began to stink. There was not so much as a can to use as a toilet, and we sat in our own and another's filth. Each of us had his own rations, but a few in our car had begun to lose interest in eating. People had begun to die in place. I concentrated hard on staying awake, and forced myself to eat from time to time. Each of us was alone in his misery. We could not make the effort to talk to each other.

Several days passed before we rolled to a stop at a station. We heard boots pounding a wooden platform and loud shouts before the doors of our cars were unbolted and flung open and we were ordered out. Painfully and stiffly I pulled myself erect. Looking about, I began to see what I had only dimly suspected in the numb last days on the train: most of my traveling companions were not asleep. They were dead. I was one of only a few in our car who had not frozen to death. I looked around me at all the dead and felt almost nothing. That I was alive in the midst of these dead prisoners was the important thing. Death was easy. If I had closed my eyes and given my weary body over to rest as these frozen men had, I, too, would have been dead. If I had not had the lucky break to be assigned to the *Paketstelle* in the months just passed, I, too, would have lacked the strength to stay awake and be alert and alive. As ordered, I got to my feet and began to move reluctant joints, working to restore my circulation.

This was Max Garcia in early 1945, 20 years old. It is hard for me to think now, decades later, of how to explain to my children that I had become almost immune to pity for the dead. I had lived the prior year and a half in an atmosphere where death was an accepted companion. The only thing of importance was life, because death was more common than life. Life was shown to have very little value. Only our own determination could give it value. If you gave in to your mental or physical suffering, if you lost interest, you would die. More than anything you had to want to live, and this became a fearful drive, causing you to seek life on almost any terms. Yet, I think, in the total scheme of things, maybe this is the way nature wants it. You do not know your destiny, and in circumstances like ours in 1944-45, you did not care much for destiny. The important thing was that you woke up in the morning; that it was another day.

KZ MAUTHAUSEN, KZ MELK AND DEATH MARCH TO *KZ EBENSEE* JANUARY - APRIL 1945

Those of us who had been *KZ Auschwitz* prisoners and who could still move were prodded by rough new *SS* guards and hurried along with heavy blows of their rubber truncheons. Our baggage was immediately confiscated. I could see that I was about to experience all over again my reception as a new prisoner at *KZ Buna* almost two years ago, except this time I thought I knew what to expect.

KZ Mauthausen was outside the town of *Mauthausen*, a small Austrian town on the Danube, near *Linz*, and about 150 kilometers west of *Vienna*. Our new *SS* guards, the *Prominenten* for this concentration camp, set upon us ferociously and mercilessly. We, the *Prominenten* of *KZ Auschwitz*, were easily singled out for special punishment, we who had well-fleshed bodies, tailor-made uniforms, good shoes, and numerous other things hidden inside our clothes. Most of us were reduced in a hurry to standard prisoners without status. There were a few exceptions, particularly the *KZ Auschwitz Prominenten* who had been criminal or political prisoners in various other concentration camps for many years and had friends among the *Prominenten* of *KZ Mauthausen*. For the most part these were men who had been exempt in *KZ Auschwitz* from having to wear the prison stripe haircut and who could wear the style haircut that was similar to that of the *SS* guards.

Predictably, we started our routine here by being herded through the camp to the delousing facility. While waiting in line to go through this process one of the *KZ Mauthausen* prisoners tending the door into the delousing facility began to yell and scream at me that here, in *KZ Mauthausen*, I would not become a *Prominente* and began to beat me fiendishly and left me lying on the ground at the entrance until some of my fellow *KZ Auschwitz* new arrivals helped me back onto my feet. It was undoubtedly the worst beating I ever received during my entire imprisonment. I'm convinced that the nausea, pain and dizziness that gripped me after this unwarranted attack were symptoms of a brain concussion. My memory of what happened afterwards remained vague. Our clothes were taken from us and we were shoved through the familiar processes of running through scalding hot showers and the scrubbing of all our hairy parts with Lysol-filled brushes. Lined up naked on the grounds of the camp in the ice and cold of January, we awaited the recording of our tattooed numbers, were issued new *KZ Mauthausen* prisoner numbers (116739 for me) and, finally, ragged old clothes. I was now back again where I was at the start of my imprisonment, with only a pair of wooden clogs, a nondescript jacket, trousers that fitted not at all and an ill-fitting cap plus the pieces of cloth that had our new prisoner numbers stenciled on them; We were responsible for getting them sewed on as quickly as possible. We got into these garments very quickly and then huddled together, shivering, trying to keep warm. When some of the *KZ Auschwitz* prisoners realized what this beating had done to me they tried to help me. Some of this I remember clearly but often my mind was fogged, my memory fuzzy.

When I saw *KZ Mauthausen* during the third week of January 1945, the week we arrived from *Gleiwitz*, it appeared to be a holding and dispersal center for incoming prisoners. Prisoners jammed the camp and filled the Blocks to overflowing. Our food rations seemed more scanty than I last remembered them in *KZ Auschwitz* before my long stay in the hospital there. My gut once again started a useless rebellion against unrelieved hunger. For me, hope had turned to despair, apprehension to mortal fear. Like every other prisoner, I responded mechanically to orders and followed the prisoners around me. Rubber truncheons drummed on our backs, heads, and legs as we were herded out of our Blocks for the daily Roll Calls or pressed into soup lines. Everything was done in double time. The beatings had made me very tired, worn out really. I noticed very little about the routines of the camp or how it was set up.

And so we waited glumly while our prisoner numbers were verified against whatever personal records came through to the *SS* administration of *KZ Mauthausen*. The *SS*, having a deadly fear of communicable diseases, kept us apart from the other prisoners in the camp. For nearly two weeks we were kept in quarantine in an overcrowded Block, beaten and abused routinely, and not allowed to mingle with other inmates of the camp. After we, the former *KZ Auschwitz* prisoners, had been officially re-identified we were assigned to outlying sub-camps where our labor was needed. The day my prisoner number was called out, I found myself on a truck filled with other prisoners being driven to a sub-camp not too far away, located on the edge of the town of *Melk* on the Danube and due east of *KZ Mauthausen*. Although we knew that the war was ending and I was leaving *KZ Mauthausen* I despaired of being liberated before the war would end. I was struggling to believe that I could live that long. I barely looked up at the buildings and grounds of *KZ Melk* as our trucks lumbered to a stop inside the gate. We prisoners filed down from the trucks and steeled ourselves for the usual blows that accompanied orders given to us. No blows came. Almost immediately we were assigned to *Arbeitskommandos* but we were not beaten or otherwise abused.

My memory of *KZ Melk* is almost non-existent. I do not recall what Block I lived in, where I worked, how I got there, what kind of work I did. All that I know about *KZ Melk* I have been told by other prisoners who survived the war and from what I have read. But we must not have been abused or overworked, because I did gain strength and even hope while we were there. We had been in *KZ Melk* since the early part of February 1945. Suddenly one morning in April we were told that we were going to be moved. We all lined up and were led to the upper bank of the Danube and then guided down to the Danube's edge where several barges were waiting for us. Where before we had been taken to *KZ Melk* by truck, this time we were being evacuated by barge. As we were taken west we passed *KZ Mauthausen* which was visible on top of the hill and looked from the barge as if it were a fortress which, indeed, it had been. What was so very amazing was the fact that I suddenly woke up from the fog of my concussion, was again fully alert and from that moment on I remembered everything.

We halted in *Linz* at one of the bridges. Filing off the barges we were told by *SS* guards that we were about to start on a march of a few days to the next camp. Many of us saw this as a good sign that the end was at hand, that there was a possibility of our being overtaken by the Red Army at any moment. I was excited. This was my third move within four months. Marching up the steps to the street level each of us was given a loaf of bread, a little margarine and a piece of salami. This was an unheard-of bonus, even for a long march, and then we moved through town in the direction of *Gmunden* on Traun Lake. At the other end of that lake was *KZ Ebensee*.

I started this march confidently now that I was awake again, but just in case liberation was still further off than I was hoping I kept a firm grip on my loaf of bread and my salami. The terrain was not difficult and I was in reasonably good shape under the circumstances, so I thought. This death march took all of six days and nights and we slept, or tried to, along the roadsides, stopping at the edges of streams, or rivulets, or at farmhouses for water. It was the middle of April 1945 and very, very cold. I do not believe that all of us who set out on this death march actually made it to *KZ Ebensee*. Within 24 hours the strength of many prisoners started to flag and our march really became a shuffle, even though it was all down hill. General weakness and exposure took their toll, but mentally quite a few of us remained alert. We believed we had the stamina to outlast our captors. I was a survivor among an army of survivors. Few of us had developed close friendships, but we all gave a hand to stragglers, those older than we or the weaker ones who were having difficulties keeping up. When we moved too slowly the *SS* guards prodded us to move faster. Those stragglers who could not keep up with the pace of shuffling were summarily shot by *SS* guards at the rear of the column.

At the time there were only two ways to get to the village of *Ebensee*: by way of *Gmunden* on a two-lane road along Traun Lake or from *Bad Ischl* on a two-lane road that followed the Traun River. We came by way of *Gmunden*. In order to get to *KZ Ebensee* each death-march column – and there were quite a few of them at that time – had to pass through the main street, *Hauptstrasse*, across the bridge over the Traun river. After we passed the railroad station and turned right we were shocked to see ahead of us a steep cobble-stoned road to the camp which, with our wooden clogs, our general weakness and the weather conditions prevailing then, was a cruel thing to climb. We were exhausted but inwardly, I'm sure, most of us were triumphant that we had made it.

Through the main gate we went and onto the *Appellplatz* of *KZ Ebensee*, a sub-camp of *KZ Mauthausen*, and I, personally, felt that we had scored a major victory over our enemy. My euphoria was soon punctured. I looked about me at an already overcrowded concentration camp. A sea of gaunt and filthy inmates eyed us hopelessly. One more time we were sent off to the usual delousing showers, scalded, scrubbed with Lysol, chilled to the bone. After we had received our "clean" jackets and trousers we were packed into filthy, overcrowded wooden barracks and assigned to sleep in bunks four-tiers high. Food rations were meager and of very poor quality, the worst of any concentration camp I had been in. We could not rest and starvation dogged us all. In addition, a most sadistic bunch of *SS* men ran this concentration camp. Treated like a menagerie of hated animals, driven mercilessly and beyond our strength to work inside a mountainside factory, we lived, each of us, on hope of imminent liberation. Many were the prisoners who gave up that hope, and then their bodies. Daily the *Totenkommando* came around to carry the dead off to the crematorium. I got through the nightmarish days and nights of *KZ Ebensee* one by one. It was good that I did not know then that the liberation described in the opening chapter was still about three weeks away.

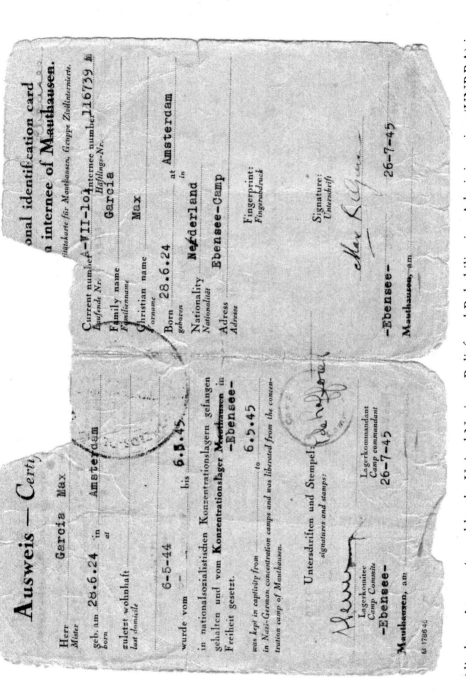

My 'discharge' paper issued by the United Nations Relief and Rehabilitation Administration (UNRRA) in *KZ Ebensee* showing that I had also been a prisoner in *KZ Auschwitz*.

PART 4

Serving American Forces in Europe

THE 319th INFANTRY REGIMENT 1945 – 1946

The officers and men of Headquarters Company, First Battalion, 319th Infantry Regiment, did not expect my return from Holland (as described at the end of Part 1), but when I was back among them they accepted me as if I were back from military leave. Gratefully, I resumed duty in Intelligence and Reconnaissance. My former bed awaited me in the pretty German house that had become our I & R quarters.

The quiet routines of the 319th continued as if I had not left. We rotated duty, cleaned quarters on schedule, attended drills and orientation movies about fraternization and venereal diseases, walked the downtown streets, and played baseball and catch for exercise. Evenings were spent in a makeshift enlisted men's club, or at American movies, or scheming to meet local girls. On Sundays our regimental band played for both GIs and townspeople in the *Bad Worishofen* park bandshell. Groups of GI musicians spelled each other, playing the latest American big-band tunes in various styles, drawing crowds of summer strollers as their admiring audience. After the U.S. Army moved into *Bad Worishofen*, the musicians played jazz and big-band combos in a club-like setting. Occasional entertainers from the States brought out the whole outfit as an audience: our day-to-day entertainment staples, however, were the old recorded favorites and new record releases provided by the USO. But of all the benefits of the USO, the most popular was that GIs could meet girls there. These meetings took place under chaperoned conditions, but what went on when the club closed for the night was up to the couples.

"Fraternization," as intimacy with girls of occupied enemy territories was called, although forbidden by Army policy, was the only real game in town. Everyone had a German girlfriend who wanted candy bars, cigarettes, small luxury items, and the company of young men in army uniform – everyone, that is except me. I was called upon right and left to interpret between American men and German women, or to speak to a particular German girl on behalf of some GI. I met many a woman looking for companionship, and yet

I could not bring myself to want intimacy with any German woman. I responded stiffly to their overtures and turned away from them in disgust. The women kept smiling and my friends either laughed at me or worked on me with persuasive arguments. "Hell, Max, the Germans were America's bitter enemy too, not just yours, and we're damned glad we finally brought them to their knees. But why bring the women into it? Women are the same everywhere. They're not fighters. They want to be given things and treated right, and then they'll do right by you." After a few weeks of trying to counter arguments of this nature just as I was beginning to figure out what women were all about, I lost my fastidiousness and my virgin state all at the same time. Sexual encounters were everywhere for the asking, and I joined the merry-go-round of fraternization with available German girls.

Possibly to give the occupying army something else to think about, and to re-instill habits of military discipline, the Commanding General of the 80th Infantry Division ordered a divisional field parade. Our Regiment, the 319th, had paraded down the main streets of *Bad Worishofen* and *Mindelheim* like any other military unit. The GIs had marched with shouldered rifles, flags flying, shoes polished, bands playing. The townspeople had turned out at curbsides to watch. But the field parade was an American phenomenon I had not heard of. Conceived as an instructive exercise drill for units in the area, some thousands strong, the parade was an enormous logistical undertaking. Once the date was set, officers buried themselves in the details of planning the convocation of all units and their equipment, of scheduling their exercises, their individual rendezvous stations, their feeding and their departures.

Because the parade was held on our home territory, the men of the 319th were delegated to find a suitable site. We found flat pasture land that fully met our requirements. Accompanying a delegation of our unit, the First Battalion, I told the farmer-owner that his land was being requisitioned for a brief period and that he could graze his cattle there only when American troops were not using it. We ripped up his fences so that tanks, armored trucks, and artillery vehicles could enter. We staked out the field, marking the spots where various units would station themselves. Spectators to the field parade were welcome but no one ordered the local population to attend. Even so, on the scheduled day, Germans left their nearby villages and towns and streamed into *Bad Worishofen* to watch the massing of the units on all the streets of the town, and then followed them onto the parade ground. Each unit of the 80th Infantry Division, with all its equipment, was ordered by the Commanding General to pass in review. One by one the units marched and rolled past the reviewing stand in a continuous flow, an impressive spectacle of energy and power. All units had come together in the early morning hours from their scattered bases in the surrounding countryside. After passing the reviewing stand, they left the area in a pre-assigned order to return to their home territories. The Germans, too, filed quietly back to their homes.

Routine settled in again. I looked for chores to do to keep myself busy. Idleness was not for me; it allowed my mind to wonder about tomorrow and grow anxious. Max Garcia, needed aide to the 319th, was how I preferred to see myself. I had no other identity and wanted no other. I had spent my young manhood working to survive. It suited me now to work at serving in any way I could these openhearted, strong Americans who had given me food, shelter, and open companionship. If anything was wanted or needed in the Battalion, I would find a way to get it. I was kidded about my survival tactics and my old-world ways. I would shoot back wisecracks about the foibles of American GIs, but was genuinely glad to be called upon to interpret, or to explain some local matter, or to apply my knowledge of *organisierung* to obtain a hard-to-get article. Called "the Dutchman," I was fairly well known in the outfit.

Back in *Aich-Assach* I had acquired my first camera. I began to take snapshots of the men of my Company, a hobby I continued in *Bad Worishofen*. I snapped pictures of them in march and drill. I snapped my friends at rest, in quite different moods. There were Marksberry, McDonald, Pritchett of I & R; GI friends Beer, Kullowitz, McCarthy; officers Miles, Salomone, Regan, Poppen, McWhorter and Sergeant Schmalz. Some of us toured nearby towns and villages in our off-duty hours. My curiosity and my camera then turned to interesting local buildings, notable details and wall painting, sculptures, parks and fountains. I looked inquisitively at structures quite different in character from the close, narrow buildings of Dutch and Belgian cities.

One day I was called to the command post. Some of the officers, Lt. Col. Clark among them, drove me out to their new club, which was being established in an old country inn. They showed me their remodeling work, then called my attention to the bar that was being constructed. The club was to open the forthcoming Saturday evening, they told me, and when it did they wanted the bar to be equipped in a typically American way, meaning, Clark explained, that not only drinks were to be served there but also bowls of hardboiled and pickled eggs.

No one had seen a fresh egg since our arrival in *Bad Worishofen*. The enlisted men had grumbled continually about the reconstituted powdered eggs served daily for breakfast. Now the officers longed at least for a few fresh eggs for the opening of their American-style bar.

"Max, it would sure be great if you could find us some fresh eggs," said Col. Clark." "There just have to be a few chickens hidden around here somewhere."

"Yes, sir. If its eggs you want, I'll bet I can find some," I answered. One of the cooks was assigned to drive me in a jeep wherever I wanted to go. We drove around and visited a number of small farms. When I asked where laying chickens might be found all farmers shook their heads. We drove back to *Bad Worishofen*, discouraged, but vowing to take our search farther the next day. Driving down one of the streets of *Bad Worishofen,* I spotted a building that aroused my curiosity when I noticed that a number of women were entering and leaving it regularly. We parked the jeep and watched the women and the building they were entering. When the women entered the building they carried folded bags. When they left the building those bags held something very delicate because they carried those bags very carefully. Eggs, I thought. They carry those bags just as our customers did in *Amsterdam* when they bought eggs at our poultry store on the *Diamant Straat.*

"Wait here," I told the cook. "I think we've got something." I jumped out of the jeep and walked into the building. Many women were lined up inside, and what they were there to buy became immediately very obvious. This place was an egg warehouse. Eggs were stacked from floor to ceiling. I could hardly believe what I saw. I walked out of the place nonchalantly and then, when outside, I ran to the jeep to tell the cook what I had found.

"You know why we are eating powdered eggs?" I asked. "Because the God-damned Germans have stockpiled every egg in Germany, that's why. That place is full of eggs."

I told the cook to get a truck while I went inside to take over the warehouse. "Max, you're crazy." the cook said. "We can't do that. All we need is a few eggs. The officers will never go for stealing a warehouse full of eggs."

"Then don't tell them." I replied. "Just bring back a truck and some of our men and we'll load up."

We argued. I convinced the cook to go after a truck, I re-entered the warehouse and ordered the owner to cease selling any more eggs and to send his customers home. I told him his egg supply was being confiscated for the use of the American Army.

The owner looked at me with amazement, then spluttered, "These eggs are my property. You can't just take them."

"Mister, you seem to have forgotten who won the war," said I, warming to combat and all this in German! "You stole from me when you occupied Holland. You stole everyone blind in every country you occupied or passed through. Don't tell me we can't take your eggs. Get those women out of here!"

We shouted at one another. The women joined in, screaming at me furiously. The truck I had ordered seemed a long time in coming, and I felt progressively more nervous waiting for it among these people. But I held my ground. Reluctantly the women began to leave. Finally the jeep returned with a truck behind it. There had been more arguments at the Command Post, the cook told me, about the probable disapproval of Military Government. Unbelievable, I thought. I had been asked to go find some eggs and when I did, the Americans did not know whether they should take them.

Nevertheless, we loaded our truck to capacity.

We drove onto the Company street where an amazed crowd of GIs watched the unloading of our truckload of eggs. Crazy Garcia has done it again, they all said. The officers would have more eggs than drinks at the opening of their club bar, and plenty of eggs would be left for the enlisted men.

Our commanding officer, Lieutenant Colonel Arthur H. Clark, who had allowed me to cast my lot with the 319th Infantry Regiment. while in *Aich-Assach*, came out from his office to survey our haul. I could see that he was amused but at the same time concerned about how he was going to explain such a heist to Military Government. I could not understand these Americans, and said so.

"Why?" I asked, "Aren't the officers of Military Government coming to the Officer's Club?" "Yes," Colonel Clark replied. "Are they not going to eat eggs?" I asked. "Touché!" Colonel Clark answered. "You've made your point!" What was all the agony about? What had I learned in my life but that the strong always took from the weak, the victor from the vanquished. The Americans themselves had not hesitated to commandeer housing and land, to bribe women to their uses with food, cigarettes, and clothing. Yet now they were getting balky about taking a supply of eggs. No German or Russian occupation forces would have hesitated for a single moment.

What I didn't understand at the time was that the Americans did not see themselves in the permanent role of military conquerors but as developers of a fair policy of local self-government so that they could go home. Right or wrong, with guilt or without, everyone ate the eggs I had provided. After all, everyone agreed, what could be done about the ways of their dedicated Dutchman.

On Sunday morning, following the officer's Saturday-night club opening, the cooks provided a festival of fresh eggs for breakfast. Whatever the preference of the GI – scrambled, boiled, sunny-side up, over-easy, poached – that's how his eggs were prepared, and in any amount requested. Some ate six at once. There were eggs for breakfast, lunch, and dinner for days, cooked ungrudgingly in any style by cooks who were glad to be able to serve a dish so popular with the men.

The next time the officers asked me to procure a supply of something they gave me money to pay for it from the Soldier's Fund. What they wanted next time was wine for the whole unit. The officers had heard that wine was available cheaply in the French Zone of Occupation at the German-French border. What with my reputation for bringing home the bacon (as the Americans called it) and my ability to speak French and German, I was the logical choice to assist a wine-finding detail to the border.

A young and eager second lieutenant named Charles McWhorter was placed in charge of this expedition. Two enlisted men also accompanied us, one driving our truck and one in the jeep in which the lieutenant and I rode. We drove North to *Wiesbaden*. We found no cheap wine in quantity, but we enjoyed looking around, like four tourists, at the fine old towns we passed through that had not suffered any significant damage from the war. Some buildings in *Wiesbaden* had been reduced to rubble only a few months earlier. Men in all kinds of military uniforms and vehicles clogged the streets. We had no trouble finding Bachelor Officers Quarters (BOQ) for Lieutenant McWhorter, and a USO club for the rest of us, where we spent the night. In the morning we pooled the information we had gathered the night before while drinking with Frenchmen and Americans. We headed due South to *Baden-Baden*. There, as advised, we found our wine suppliers. We bargained, bought, and loaded up. Back on the Company street the following evening, volunteers were very eager to help unload our precious cargo.

Not long after that trip, Colonel Clark received orders to go home. I hated to see him go. There was a formal distance between his high rank and my auxiliary status, but he had taken me in at *Aich-Assach*, had kept his promise to me, and had seen to it that I was treated well even when I had made mistakes. A celebration was planned in his honor at the Officer's Club on the evening he was to leave. Along with his driver, I was delegated to accompany him to his train in another town after the party. At the appointed hour of departure, his driver and I entered the club to pick up the Colonel. Everyone was still celebrating. Everyone was drunk. Colonel Clark, the center of attention because he was the first one of the unit to be designated to go home, was hardly sober. Gently we pulled him away from the celebrants and, reminding him he had to make his train connection, we helped him into the back of his waiting staff car.

Sitting next to the Colonel during the long ride to the railroad station, I summoned the courage to tell him that I would always be thankful that he had taken me into his First Battalion at *Aich-Assach*, and that I was going to miss him. To my astonishment, Colonel Clark turned to me and said that he was going to help me get to the United States. He knew how much I wanted to go there, and he wanted to help. I was deeply moved, and tried to express my profound gratitude. Then I checked myself. I realized that the Colonel probably would not remember for long what he had said to me. I poured coffee from a canteen for Colonel Clark to drink, to help sober him up for the train ride ahead. We made the train on time, shook hands all around, and wished one another well.

I tried to imagine what it would be like to be in Colonel Clark's shoes and able to leave devastated Europe because his tour of duty was up. He would return to his family in prosperous America, to *Buffalo*, where everyone was free to do as he liked, where everyone was rich and drove his own car.

By late autumn 1945, the 80th Infantry Division was ordered to Czechoslovakia. Our Regiment packed up to travel military-convoy style across Bavaria to Northern Czechoslovakia. Our 319th Infantry Regiment was assigned to the area around *Eger* (now called *Cheb*), Czechoslovakia. To my relief, there had been no question about my coming along, I was an accepted, if unofficial, member of the 319th. The 80th Division had been sent in to replace another American occupying force in this territory until an agreement could be worked out with the Soviet Union to restore Czechoslovakia as a fully independent nation. In 1945 the Red Army of the Soviet Union occupied most of Eastern Czechoslovakia. The Americans occupied the Western borderlands, the Sudetenland, which the Third Reich had annexed in 1938, a move that was welcomed by the German-speaking population of that area. While the Czecho-slovakians looked upon the Sudeten Germans as traitors for having joined forces with the Nazis, the Sudeten Germans looked upon the

Americans as their liberators. By now the Czechoslovakians and the Sudeten Germans had a fierce hatred for each other, and the Soviet Union considered all of us their enemies. Thus our occupation duty in Czechoslovakia was a far more nervous assignment than duty in Austria or Bavaria had been.

Czechoslovakia had not existed as a nation until the end of World War I when it became an independent nation as one of the successor states of the defeated Austrian-Hungarian Hapsburg Empire. It consisted basically of Bohemia, Moravia, and Slovakia. In World War II, Czechoslovakia was swallowed up by Hitler – the Sudetenland first, the rest of Czechoslovakia later. At the end of World War II the Allies persuaded the Soviet Union that they, jointly, should restore Czechoslovakia as a free, independent, nation by withdrawing all their military units on the very same day. At last this was agreed to.

However, before all this took place in February 1946, the 319th upon arriving at their designated localities in Sudetenland immediately assumed a posture of military readiness. The rookies who had come into the Regiment to replace the homeward-bound combat veterans were drilled daily and put through maneuvers alongside the regulars. Neglected rifles and guns were oiled. Telephone lines were strung between all units of the 80th Infantry Division. All vehicles were brought to a state of readiness and all heavy-duty combat equipment was also ready just in case.

In time we became familiar with the customs, problems, and people of our Sudeten locale. I met some of the citizens of *Eger* soon after our arrival when I was assigned to find a baker to prepare our unit's bread, rolls and cakes, and soon I began to pick up some Czech words. Like everyone else in the unit, I also found words with which to pick up Czech girls. But when I discovered that almost all of them were Sudeten girls, I could converse with them in German. Manless since the departure of the Nazis, and deprived of the favors they had received during the Nazi occupation, nearly all these Sudeten girls were now eager to fraternize with the Americans. Hated by the few Czechoslovakians still living in their area, these girls looked to the Americans for sexual companionship and the amenities that usually followed.

The whole battalion was soon overrun with girls. The officers were as vulnerable as the men. Although division headquarters had ordered them to issue restrictive orders about fraternization, they failed to follow up on them. To get around these restrictions which prohibited women and girls in enlisted men's quarters, the GIs hired their newly-obtained girlfriends to clean their quarters, paying them in Army scrip. In this way, the women and girls entered upon a paid domestic arrangement that was condoned by the officers. In fact, the officers cooperated with the enlisted men to the extent of giving notice well in advance when there would be inspections in the enlisted men's quarters.

We performed our occupation duties as ordered; but, just as in *Bad Worishofen*, we reserved our greatest energy for eating, drinking, dancing, making love, and changing partners. No doubt the occupiers of the Soviet Union, not so far away from us, were playing the same game.

I ate my first Thanksgiving Dinner with the officers and enlisted men in *Eger* with the 319th . It was an orgy of formal dining courses, the like of which I had never seen or tasted. My preoccupation with food, a habit since my days in the concentration camps, was intense. Since I became attached to American forces directly after my liberation from *KZ Ebensee*, I had always cultivated a close relationship with the cooks and their kitchens and enjoyed their assignments to obtain local foods from local suppliers. Noticing the arrival of large, extra cartons of foodstuffs at the start of November, I hung around the kitchen to find out why supplies were increasing. The cooks told me about the history and traditions of the American Thanksgiving Day. I watched them cut, cook and bake for days. Yet I was not prepared for the extravagance of the celebration, even at our distant outpost.

On the appointed day, the men were summoned to the mess hall, which had been converted into an elegant dining room. The tables were covered with white linen, decorated with candlesticks and centerpieces of fruits, nuts, and flowers and the tables were laid out with individual place settings. Serving tables were covered with an unusual array of food. Prayers were offered. Then we dug in. I tasted everything: turkey, stuffing, candied yams, cranberry sauce, peas, carrots, beans, corn, all in sauces or butter, salads, rolls, relishes, pickles, then pumpkin, mince or apple pie.

About a month later we consumed a similar feast in celebration of Christmas. Throughout that season, from Thanksgiving to New Years, American GIs received, and shared, great boxes of home-cooked baked goods and candies, as well as small gifts and I thought about our days in the *"Paketstelle"* in *KZ Auschwitz*.

For the New Year, I jumped into preparations for another wild party, this one under very different circumstances from the one thrown at *KZ Auschwitz* the year before. We rented the large meeting room of a local organization for the occasion, and I hired a German brass "oompapah" band. Liquor rations had been saved up since Christmas.

On New Year's Eve, the Mess Sergeant and I set up serving tables, stocking them with rows of popular American brands of liquors, soft drinks, mixers and cans of fruit juices. There was very little beer because the beer-producing areas, such as *Pilsen* were occupied by the Red Army.

In my efforts to Americanize I had tried but had not succeeded in developing their capacity for downing hard liquor. This evening was no exception. We had been asked to attend the party in full-dress uniform, and had permission to bring our *frauleins*. Because I was planning to help, my girl and I arrived early. Also, I owned no full-dress uniform. We mixed our liquor with various delicious fruit juices. We danced; we socialized, and drank more cocktails. By the time most of my friends arrived, I was sitting down and could not get up. Well before midnight I suffered the humiliation of being half-carried, half-dragged back to my bed. I awoke hours later to find a furious girlfriend sitting reluctantly by my side. As her ticket to the party, I had been a wipeout.

On off-duty hours, many GIs took tours to local resorts and places of interest. I joined excursions to nearby *Franzensbad*, then to *Marienbad*, where we relaxed in elegant hotels and restaurants, bought souvenirs in pleasant shops, bathed in their famous spa waters, and sipped "therapeutic" mineral waters. The USO arranged a special tour to the venerable capital city of *Prague*, which was in the Red Army's Zone of occupation. My request to join that tour was turned down because of the possibility of my being identified and detained by the Red Army as a Displaced Person.

Soon after the plan for leaving Czechoslovakia had been agreed to with the Red Army, the 80th Infantry Division received the long awaited orders to proceed to Embarkation Camp *Aschaffenburg* in Germany for repatriation home. A joint farewell military parade was held on the main street of *Konigsworth*, a historic combination of Czechoslovakian, Red Army and American units. Officers of these three services and representatives of the Czechoslovakian Republic and civilian authorities of *Konigsworth* watched us from a reviewing stand.

Sadly, as soon as the presence of the Western Allies had disappeared, the Soviet Union lost no time in bringing Czechoslovakia under their political control. The forced suicide – tossed out of a window – of Foreign Minister Jan Masaryk signaled the triumph of Moscow-dominated communism in Czechoslovakia. From that time on she would be counted among the puppet states of the Soviet Union.

When the units of the 80th Infantry Division arrived back at each of their stations after they had paraded in *Konigsworth*, they immediately began the task of dismantling everything and packing the trucks that would take them out of Czechoslovakia to *Aschaffenburg*.

Because of the slowness of such a move on the roads of Germany, we had been ordered to be ready to move very early in the morning and word had spread quickly among the Sudeten German girls, all of whom now were afraid to remain in Czechoslovakia. We helped them climb into our trucks for the long but not unpleasant ride into the heart of Germany. Once at *Aschaffenburg*, the entire Division was placed in quarantine within the tent camp while the girls stood outside the barbed-wired fence and waited in vain. They had no money, no food, and no prospect of fraternizing further with these Americans.

Max R. Garcia as a member of the Nurnberg C.I.C. unit, 1946.

Camp *Aschaffenburg* was a "repple-depple," or Replacement Depot, but now it had become a processing camp for home-going veterans. Medical examinations were conducted and treatment provided where required, prevention shots were given and personal records were brought up to date. No passes were issued for any reason while we were there. Time dragged and days turned into weeks. The men played cards, lay on their bunks, smoked, or hung about the USO, awaiting orders for shipment home. I waited too, but not for shipment to the States. Back at our place of residence, near *Konigsworth*, I became very anxious when official orders came through for the Division to be sent home. As usual, I had postponed thinking about what I would do next until I was forced to face up to it.

I went to see Captain Jesse R. Miles, under whom I had worked since *Aich-Assach*. To my relief, he told me that as a career army man he was not due to return to the States, and that his plans included taking me with him to his next assignment. I told him about Colonel Clark's inebriated promise to me, and asked if he thought it were possible that the Colonel might help me get to the States. Captain Miles surprised me by affirming that he knew of the Colonel's intentions, that they had discussed the matter before the Colonel departed. Colonel Clark had asked Captain Miles to look after me until arrangements could be worked out. My head reeled! So this had not been the sentimental talk of a friendly officer in his cups. Even if I never reached the States, the humanity of the Colonel's efforts for me was overwhelming. I had hardly dared hope that the generous efforts of an American officer would give me a future in the United States.

THE C.I.C. 1946

Captain Jesse R. Miles took me with him from the *Aschaffen-burg* replacement depot to *Scheinfeld*, Bavaria, near *Nurnberg*, where he had been assigned to duty with the 18th Infantry Regiment of the First Infantry Division. We found his new unit headquartered in a hilltop castle overlooking the town.

Captain Miles reported to the Commanding Officer while I sat in the Staff Car. Some minutes later he returned to escort me into the ornate office of the Colonel in charge. The Colonel was a short man, even shorter than I (I stand at 5' 6"), who had a scrappy manner and had two German Shepherd dogs at his side, but the officers discussed my situation amiably enough. Captain Miles went so far as to explain that he was acting as my guardian for a colonel who was hoping to help me immigrate to the States. He outlined the work I had been doing for the 319th and asked the colonel if he would try to find some work for me in his own I & R section. Without batting an eyebrow the forbidding looking colonel agreed, and to my relief I started pulling routine duty once more. But I & R work had become dull. On-the-spot-interpreting was almost never needed. The bureaucracy of peace was enlarging daily, with ever more specialized agencies engaged in the governing process. I & R men at the Regimental level had to scratch hard for something to do.

Bitter winds blew snow about the turrets of our castle and down into her courtyards. We kept our coats on in the castle's vast, cold rooms. Within a few weeks I no longer saw details of the interior that had so impressed me on our arrival: marble staircases and statuary, richly polished woods throughout, massive and ornate furnishings, and, in one large hall, individual ceiling frescoes framed within heavy intersecting beams. Heedless of the opulence, our Regiment had the castle rooms and halls festooned with communications wiring, and the picturesque courtyard was filled with trucks and jeeps.

Often, on off-duty hours, we drove down to *Scheinfeld* and though her classic entrance-tower gate in order to stroll about this quaint Bavarian town. Evenings we gathered to drink and socialize at the local enlisted men's club. At one such gathering I met and talked with a GI who became extremely interested in me when I mentioned my background. He asked me many questions about what I had been through and when we parted I realized that he had learned a great deal more about me than I had about him. Within a few days he sent me an invitation to a dinner sponsored by the local unit of the Counter Intelligence Corps. Pondering the reasons for such an invitation I became wary enough to seek out Captain Miles. I asked him what he could make of a GI pumping me for my story, and then asking me to dinner with other C.I.C. agents. I feared a trap and that my attendance at the dinner would result in my being sent to a D.P. camp or back to Holland.

Captain Miles was surprised to hear of the C.I.C. overture, but he looked at the invitation and thought about the fears I had expressed. He said he doubted that the C.I.C. was interested in hunting down D.P.s who were not war criminals. He suggested that I look upon their invitation as an interesting opportunity for myself and possible turning point in my life. He reminded me that I was not doing much at that point besides waiting to hear from Colonel Clark, and might as well be doing some useful work among interesting people while I waited.

I went to the dinner, joining a small group of young men dressed in officer's pinks, but showing no rank. We talked together as a number of drinks were consumed, followed by an excellent dinner. By dessert I had told my story once more before the assembled group. In answer to my questions they told me a little about the work of the C.I.C. They were primarily interested in rounding up Nazis and overseeing the establishment of local governments under American Military Government. One person popped the question: Would I consider joining the C.I.C.? My language ability and my I & R training were just what they were looking for, he explained, but in addition they had to be assured that I had the motivation to dedicate myself to their kind of work.

I told them that I was not sure, that I would like some time to think about it. Not yet a year out of concentration camps and often barely disguising angry, vengeful impulses towards Germans, I knew I could hunt Nazi war criminals with dedication. On the other hand, the camps had taught me to be wary as a hunted animal myself. I still suspected the C.I.C. might be interested in rounding up D.P.s still on the loose. Men wandering homeless were a constant problem to occupying forces, and the Americans might be looking to the day when I would be left behind. I did not want to risk being processed back to Holland, particularly with my new hope of emigrating to the United States. I had seen Holland after the war. I, a Jew, would never be at home in *Amsterdam* again. If I were forced to return what would I do in that war-devastated country to live? I could see the writing on the wall. I would be a diamond polisher, a surviving Jewish diamond polisher, who would teach the trade to a new generation of gentile polishers.

In the end I trusted to Miles' opinion and overcame my fears. I made an appointment with the C.I.C. contact man, telling him that I would take the job provided I was given the same guarantees I had demanded of the 319th. They had to promise not to abandon me if their unit was to move on or they were returned to the United States. They had to make some provision for my care and safety. The C.I.C. man gave me his solemn word that I would be looked after. He asked me to report for duty the following week.

I began to pack my belongings and to say my farewells to the officers and men of the 18th Infantry Regiment. The time was late March 1946. During that week Captain Miles received a letter from Colonel Clark, postmarked *Buffalo*, New York. Captain Miles ran to my room and showed me the Colonel's signed affidavit, dated 7 March 1946, sponsoring my emigration to the United States. I was overcome. Colonel Clark had kept his promise to me, a homeless Jewish refugee. My gratitude and astonishment gave way to pure elation. I turned to Captain Miles and asked him when and how I could plan to leave.

News had reached us by then that President Harry S. Truman had authorized in December, 1945, the admission to the United States of 42,000 qualifying Displaced Persons. Captain Miles reminded me that to qualify for emigration into the United States I had to have a visa from my country of origin, and that my case could well be complicated by the fact that I had refused to return to my homeland or register there, or anywhere, except for my stay in Germany with the Army of the United States of America. In addition, I had just committed myself to a new duty assignment with the C.I.C. We talked about my prospects of obtaining a visa, and eventually I agreed with his analysis that if I worked for the C.I.C. for a while, they could probably help me obtain a visa and passage to the States faster than he or I could. I agreed to honor my commitment. Captain Miles drove me to the local office of the C.I.C. on the appointed day, and Captain Miles assured me that we could stay in touch.

At their offices, instead of being invited to unpack, I was hustled with my baggage into a car and driven immediately to *Bamberg*, Germany. I had been given only the briefest of explanations: six weeks of introduction and training at the *Bamberg* Station was standard operating procedure. It sounded logical, but the silent ride to nearby *Bamberg* was long enough for old anxieties to arise that I might be stepping into a trap.

To my relief, I was greeted warmly and officially at the other end by a couple of officers who called me by my name and let me know that they had been expecting me. They introduced me around, showed me to my room, and gave me a briefing on the house rules. Though I had never met a single one of them before my arrival at the *Bamberg* Headquarters, every person I met made an effort to put me at ease.

As the C.I.C.'s newest recruit, I joined a curiously assorted group of trainees. Some were American, some European. A few were women. Most of us were in our twenties, but a few were as old as their forties. I could tell where most of my European companions came from by their accents, but we were discouraged from asking personal questions about one another. Only administrative officers knew our personal histories. Encouraged to keep to ourselves and to avoid fraternizing with even American forces, we settled down to learn and work together. We all were now dressed in identical officer's uniforms conspicuously unmarked by rank. We were trained in setting up files, in firing revolvers and the M-45, and in standard military driving procedures. We were instructed in interrogation techniques and various aspects of reconnaissance and counter-intelligence. Much of the material we covered I had learned earlier as an interpreter but never in such scientific detail. I trained no more than four weeks when I was told to pack up for assignment to the *Nurnberg* office.

By early May, 1946, a C.I.C. driver delivered me to the door of an imposing city mansion that served as our headquarters there.

Again I was warmly received and shown around our vast quarters before being escorted to comfortable rooms across the street in yet another building that served as our residence. Staff members welcomed me cordially, treating me like an equal in rank and experience. If I was somewhat unsettled not to know who had authority over whom here, I pretended not to be concerned, and within a few days or so I no longer cared. I became transformed, as if by magic, into a real officer relaxing in his private club.

I was briefed in the specifics of our work. We were charged with picking up intelligence about actions that might be against the interest of the U.S. Army. We were to ferret out Nazis who ranked in the *SS*. We were to cooperate closely with Military Government to restore the rudiments of local government. Black marketing and local law enforcement, usually outside the jurisdiction of the C.I.C., were to be followed up if an intelligence angle was suspected.

I started duty by assisting with office interrogations. *Nurnberg* had its share of Frenchmen, Belgians, and Dutchmen who had supposedly been brought to wartime Germany as forced laborers, but some of them were Nazi sympathizers who had agreed during the war to work in German factories. Most of these people now wanted to go home. It was our task to determine which of them were Nazis, so that they could be processed through military courts or to be turned over to their home government for justice.

One of my first assignments was to assist in the interrogation of a young Dutch couple who claimed to have been brought to Germany as forced laborers. I listened for about 10 minutes to their interrogator and the couple who spoke to each other in German. I caught them in a lie about some of their details and stopped the questioning to call for a consultation with the interrogator. We left the room to decide on a strategy, then returned to the room and continued the questioning of the couple. Suddenly I broke into the exchange, speaking Dutch, and told the two they were liars and Nazi sympathizers. Taken off guard, the two became flustered, capitulated, and confessed. They begged to be able to return home, stating that they had been too young to know what they were doing, that they had learned a bitter lesson by their acts. I wrote a report on the case, after which the young Dutch couple were turned over to Dutch government representatives in *Nurnberg*.

When we were doing undercover work we always wore civilian clothing, and a number of us also shared the use of a beautiful Mercedes-Benz convertible that had been "liberated" (their word for "*organisiert*") by the Americans. We agents were an almost comical giveaway as we rode around town in that convertible, civilian clothes notwithstanding. Everyone knew the Mercedes belonged to the C.I.C., and that the Americans were almost the only ones in town with enough gasoline to drive such a car. I drove the Mercedes at every opportunity, feeling like a king as I slid onto the smooth leather seat beneath the steering wheel. Looking out over the great headlamp, I would roar through the streets of *Nurnberg*, dodging pedestrians, bicycles and horse-drawn carts. I did not need so much as a driver's license to get anywhere I wanted to go in that car.

One day we received a tip that a wanted *SS* officer was on a certain train that was due to arrive at the main *Nurnberg* railroad station and it was expected that he would be wearing civilian clothes. We had a very good photograph of him. A contingent of us agents, in civilian clothes, packed our revolvers and sped to the main railroad station in our well-known Mercedes. We elbowed our way through crowds of homeward-bound ex-POWs, and met the train on which our fugitive was supposed to arrive. We thought we had spotted him and shouted at him to stop. The man turned swiftly into the crowd, and we fired over their heads in his direction. Everyone dove to the platform, but search as we did, we could not find our man again. Still, we climbed back into the Mercedes in good humor. The chase had been great fun, even if our quarry had eluded us, we knew we had given him a good scare and that he would have to keep on running.

On another occasion I was sent, by myself, in one of our jeeps, to pick up a former *SS* officer who had just been identified. The address I was given was that of a butcher shop. The store was open but no one was in the sales area. No one entered or left the store as I sat there in my jeep watching the door. I began to sweat as I started to think about the fellow I was after, an *SS* butcher, who would be working in the back of the shop holding, no doubt, a cleaver in his hand. Finally I entered the shop and rushed into the back area, revolver in hand. There I found the man I was after sitting quietly at his kitchen table. I flashed my credentials and announced his arrest. He surrendered without saying a word and made no effort to resist me or overpower me as I drove him, sitting beside me in the front of the jeep, to our office.

Once I was on night duty when I took a telephone call that multiple murders had been committed at a nearby Polish D.P. camp. The C.I.C. was expected to investigate such cases to determine if subversive activities were involved in the crime. It was about 10 o'clock in the evening when I drove across town to the camp. I showed my credentials to the Military Police who were already there. They escorted me to a cordoned off barracks and led me inside to a sickening scene of splattered blood and brains. My stomach churned and I tried hard not to gag. Soon I pulled out my notebook and began to write up what I was seeing and what I had learned from interviewing witnesses.

I learned that the D.P.'s at the camp, while awaiting repatriation, were employed as guards at military installations, receiving in exchange occupation chits and cigarettes. To increase their earnings, many of them worked the black market on the side. The D.P.s wore blue-dyed American uniforms and were housed together in old German military barracks such as the blood-spattered one in which I stood that night. The place was divided into two-bunk cubicles, each with enough extra room for a single chair. Clothes were hung on nails in the partition walls, which were about an inch thick.

According to witnesses, two of the three dead men I had found there had been feuding for weeks over their operations in the cigarette black market. One of them worked himself into such a frenzy of anger he had gotten himself a rifle. That evening he had aimed the rifle at the head of his enemy whom he knew was sleeping on the bunk directly adjacent to the partition. The bullet killed not only his enemy in the next cubicle but the fellow who was sleeping in the other bunk in that cubicle. When he realized what he had done, the man placed the muzzle of the rifle in his mouth and blew his brains out.

Back at headquarters I reported my findings to the duty officer. I had no evidence of subversive activity, but rather of frustration, passion, and remorse. I added that I was still sick to my stomach over what I had seen. The duty officer laughed out loud and told me to forget it. He suggested that I eat a good bowl of spaghetti to help me get over it. At breakfast in the morning, agents who had heard about my report greeted me with taunts and laughter over my squeamishness.

Sent out solo again to look into a report of wholesale thefts at a Quartermaster Corps supply depot, which was also guarded by D.P.s, I poked about so that I might observe what was going on. I was spotted by the commanding officer of the depot, a colonel, who summoned me to his office and asked me to identify myself. After I showed him my credentials he demanded to know my rank. I told him that C.I.C. agents are not allowed to divulge their rank. He threatened to throw me off the base. I told him that throwing me off the base would only create more problems for himself than the presumed thefts from his depot. He had no thefts, he maintained, and had no pilfering. I replied that in that case he should have no objections answering my questions. He now told me he would not answer any of my questions unless I told him my rank.

I felt defeated. I felt that his piercing stare could see through my C.I.C. uniform to the rankless D.P. underneath. I turned on my heels and headed back to headquarters where I informed the officer of the day of the failure of my mission. "Max," I was told, "your mission is to get that colonel to give you his cooperation." I was assured that I had the authority to question even an American colonel, and I was ordered to return at once to his office to press my inquiry and to call headquarters if the colonel gave me any additional troubles.

Back at the colonel's desk I tried once more to insist that he answer my questions, but again without success. As instructed I called headquarters and ordered the colonel to take the phone. I never learned what he was told but as I stood there his face turned ashen and when he sat down he now was compliant. He answered my questions in detail, and allowed me to conduct a full investigation. I no longer doubted that the C.I.C. had an effective hierarchy. Organizational authority, I now fully realized, reached as high as was needed.

A few months later I was placed in charge of a *Kreis*, which is similar to an American county. In addition to my regular duties I now drove regularly to my assigned *Kreis*, where I worked in cooperation with the local military government and the local police on any problem arising within the C.I.C.'s jurisdiction. One afternoon as I drove my jeep back to *Nurnberg*, large raindrops splashed down on my head. I struggled into my rain poncho while continuing to drive rather than stopping and taking the time to lift the jeep's top over my head and secure it to the jeep. The rain increased, distorting my view through the windshield. I reached forward to activate the manually-operated windshield wiper, and in doing so I swerved to the left and caught the shoulder of the road with my left front wheel. The jeep careened off the road and rolled over twice into the ditch below. The next thing I heard were a couple of men's voices talking above me, asking me in German, if I was alive. "Yes," I answered in German. "Can you help me get out?"

My rescuers pushed and shoved the jeep on its side. I crawled out and walked about in a circle, checking the movements of my arms and legs, my back and neck. I patted my holster frantically making sure that my revolver was still in place. Headquarters did not gracefully accept agents' excuses for losing their hardware. The Germans urged me to lie down because I had a cut on my forehead, but I felt fine and persuaded the Germans to help me finish rolling the jeep back onto its wheels. As we worked to stabilize the jeep I could not help thinking how I had once again managed to escape serious injury and silently congratulated myself on this latest proof that I had had a better than average share of good luck. In a jeep the passenger seat is secured to the bottom of the jeep with hinges and thus folds forward. I had been thrown over into that seat as the jeep rolled and the seat promptly folded over me, protecting my body completely.

We got the jeep back onto the road. It had taken the brunt of

the smashup, but it started up well enough. I thanked my rescuers for their help, and while the hard-driving rain continued, I was
able to guide the jeep slowly back to headquarters where I had to
fill out a flurry of forms in order to get windshield, headlamps and
fenders repaired.

An agent like myself – voluntarily employed D.P. – was paid
very little. But we had sumptuous living quarters, good food, cars,
and girlfriends, worked half days on Saturdays, and had Sundays
off. Between the excitement of our daily duties and the privileges I
enjoyed while impersonating an American military officer, I thrived
on the city life my friend Jesse Miles had urged me to try. It did not
seem strange to me that I began working the black market in order
to earn the pocket money to keep up with my peers. As pseudo-
officers, we were compelled to use the officer's club. There the C.I.C.
had its own table, set off from the other officers, who looked upon
our rankless group with suspicion. They did not know who we were.
They did not like our foreign accents. We wore their uniforms but
did not fit their mold. We often ate at the officers' club and we drank
there during our hours of spare time. My particular addiction was
Coca-Cola, to which I had been introduced by the Americans soon
after my liberation. I drank *Cokes* like water. At the officers' club
we paid far more for our refreshments than we would have at the
enlisted men's club, a place off limits to the C.I.C. As we drank and
joked together, I learned the backgrounds of some of our people.
There were former journalists, police officers, Americanized sons
of Germans who had fled the Nazi regime, and patriots of long
American lineage. One other agent and I were the only Displaced
Persons in the *Nurnberg* unit.

To raise pocket money, I took some of our rations of cigarettes,
stockings and soap issued to pay off informers, and traded them in
the black market. The C.I.C. thought nothing of it. The black market
was a Military Police problem, and one which was only arbitrarily
tackled. Then I began to deal in German marks for American dollars for some of my American friends. With the commissions I made
on money changing, I began to accumulate a small nest egg.

On summer Sundays, my friends and I took our girlfriends to

the mountains. We picnicked together, then hiked off with our girls in separate directions. The Americans taught me fly-rod fishing in clear streams, but I never did enjoy fishing, even in the days when my father had taken me out to the Amstel River. We caught trout and pan-fried them at day's end on the stream's bank or had them for breakfast if we had made it into a weekend overnight. No fresh fish ever tasted better.

SUMMER, 1946

From time to time during my tour of duty with the C.I.C. in *Nurnberg*, I took weekend trips to visit Captain Jesse Miles in *Scheinfeld*, about 58 kilometers away. By now the Captain had been joined by his fiancée, Ruth, whom he had met months earlier when we had been stationed in *Bad Worishofen*. I had met Jesse's girlfriend there as well and so enjoyed visiting and exchanging stories with the two of them. Jesse, as I had by then been permitted to call him, also patiently answered my many questions about what life in the United States was like. I was eager to leave Europe for my new home. By midsummer, I told Jesse that I thought I had worked for the C.I.C. long enough to request their permission to go after emigration via Holland. He agreed that the time was probably ripe.

I sought an interview with my superiors at C.I.C., presented my affidavit from Colonel Clark, and asked for a week's leave in order to seek a visa through the American Consulate in *Amsterdam*. I explained that I expected the Americans there could help me because I had worked for American forces instead of returning to Holland. Permission was granted, provided I travel at all times with another agent of their choosing.

An American agent I had not met before was assigned to travel with me. We were given a jeep and a leave of one week. Under no circumstances, we were warned, was I to be left behind in Holland. We were ordered to shoot our way out, if necessary, and to emphasize the point, we each were given an additional box of bullets for our revolvers. I was surprised at the security arrangements in my behalf, but made no comment. Perhaps all agents traveling outside of their local territory were well armed and with one or more companions because of the danger of being intercepted by Soviet counterintelligence agents (who were known to be active also in the postwar occupation zones). Perhaps my status as a D.P. made me particularly vulnerable to kidnap by enemy agents. Perhaps that same status made me suspect to my own C.I.C. officers. I did not know.

Once in *Amsterdam*, we conferred with American consular officers who looked over my papers and listened to my explanation of how I had served with U.S. forces since my liberation from concentration camp *Ebensee*. Yes, I was born in *Amsterdam*, Holland, I answered to their query. No, I had not returned to Holland since the end of the war nor had I been repatriated. No, I had no family in Holland any longer. No, I had no permanent address in *Amsterdam*. I was a Dutch national who had survived a number of concentration camps and upon my liberation had served the American forces in Austria, Germany, and Czechoslovakia. They could not help me even though I was a native born Hollander because I had not returned to Holland after the war. They suggested I apply in *Munich* for a visa as a Displaced Person.

My companion and I walked silently out the Consulate's door. I could not get a visa in my native country from which I had been forcibly removed. I had struggled to stay out of the refugee camps of the disenfranchised masses called Displaced Persons. I had rebelled at having such a label pinned on me but if accepting that label would get me a visa, then I would do it. Talking over my situation, my companion and I realized that we would have to return to *Nurnberg* and request permission to apply for an immigration visa in *Munich*. But with a few days' leave left, my companion – an affable fellow and interested in seeing as much as he could of Europe – agreed with me that we might as well see the town together.

I gave my companion an intimate tour of *Amsterdam*, all the while pretending to be an American myself. When we checked in at a downtown hotel, I registered my address as *Buffalo*, New York, the home of Colonel Clark. I pointed out landmarks and places of special interest as we walked and drove through the city's streets.

Then even I became a tourist as we rode down the canals in a tour boat, and drove out to the fishing village of *Volendam* where the entire community went about their daily chores in traditional costumes. We also caught a ferry to the island town of *Marken*, another such fishing community with entirely different, more flashy, traditional costumes.

My family had never traveled to such provincial parts of Holland, even though these villages were not far away from *Amsterdam*. I took as much delight as my companion in watching and snapping pictures of costumed natives working their boats, gardening, washing clothes, mending fishing nets, tending farm animals as if the 20th century and the war, just over, had not touched them at all. In *Amsterdam*, I showed my companion my old neighborhood, my school, the Miranda swimming complex, and the former apartments, of various relatives and friends. I avoided taking him into the old Jewish section. I made no efforts to contact the Jewish community. However, we drove to the flat of my boyhood friend, Appie Klaverstijn, on the hunch that I would find him still living there. Because his parents had a mixed marriage – his mother Jewish, his father gentile – I thought they might have been spared. My reasoning had been correct. Appie and his parents were at home, and a new member of the family as well, for Appie had taken a wife. We greeted one another emotionally, and I introduced my companion as an American serviceman. Our C.I.C. connections were not mentioned.

As a treat we drove the Klaverstijns out to the nearby seaside resort of *Zandvoort*, where our families had participated in many a holiday outing. We walked the beach and talked together through most of the afternoon. From time to time I would translate for my companion the gist of our conversation so he would not feel left out. Since our boyhood days Appie had become a competent diamond polisher, a fact that surprised me since his father had never worked in that industry. However, I learned that his grandfather and uncle on his mother's side had both been skilled polishers. In addition, before the war, his father-in-law had been a well-known member of the diamond exchange. The Klaverstijns were still in a state of shock over the disappearance of the Dutch Jewish community, as was I, but we found few words to convey our thoughts on this painful subject. Instead, I told them about the concentration camps I had been in, and had survived, and about my service with the American forces that had liberated me. I told them of my resolve to emigrate to the United States rather than return to Holland to live. Appie told me that the queen was calling up men of our age, class 1924, to fight in Indonesia, and that confirmed my decision to seek a new life elsewhere. Later in the day we drove back to *Amsterdam* after taking our leave of the Klaverstijns.

Driving with my companion through familiar streets one afternoon I was stopped by a traffic cop when I tried to make a left turn from the *Ceintuurbaan* onto the *van Woustraat*. He began shouting at me in Dutch for violating a traffic regulation. I understood him very well but shrugged my shoulders and asked him in English what I had done wrong. He told me in Dutch that all Americans drove like wild cowboys, an image of myself that I enjoyed very much, but I put on a thoughtful expression and told him that I didn't understand a word he was saying. A few helpful *Mokummers* – the nickname for those who lived in *Amsterdam* – gathered around to help with interpreting, and in this way I pretended to learn what traffic regulation I had violated. As my companion struggled to keep a straight face, I apologized to the traffic cop through my helpful interpreters for embarrassing the reputation of the American Armed forces. The exasperated traffic cop sent us on our way.

We had seen enough of *Amsterdam*, but since we were not expected back in *Nurnberg* for a few more days, I suggested we go on to *Antwerp*, another city I could show in detail to my companion. It only took a few hours to drive to *Antwerp* and soon we found our way to the Bachelor Officers Quarters where we requested meals and sleeping accommodations. Our C.I.C. credentials were scrutinized at the desk and we were told to wait.

Strange, we commented to each other, that we should be asked to wait. However, we waited for almost an hour before we asked the desk clerk if we could enter the dining room to eat while we waited. Admitted to the dining room after a backroom consultation by the desk clerk and someone not visible to us, we were allowed in and when we were in the middle of our dinner the Commanding Officer of the BOQ introduced himself and joined us at our table. A polite interrogation began:

"What are you boys doing in *Antwerp?*"

"Passing through."

"Where are you headquartered?"

"*Nurnberg.*"

"Did you come here from *Nurnberg?*"

"No. We came from *Amsterdam.*"

"What took you to *Amsterdam?*"

"We can't tell you that, sir."

"Why did you come to *Antwerp?*"

"Passing through, as we've told you. We want to see the city and *Brussels* as well, before we return to *Nurnberg.*"

"A likely story!" the C.O. retorted. "As a matter of fact you are not allowed to leave the BOQ tonight, nor can you go to *Brussels* tomorrow. Both cities are closed to unauthorized American personnel by American Military Government." We asked on what grounds we were confined to quarters and forbidden to travel freely in Belgium, but the C.O. refused to discuss the matter. We prevailed upon him to call *Nurnberg* to verify our story. He made the call, talking with a duty officer who confirmed that, yes we had permission to travel to *Amsterdam* for a week, but no, he did not know why we had gone to Antwerp. Why don't you ask them why they are there he reported to have asked. The C.O. began to believe our story. He gave us overnight rooms, and after we cajoled him further, he gave us passes to see the town.

We spent a long night seeing *Antwerp* as I had never seen it as a boy. The next morning we tackled the C.O. again for passes to visit *Brussels* and its BOQ. He kidded us about wanting first a finger, then the whole hand, but he was in a better mood and eventually gave us the passes we had requested. The ice was broken enough for us to ask him about his suspicions of the night before. He told us that a full scale investigation was rumored to be in the works because of heavy thefts of military cargo in *Antwerp* and *Brussels*. When the C.O. got word that we were C.I.C. agents, he assumed we had been sent by Headquarters to begin preliminary investigations. We confessed that our trip to *Amsterdam* had been for the purpose of seeking a visa for me, a native Dutchman, to get to the United States, and that all the other stops on our way back to *Nurnberg* were those of tourists as we had maintained all along. We shook hands all around, grinning at each other, and left.

We visited *Brussels*, a fine old city that I had never visited before, spent the night in the local BOQ and were never again challenged as to our credentials. The next day we drove back to *Nurnberg* where we were expected by evening. There we were roundly kidded for the complete failure of our mission and reminded that even as tourists we would have failed had we not been rescued by our own headquarters.

Within a few weeks my American companion and I were authorized to go to *Munich* for another try in obtaining a visa for me. At the American consulate there we encountered the same old difficulties. No, I did not qualify as a Displaced Person because I did not live, and had never lived or registered, at a Displaced Persons camp. No, I did not qualify as a German, even though I now lived in Germany, because I was not born a German nor had I applied for citizenship. I had already learned that I did not qualify as a Dutch national, but I was just beginning to learn that by running rather than registering I had made myself a man without a country. My chances for emigration began to look doubtful, my affidavit unusable.

Rumors flowed around the *Nurnberg* office that a big operation of some kind was in the offing. At first only upper echelon agents were involved, meeting behind closed doors for long periods of time. Gradually, some of the rest of us were called together to start training, including an agent named Sasha, a Polish Jewish boy, also a concentration camp survivor and also a Displaced Person. We received specific instructions for the part we would play in carrying out an enormous raid simultaneously in the U.S., British and French occupation zones. However, the precise nature of the raid was not divulged to rank and file agents like ourselves until just before the raid was to begin.

Our operations as C.I.C. agents had so far been directed against

Nazis and Nazi sympathizers. It was inevitable that we would now begin training to round up Communists and fellow travelers. With the United States and the Soviet Union emerging from World War II as the two most powerful nations on earth, each ideologically opposed system presented a threat to the other. Even during the war Churchill and Roosevelt, and Truman, had withheld information from the Soviet Union. It was common knowledge that Stalin shared as little information as possible with his allies. Wrangles over occupational boundary lines and ideological control began before the last surrender treaties were signed.

The end of the hostilities brought the working intelligence forces of both sides to all joint occupation areas. The Allies became as worried about Communism gaining an upper hand as they were about burying Fascism. And yet the general mood among the Allies was one of impatience. Everyone had had enough of fighting, death, and deprivation. They were anxious to wind up the business of war and get back to peacetime pursuits.

Communist agents of the Soviet Union were known to have invaded the British, French, and United States zones of occupation and to be very active in gathering intelligence and recruiting sympathizers. We C.I.C. agents were therefore not surprised to learn that a large, combined, counter intelligence raid was in the offing. Many of us welcomed the opportunity to take part in an action designed to reduce communist influence in Europe. I shared the beliefs that Communism would be as disastrous for free men as Fascism had been, and I well remembered the words my father had spoken in the early thirties about brown shirts, black shirts and blue shirts.

The Saturday evening of the raid, all agents were called together while still at headquarters and were given a broad outline of what the evening held in store and what our particular duties would be. It was at that time we learned that the purpose was to pull in communists and communist sympathizers. Wearing our uniforms and fully equipped from handcuffs to handguns, we drove our cars and jeeps to a 10 P.M. rendezvous at the *Nurnberg* Stadium Hitler had once used for his rallies.

When we arrived at the Stadium we found it half filled with

military police and GIs, none of whom were aware of the nature of this action. Over the loudspeaker system the leaders of this operation announced that the C.I.C., with cooperation of the U.S. Armed Forces and the military police, would lead a raid shortly after midnight and would envelop the entire American zone of occupation.   Simultaneous raids, we were told, would be carried out in every major city in the British and French zones by their counterintelligence units. We were to travel in teams. Each car or jeep would carry four men: a C.I.C. agent, a military policeman and two GIs. We were instructed to proceed swiftly and silently with the intent of taking our subjects by surprise. Those arrested were to be escorted to strategically located roundup trucks. The arrested ones were not to be roughed up unless resistance made such action necessary.

Just before our midnight departure, our team assignments were distributed. My team was responsible for bringing in a small number of suspects, listed in the order of the arrests to be made. The instructions we received gave their names, the streets and apartment numbers where they lived, conditions to expect and the locations of the roundup trucks. Photographs of the suspects were attached. We broke quietly into apartment houses; silently we sneaked up flights of stairs, kicked in doors, and tried to overpower our subjects before they could fully awaken. Some had guns, but we gave them no chance to make use of them. We picked up both men and women, sometimes whole families, encountering little resistance. Once positively identified, our suspects were taken to the designated waiting trucks, after which they were driven to interrogation centers. The roundup raids continued all night and through all of Sunday.

At the interrogating centers teams of interrogators systematically questioned all the suspects who had been under counterintelligence surveillance over many weeks. Some were released. Many were removed to jails and there detained. Interrogations and reports took up the rest of that week and spilled over into the following week as well. My duties ended when the roundup was completed and we were able to catch up on some sleep. There was little else for us to do.

AUSCHWITZ, AUSCHWITZ... I CANNOT FORGET YOU

A superior in my *Nurnberg* headquarters had given me a permanent pass to the *Nurnberg* War Crimes Trials, assuming that the trials would interest me. However, at the time I did not have enough perspective on the trials to want to attend them and learn from them. I had been fed (unsuccessfully) into the Nazi extermination machine as into a meat grinder because I was a Jew. There had been no justice in what had happened to me. I had little appetite now for attending formal trials that were determining degrees of guilt to be assigned to the madmen responsible for it all. I wanted to get on with my life, to continue trying new experiences, to forget the past if I could. Crying over wrongs and nursing revenge would bring back only bitter memories of that recent past, a past I wanted to put behind me. The words of the Polish prisoner I had met in *KZ Buna* still echoed in my mind, "Forget your past. Forget you ever had a family. Find out how this place works and learn to survive in it. Live for tomorrow."

Nevertheless, I attended several sessions of the trials during the quiet days following our raids. I looked into the faces of several former high Nazi officials – faces and names I can no longer recall with assurance – and listened to accusations being made, the rhetoric of the attorneys and explanations for their actions. The courtroom scene was like a pretentious stage play in which the players debated, in lofty terms, some moral problems of war as if ordinary innocent people were not abused and murdered by orders from these officials. I had not been a pawn on a gigantic chessboard. I knew who had hunted me down, thrown me behind electrified barbed wires, and taught me to survive on terms I would just as soon forget. The Nazis had buried Jews with great enthusiasm and laughed with great satisfaction at the moral reduction of those who had tried to survive on their terms. When my fellow agents asked me what I thought of the trial, I told them the truth as I knew it to have been. I told them I did not know what to think. I did not understand why these trials were necessary. It was obvious to me that the whole bunch sitting in the dock was guilty as charged and should be done away with as soon as possible.

Suddenly my superiors in the Nurnberg C.I.C. office became

very concerned about the well-being of Sasha and me. They realized that as Displaced Persons the two of us were in great danger of being picked up by the counterintelligence agents of the Soviet Union. The Soviet Union was in *Nurnberg* for the War Crimes Trials, along with the British, French and Americans, and the Soviet cadre of counterintelligence people were known to be out for blood over our recent raid. It was assumed they possessed lists of our names and backgrounds. As D.P.s, Sasha and I could disappear overnight and no one would have the power to do anything about it. The C.I.C., recognizing our danger, decided it was time to help us get emigration visas for us to go to the United States.

They could have turned their heads and let us disappear with very few people being the wiser. They choose to honor their initial promises to look after us, a trait I had learned to respect greatly in Americans. During the first days of September, Sasha, who also had a sponsor's affidavit, and I were sent to *Frankfurt am Main* where C.I.C. Headquarters was located, as well as those of the U.S. Army and the U.S. State Department. Each of us was assigned a room in a hotel maintained by the C.I.C. and we were advised, for our own safety, to confine ourselves to the hotel except for escorted trips on official business.

At C.I.C. Headquarters a legal officer examined our papers and interviewed us, at length. He then personally presented our cases before U.S. State Department representatives. Papers were signed and stamped and we were quickly cleared but for our medical examinations.

At the hospital where we were examined my rising hopes were almost dashed again when I was told that my chest x-ray revealed TB scarring, and that a more detailed set of x-rays would have to be taken. Technicians took more X-rays and sent me back to my hotel to sweat out the news of the results until the next day. Calling them in the morning, as instructed, I now learned to my great relief that they found no evidence of active TB. Another hurdle was behind me.

Within 24 hours, Washington, D.C. sent through our visa numbers. We were cleared to emigrate! Our visas would be ready the following week. The legal officer of the C.I.C. put us in touch with the U.S. Transportation Agency to arrange for our passage to the United States on the earliest available ship.

SEPTEMBER, 1946

From *Frankfurt am Main*, Sasha and I were flown back to *Nurnberg* on a C-47 bucket seat cargo plane. Taking off on my first flight I sweated with anxiety until we were airborne, then thrilled to the sight of towns and rolling farmlands unfolding beneath us.

At our headquarters everyone gathered around to congratulate us on our good fortune. We had a week in which to wind up our affairs. The U.S. Transportation Agency notified us that we were booked for passage on the S.S. Ernie Pyle out of *Bremerhaven* on September 19th, and that we each owed $142.00 for our one-way tickets. To insure our safety, agents escorted us on our errands about *Nurnberg*. We arranged to draw the monies to pay our ship passage. We visited a tailor who made inexpensive suits for us out of an ersatz material in only a few days. While still in *Nurnberg*, each night a different agent hosted a party in our behalf.

Sasha and I flew back to *Frankfurt* for the completion of some paperwork at the U.S. State Department. That process took several days and during that time we stayed once again at the C.I.C. hotel. With visas and official photographs finally in our possession, we were flown to *Bremen* and confined to rooms in the C.I.C. residence to await the departure date of our ship.

On the morning of September 19th, we were driven by a C.I.C. agent to *Bremerhaven*, introduced by him to the captain of the S.S. Ernie Pyle, a converted Liberty ship, and in our presence the captain was instructed that under no circumstance were we to leave the ship in any European port. Sasha and I stood at the rail and watched expectantly as people began to board. We sailed to *Le Havre*, France, a trip of two days, and picked up more passengers. Except for a few of us, the ship soon filled with American repatriates, people who had been caught overseas for one reason or another when the war broke out. More than a year after the war was over, these Americans were just being readmitted after lengthy checking and clearance procedures. I don't know what Sasha was thinking but it was very difficult for me to believe and understand what had happened to me these last few weeks. I was actually on board a ship and soon we would sail to the United States of America by way of France. It had all happened so fast since the raids in June, or were they in July, and here we stood on the rail of the S.S. Ernie Pyle in September 1946.

Little by little Sasha and I parted company after we hit the open sea. We had not worked together nor had we spent time together until after the big counterintelligence raid in *Nurnberg*. We had not developed a close relationship and felt no obligation to stick together as immigrants although both our suits had been made by the same tailor and wearing those we looked somewhat alike. Our small Liberty ship teemed with Americans speaking European languages; indeed, they seemed to have forgotten their own. Communicating in one language or another, I found shipboard acquaintances easy to make. The ship itself was crowded and uncomfortable. To make matters worse, we almost immediately ran into a storm. As the S.S. Ernie Pyle tossed and plunged, most passengers succumbed to seasickness. They took to their bunks in the hold and mingled their helpless groans with the creaks and groans of the ship. In the midst of the storm I became so ill that I went down from the gun deck to the rail surrounding the ship, held tightly onto the rail, and vomited everything that was inside of me. The wind and seawater were blowing in my face and I felt hot and clammy, my clothes were soaked and my hair smelled of salt; I really felt sick and all I could think of was that I was going to drown, here in the middle of the Atlantic, and all that I had survived had been for naught.

The hold began to smell so badly from vomit that I could not make myself climb down into it. A number of passengers felt as I did that the deck was far preferable to the hold. On topside we could better keep our equilibrium and fill our lungs with fresh air. Although the storm continued to rage we realized that the September winds were warm and pleasant. A small group of us claimed an abandoned gun platform near the front of the ship, from which the wartime artillery had been removed. We dragged our mattresses up from the hold and placed them under the shelter on the gun platform. Some of the girls who had joined our group obligingly consented to bring us sandwiches and drinks from down below. The storm refused to let up and even those of us on topside felt seasick. When someone reported that the crew had a supply of cognac they were willing to sell, we pooled our monies and began to buy and drink the stuff with the idea of half-anesthetizing ourselves. As our little ship continued to be tossed about like a cork in a tub of water, we drank the cognac, lolled about glassy-eyed and occasionally ran to the rail to vomit.

Eventually the ocean calmed and on a glorious rainy evening the loudspeaker announced that *New York's* harbor was just coming into view. All passengers poured onto the deck to watch the Statue of Liberty come into view. We dropped anchor at the entrance to the harbor, and many of us stared in awe at the Statue until darkness fell. After the stormy ride across the Atlantic Ocean which at times I thought would be my grave, I now looked upon that symbol of LIBERTY with great humility and thankfulness.

Liberty! I stood at the gates of the nation that dared to welcome the downtrodden of the world to a haven of freedom and promise. For months I had imagined that day when I would first lay my eyes on her. It meant I was going to find my way as a free man among the most remarkable people on earth. I wanted to become an American citizen as soon as I was allowed to do so. I also believed that America stood waiting to compensate me with her caring people and her wealth for much that I had lost. Painful memories would no longer creep into my sleeping and waking hours. I would stand tall and make myself worthy of America. I wished my parents could see me. Here was their son, Max Rodrigues Garcia – to whom they had granted life many times over by their actions and teachings – who had just arrived in the land of liberty. They would have shared my gratitude and be, oh so, thankful to the Arthur H. Clark family for having made this possible.

Here, also, stood Max R. Garcia who had pledged to himself that when he set foot on American soil, he would forsake his Jewish identity. I had reasoned my Jewish Sephardic heritage was too perilous a condition to chain myself to any longer. I had escaped with my life for the indiscretion of having been born a Jew, and contemplating the Inquisition during which my ancestors had experienced a like condition, I was no longer willing to subject myself or my hoped for progeny, to the unpredictable burdens of such a heritage.

Another Max R. Garcia stared at the Statue as well: a studied copy of an American G.I., confident, tough, and looking forward to conquering on the new home front as he had abroad. The cars, the privileges, the power I had acquired as a C.I.C. agent were not far behind me. I could hardly wait to see what America itself had in store for me.

Early the next morning I pulled myself together and forced myself to go below deck to clean up. I was a sorry specimen and I knew it. The Army uniform I had worn throughout the voyage was filthy. My body reeked almost as badly as the day of my liberation. My face was bristled with stubble. I was anxious to clean myself as was everyone else who had been topside during the trip. I felt like a groom readying himself for his bride. I wanted to make myself as presentable as possible to my new country and to the Clarks. I brushed my teeth, I shaved and showered when it got to be my turn. I put on clean underwear, socks, a fresh army shirt and my new suit of ersatz material plus the shoes I had not used during the trip. My hair was neatly combed and feeling wonderfully expectant I charged up to the deck to watch the dawn gather light over the calm waters of *New York* harbor.

The harbor pilot boarded to help the S.S. Ernie Pyle to its docking place. I stood among acquaintances on the foredeck as the ship glided silently past the Statue of Liberty and an enormous banner mounted on the shore that read: "WELCOME HOME, WELL DONE." A morning fog bank obliterated all but the tops of the *New York* skyline. Buildings taller than I had ever seen penetrated a high white fog mass beneath them. It looked like a mirage. We passengers passed the cognac bottle for the last time and wished each other well.

I wiped away tears of gratitude, overwhelmed by the emotion and magnitude of it all, as the S.S. Ernie Pyle docked on September

30th, 1946. I went through immigration in a turmoil of anticipation, searching the waiting crowd for the face of Colonel Clark. But as officials finished checking my papers, a woman called for me. She introduced herself as a representative of the Travelers Aid Society, and explained that Colonel Clark had arranged for the Agency to meet me upon docking and assist me until I could be put on a train to *Buffalo* later that afternoon; He had sent money for a coach ticket.

I thanked the Travelers Aid agent and followed her, swallowing my overwhelming disappointment that Colonel Clark had not come to meet me. I knew that I was in *New York* and that *Buffalo* was in the State of New York and I could not understand why he could not have taken the time to meet the S.S. Ernie Pyle. It was not until I completed the long train journey from *New York City* to *Buffalo* and was met in the early hours of morning by Arthur H. Clark, husband to Jean, and father of two small girls, that I began to realize how far *Buffalo* was from *New York City* and how busy Arthur Clark was with his family and business.

The train ride out of Grand Central Station had been comfortable to the point of luxury for a European boy who expected coach-car seats to be upright wooden benches but now was ushered to a cushioned and upholstered seat with a adjustable back. I talked easily with some homeward-bound GIs taking the same train. Occasionally we ducked into the men's room to share whiskey and water in paper cups and laugh over army reminiscences. We had come through the war and were going home – a good feeling.

Around 2 o'clock in the morning I stepped off the train at the *Buffalo* Railroad Station to find the Clarks waiting for me. The Colonel was wearing civilian clothes, a real shock for me, but otherwise he looked as I had remembered him, tall and wearing that shy smile of his. He introduced his pretty young wife, not many years older than I, and asked that I call them Jean and Arthur. It seemed we were the only ones in the station at that time and one could hear the echo of our steps through the wide ceramic-tile floored hall.

Arthur at that time was 31 years old and I was 22. The ride to *Snyder*, the suburb of *Buffalo* where they lived, took quite a while.

I told them excitedly about the C.I.C. getting me to the U.S.A in a month's time, about my seasick days on a storm-tossed liberty ship, about my glance at the buildings of *New York City*, the kindness of the people at the Travelers Aid Society and the comfort and pleasantness of American railroad coaches. We did not talk long when we reached their home. Jean showed me to the tidy bedroom they had fixed up for me, and we went to bed.

Had my life been the kind of movie I had become used to watching, the film probably would have ended here: after many hardships, the orphaned boy finds a family, is welcomed to the land of his dreams, and lives happily ever after. Instead, I awoke in the morning to a continuation of my life and its accumulating collection of problems, not the least of which was the wide difference between my expectations and the realities that faced me.

"Liberty! I stood at the gates of the nation that dared to welcome the downtrodden of the world to a haven of freedom and promise." – Max R. Garcia

PART 5

The Immigrant

1946 - 1947

In the morning, Jean introduced me to the Clarks' two wide-eyed little girls, Lynda, five years old, and Barbara, two. Jean showed me around the spacious, well-furnished rooms of their home, and then took me outside. The house was one of a block of solid residences centered on well-tended lawns and fronting on a wide, tree-lined avenue. They owned a Canadian summer home as well, Jean told me, with a beachfront on Lake Erie.

The Clarks took me to visit both their sets of parents, all long-time *Buffalo* residents. The senior Clarks lived on the ground floor of an even larger house than their children's, on a wider street, and in an older but elegant residential area. Jean's family lived in a fine home nearby. I was a long way from home. Even the wealthiest members of my large *Amsterdam* family had not owned homes except, perhaps, one of my mother's older sisters who was married to Michel Cohen de Lara. Buying a home was a goal none of our tribe had even dared to contemplate, but for Americans owning a home appeared to be the norm.

While I was with the C.I.C. I had sent my savings (black market income) to *Buffalo*, and Arthur had opened a small savings account for me. It was from this account that Arthur had forwarded a money order to pay for my ship's passage. By the time I arrived in *Buffalo* a few dollars still remained in that account and Arthur suggested that we use them to shop for some new clothes. Except for my hastily tailored ersatz suit, the rest of my garments were all army-issue, including my shoes. Arthur drove me downtown, through the heavy traffic of the city's center core. My GI friends in Europe had not been exaggerating. Every family in America seemed to own a car. We shopped in enormous department stores filled with great stocks of clothing. I could not help staring as we walked from one amazing emporium to another. Arthur advised me about style as we selected shirts, slacks, underwear, socks and shoes. By late afternoon, I was dressed in my new clothes, and proud to think I looked as American as anyone passing me on the street.

A few days later Arthur took me on a tour of his father's small chemical plant, in which he was a partner. After dinner one evening Arthur encouraged me to discuss with him and Jean my plans for the future. I told them I thought I should enlist in the Army right away because of a law, still in effect, that gave immigrants the right to full citizenship within 90 days if they enlisted in the armed forces of the United States. In that way, I explained, I would have an advantage of citizenship within a short time, and I could serve in work familiar to me while I got used to American ways. I would be in a better position to decide what to do next.

Arthur would not hear of it. Absolutely not! I had never tried civilian life, he pointed out, and he thought it was important that I learn to get along as a free man in an unregulated society. I could not tell him, because I hardly grasped it myself, that I was becoming frightened at the concept of such freedom, and even more so of finding my way in a classless society. I had been raised to understand the limited horizons of the European workingman. Even in the Army, I had noticed, the sons of American plumbers, factory laborers, small grocery store owners, were well-off – some even rich – by my standards. They had showed me pictures of their homes, their cars, their bathing-suited girlfriends, and they had told me about their plans for going to college and interesting careers when they got home. I greatly admired my American friends' bold confidence that the future was theirs; but for myself, secretly, I had no such confidence. How was I going to transform myself from an unschooled workingman to the trained professional I dreamed of becoming?

Nevertheless, since Arthur wanted to hear about my aspirations, I told him I had not given up on my idea of one day becoming an architect, but that I did not know how to go about financing my education. Arthur told me I could work to be anything I wanted, but that he would be unable to underwrite my education as he had children of his own to bring up and educate. What he did propose, to fulfill his sponsorship pledge to keep me off welfare rolls for five years, or until I got my United States citizenship, was to give me a job in his chemical plant, and to stand behind me with whatever help and advice I needed. He hoped for the sake of my development that I would choose to start there rather than in the army.

I had not known what to expect, but I was learning. I had not come to America to work in a factory, not even Arthur's. If he saw this as a first step to a larger experience, I did not. I believed that to work in a factory was to accept a ticket to stay in the working class. If Arthur was being generous in discouraging me from entering the army, receiving quick citizenship and a quick end to his responsibilities, I did not realize it. I had been given so much by the Americans in Europe after my liberation – cars, prestige, ready access to things I wanted – that it had not occurred to me that I might have to start with less in the homeland itself.

Right from the start I resented the factory job. I worked on an assembly line with a number of girls who had been employed there for some time. When I discovered that I was being paid more than they, even though I was less skilled then, I resented that too. The unfairness of it! We sealed packages of domestic chemicals in commercial wrappers as they came down a conveyor belt, and then packed the finished products in shipping boxes. The girls chatted about their friends and their problems; I was an outsider with foreign ways and a foreign accent.

I had arrived in the States a cocky youth full of dreams of instant successes. In the factory, I soon grew unsure of myself, and hesitant about speaking. At the Clarks' home, Jean shrank from my company. She found my manners crude and my army-learned English coarse. Arthur advised me to improve my manners and my language, even to attend night school in English, because Jean was concerned for the sake of the children about my many crudities. I became even more shy of people and withdrawn, but hostile in conduct. An ungrateful employee, I was also a problematical grown son to an already burdened young mother of two children. The Clarks and I were crowding one another. Within a few weeks I took a small room by myself close to the downtown area of *Buffalo* and nearer to my assembly line job. The Clarks invited me to take Sunday dinners with them in order to stay in touch.

The nights were lonely. The assembly line job went no better. The migraine headaches I had experienced from time to time since boyhood returned. One day I walked into Arthur's office and told him I was quitting, that I could no longer work on an assembly line. I thought him unfair to pay me more than his better skilled girls. Arthur reminded me that he had promised to back me up financially until I became a citizen and that a factory job was his way of doing so. He had hoped that I would save my money and that within a few years I could be off to a good start in whatever direction I wanted to go. I told him not to worry about me that I could take care of myself.

I landed a job for the Christmas season in the toy department of Adam, Meldrum & Anderson, a large *Buffalo* Department store. There I worked in a fairyland of toys, and enjoyed playing with the hottest selling item of that season, a little machine that melted down various colored plastics for pouring into variety of design molds. The job was much more to my liking than the assembly line. I began to open up to people again, to joke and enjoy myself. An assistant buyer invited me to his home for my first family Thanksgiving in America. Wherever I went, I listened well and tried to improve my vocabulary. I imitated the American way of speaking, trying hard to lose my Dutch accent.

In January the Christmas season job ended. I became a busboy at the Statler Hotel, working from 4 P.M. to 1 A.M., setting and clearing tables, replenishing water and ice in glasses, and so on. Dinner was included as part of my salary. I moved to a room at a nearby YMCA so that I had only a short walk to my job.

The winter of 1946-47 was bitter cold and, to hear everyone talk, it was typical. The winds blew in from the north and from the Great Lakes, bringing with them more snow than I had ever seen in one place. Walls of snow so high I could not see over them rose beside the shoveled sidewalks around the hotel. Arthur, to whom I still talked occasionally, urged me to get out and participate in winter sports, reminding me of stories I had once told him about ice skating on *Amsterdam* canals. But I no longer felt like a boy in the mood to play, and was not inclined to set foot outside except to walk to work or do necessary errands. If Arthur wondered what had become of his one-time resourceful aide to the 319th, I wondered how to fit into American society. What I knew about surviving, Americans knew about playing. They turned every season into a celebration complete with appropriate sports and family gift-giving holidays. Everyone had a house, a car, and sporting equipment for each season. I looked on but did not know how to join the party.

Because of my night work and the bitterness of the weather, I spent most of my days at the movies, feeding my dreams, staying warm. I worked every night but one, even on Saturdays and Sundays. This, too, filled me with resentment for I had the strange idea that Americans should not have to work on weekends. I was fed up enough to quit my flunky job with its long evening and night hours, but soon I was forced to take a similar one. I became a short order cook at a White Tower diner, grilling hamburgers and eggs on the night shift from 10 P.M. to 6 A.M.

I bought *New York City* newspapers and began planning to move there, where I assumed I could fairly easily find a job as a translator, perhaps in the export-import business. I did not tell the Clarks about my plans but saved my earning until I could afford a bus ticket.

I was probably an exceptional immigrant Jew to arrive in *New York City*: I made no effort at all to contact its Jewish communities or aid societies. I checked in at a "Y" and began tramping the streets in search of a job. In a day or two it became apparent that I was not educationally qualified for a translating job, or, in fact, for any job I went after. The busy streets and towering, cold buildings were intimidating. My money dwindled alarmingly. No one spoke to me except to transact business, and I grew desperate. Finally, I was accepted for a job – that of a door-to-door magazine salesman.

Four or five of us salesmen were driven daily to New Jersey, where each of us was assigned to a sales area of a few city blocks. You're a natural, the boss had told me. Just tell your prisoner story and you'll sell hundreds of magazines and earn big commissions. For weeks I trudged up apartment steps and tried to get at least a foot in the door by starting my story. I did not sell many magazines but I learned there were some very lonely housewives. Sometimes women responded to my sincerely-spoken story with seductive smiles, but no subscriptions. Some even opened up their robes to reveal parts of their nude bodies. With each such incident I fled in confusion, ignoring the advice of my co-workers: "If they want it, give it. You'll get bigger commissions, idiot, and some fun besides." I quit, demanded to be paid off, and was left stranded somewhere in New Jersey.

I was a beaten man. For a young immigrant in a hurry, America had turned out to be cold, inhospitable country where my efforts were answered with indifference. My thoughts went back to Europe, to people and customs I understood. I looked at the money in my hand and took the bus to the nearest big city, *Philadelphia*. There I spent the night in the bus station. In the morning I went to the recruiting office and signed up for 18 months with the United States Army. I called Arthur to tell him of my enlistment. He pleaded with me to come back to *Buffalo* and try to work out things there. Much as before, I explained that I needed to join the Army because I was familiar with Army life and because I hoped it would help me prepare to live in the United States. I could not yet cope with living and working by myself. I think Arthur began to understand how I felt. He wished me luck, and told me to stay in touch, words of friendship that I badly needed.

I was inducted on March 10th, 1947, and sent to *Fort Jackson*, just outside *Columbia*, South Carolina, I started basic training in a Southern army camp. The wartime law granting American citizenship after 90 days to immigrant enlisted men had expired at the end of December, 1946. As I started my enlistment in 1947, nearly everyone who had served in World War II was getting out of the army. There was little glory in joining up. The honors and the thrills were gone. The only veterans left in the army were those who had decided to make a career of military service. A Captain, for instance, would accept downgrading to Master Sergeant, a Master Sergeant to Buck Sergeant.

Central South Carolina, where I was stationed, was not at all like upstate New York where I had lived during my first months in the United States. The climate was hotter, more humid, and people seemed to live closer to the land. South Carolinians moved slowly and spoke with a drawling accent I often strained to understand. They ate a different diet from Northerners. Their towns held little interest for an *Amsterdam*-born GI who was stationed among them.

To my amazement, Southerners followed strict rules for the separation of black and white citizens that I had not observed in the North. In the towns, blacks had to drink from separate and specially designated fountains, use separate public toilets, eat in separate restaurants, take seats in the back of public transportation. In *Columbia*, the capital of South Carolina, there was as unwritten understanding that no blacks were to be seen on the streets after sundown. I had not thought it possible that in the United States some of its citizens could be discriminated against much as we Jews had been under early Nazi occupation. I asked around, incredulous, and learned that discriminatory policies against blacks were standard practice in Southern states.

At Fort Jackson I began eight weeks of basic training in the company of young recruits; but unlike the recruits I already understood army life. The war-trained buck sergeant understood me as well. They know where I had come from and that I was a war veteran of sorts who had never taken basic training. I trained and exercised no more than I had to. I produced my old camera and requested permission to become company photographer. The sergeant allowed it. When we were ordered to the parade ground, I could often be found on the sidelines taking pictures of our company in action. I could also wangle a pass to *Columbia* (where I found nothing to do) when my fellow recruits were confined to base. In just such ways I took up my comfortable old game of wheeling and dealing to try to improve my position.

As basic training neared an end, the recruits were allowed to choose a school for further military training. I requested C.I.C. school with one goal in mind: I wanted an overseas assignment. I was homesick for Europe. In America, I did not "belong" in the same way I had belonged with American troops overseas. I had looked around, and had thought until my brain ached, about what I might do to make a place for myself in the new country. I had to admit defeat. I was lonely, and longed to be back among people, customs, and idioms I understood. I had little in common with the beer-drinking, comic-book-reading American kids who made up our company.

In order to qualify for C.I.C. school, I passed a battery of tests. I was notified of my eligibility except for one requirement, I had to be a citizen. My request for C.I.C. school was denied. My alternative request for training at the Military Police School of the Criminal Investigation Division (C.I.D.) was granted.

The C.I.D. Military Police School was in Carlisle Barracks, near *Gettysburg*, Pennsylvania. Once a cavalry school, Carlisle Barracks was a pleasant old army post of brick buildings set among rolling green hills. As a lone private among corporals and sergeants, I attended daily classes for more than a month. Near the end of our training rumors began to circulate, as they always will in military life, that our entire class was to be sent to Germany. I was elated, and went about my routines in good spirits. We were ordered to undergo physical and dental check-ups as a preliminary to our being sent overseas. The physical was no problem for me, but I steeled myself for what was to be my second encounter with a dentist since my attendance at Middle School in *Antwerp*. Dating from that time, I had a phobic fear of dentists and the pain they caused. My teeth were in poor shape, badly out of line and riddled with cavities. They gave me problems I preferred to deal with by closing my mouth and thinking about something else. Submitting to a dentist had long been on my list of situations to avoid; but, if I were to go overseas, I had no choice. In *KZ Auschwitz*, or any of the other concentration camps dentists were not used to keep the dental condition of their captives healthy.

The young army dentist who ordered me to open up so he could have a look, poked about my mouth for some time, then lifted one foot onto the chair I was sitting in, leaned on one of his elbows on that knee, and let me have it:

"You hate dentists, don't you, Soldier?"

"Yes, sir!"

"Well your luck has run out. We're going to pull six teeth and fix up a number of cavities."

I had already thought of a way out of this predicament.

"If you don't mind, sir, I'd rather go downtown to have my teeth fixed by an experienced private dentist. I understand they will use general anesthesia if I request it."

I recognized the young dental officer as Jewish, and, perhaps he saw that I, too, was Jewish. I made no sign, but when he began to argue with me about the stupidity of neglecting my teeth, then wanting to pay a private dentist from my meager monthly paycheck when he could do the same work for me without charge, I began to have confidence in him. He told me that the use of novocaine, a local anesthetic, was standard dental practice in the army, and that it would be effective. I let him shoot my mouth full of novocaine and let him do all the yanking and drilling work he deemed necessary. The work required several sessions, and submitting to it took as much courage as I could muster, courage I would have lacked had I not instinctively liked the dentist and wanted so desperately to go overseas.

Our class graduated in July 1947 and received orders to ship out to Germany. Ironically, two nights before we were to leave a telegram arrived at the school informing them that I was to be excluded from being shipped to Germany. No reason was given. When my classmates pulled out, I was still in Carlisle Barracks, a bitterly disappointed recruit, awaiting stateside reassignment.

I was sent to *Fort Lee*, Virginia, to serve in a special C.I.D. detachment. In less than a week I was transferred out of the C.I.D. detachment and assigned to the regular military police. Reason given: I was not a citizen. As a member of the regular military police I was assigned guard duty on the ground towers of a prisoner stockade and stood watch in rotation with the others. I paced about the towers while the inmates paced in the compound below. Sleep came hard during my off-duty hours. When I dozed, I slept fitfully, sometimes awaking to my own screams, my body soaked with sweat. The two hours I served on the guard towers were stretches of gloomy introspection. My off-duty hours were spent alone. My bunkmates eventually complained that I screamed in my sleep and was so restless no one could sleep; I was sent to a camp doctor, who listened to my history and examined me, then sent me on to three other doctors, one after another, whose specialties I did not know. As a result of their consultations, I was relieved of guard duty on the stockade towers. My commanding officer had been advised that my history as an ex-concentration camp prisoner made me a potential threat to prisoners in the stockade and others because of the possibility of my acting out problems of reversed identity.

New orders were cut for me, and I was assigned to a post in Maryland. No sooner did I arrive there than I was told to put in for a transfer. Reason given: I was not a citizen. In this instance, lo and behold, the army had assigned me to a top-secret post. Until my transfer could be arranged the security officer gave me a colored tag to wear around my neck and assigned me to a barracks with others who were awaiting transfer or discharge.

The post was a coding and decoding center that served the entire East Coast. Everyone on this post wore color-coded tags and identification photographs around their necks. Free movement and talk about one's work were not permitted. Individuals passed from one area to another according to the color of the tags they wore. There was absolutely nothing for me to do. The post was situated in the country, well away from the nearest main roads. I sat around for a week before I finally approached a sergeant and begged him for work of some kind so that I would not go out of my mind. The sergeant thought about my request, then suggested that I take duty on a supply truck that ran between the post I was on and Fort Belvoir, Virginia, to pick up rations. I went out on the supply truck about three times a week. The rest of the time I played cards or chess, and went to every movie shown at the post theater.

Weeks went by and still there were no new orders. I requested a weekend pass to *Washington*, D.C. The commanding officer mulled the idea over for a while because I was not a permanent member of that post, but he finally consented to issue me regular weekend passes to *Washington*. That's how I became acquainted with the capital city. I visited the federal buildings, congressional chambers, and other points of interest like any tourist. I also met hostesses at the U.S.O. there, and began to spend most of my weekend time at the servicemen's club, socializing, dancing, and consuming refreshments.

After two-and-a-half months, I was still frittering away weeks on that post while weekending in D.C. One weekend at the U.S.O. I met and talked at length with a GI who worked in the Army Medical Library in Washington. He learned that I could read and speak a few European languages. When he heard that I was a soldier in search of an assignment, he encouraged me to try to get into the Army Medical Library, where, he assured me, linguists were badly needed. His description of duty at the Library sounded inviting, and the idea of working in *Washington* appealed to me.

When I returned to the post I finished my usual Monday-morning supply truck duty before trotting off to the post's administration building to tackle a sergeant on the subject of my transfer.

"Sergeant," I said, "I have a lead on a translating job at the Army Medical Library in *Washington,* D.C. Since I am not wanted on this post and have no other orders, I would like to request a three-day pass, in mid-week, to follow up on that lead."

The sergeant stared at me. "Garcia, don't you know you can't do that? You just can't go out looking for a job in the army. The job has to come to you, very probably, with orders."

"Yes, sergeant, but look what's happening to me with all these proper orders. I keep getting assigned to posts where the army can't use me because I'm not a citizen. I'm trying to tell you that I've found a place in the army that could use my training, citizen or not."

"You'll have to wait, Garcia," said sergeant. "I'm sure your orders are on the way, and reassignment is not far off."

After a few more weeks without orders I returned to the sergeant in a desperate mood. This time I persuaded him to approach a lieutenant with me about trying for the library position in *Washington.* Together we went through a similar routine with the lieutenant that I had already been through with the sergeant. "Okay," he agreed, "let's give the soldier the three-day pass and see what happens. Maybe he can get himself reassigned by his own efforts. We sure as hell haven't been successful at it." The lieutenant had seen the logic of my request.

I went to *Washington* and found the Army Medical Library on Constitution Avenue next to the Smithsonian Institute. My friend, when I found him, took me immediately to his commanding officer, a captain. I discussed with him my qualifications for translator-clerk job with the library, and briefed him fully on my predicament. The captain picked up his phone and called someone, apparently on a higher level, giving him my serial number and asked that I be transferred to the Army Medical Library, He said that he would wait by his telephone for an answer and hung up. We talked about the nature of the work I would be expected to do, and waited for the telephone to ring. A call came within a half hour and cleared me to transfer as requested. The Captain told me to go back to the post where I was stationed and wait for orders.

At the post, my story that I had successfully managed my own reassignment was met with good-natured skepticism. I sweated out a week-and-a-half more waiting, and then had the satisfaction of receiving orders of my transfer to the Army Medical Library.

The library assignment was a plum job. The usual army routines were absent. I worked in the reference division with a small detachment of about 10 men, learning clerking duties, translating title sheets of foreign books into English, assisting civilians who drifted in and out. I worked, too, on translations of captured German documents. Because we had no post, we got "rations and quarters," that is, we received monthly pay plus a weekly allowance for food and lodgings. There was no reveille. There were no inspections. I lived in a Northwest *Washington* boarding house, near DuPont Circle, where I took two meals a day, seven days a week. I met my fellow boarders, many of them students at nearby George Washington University. A little at a time, I brought some civilian clothes to wear on weekends when we were off duty. My life began to warm up.

Acquainting myself with university students, most of whom were younger and appeared no smarter than I, I began to realize that I could go to college, particularly as I had enlisted under the "GI Bill," which extended educational benefits to servicemen based on length of service. I enrolled in the U.S. Armed Forces Institute and started night school equivalency classes toward a high school diploma.

In the spring of 1948, I was offered the rank of corporal in the Army Medical Department with the stipulation that I reenlist for another two years. I would be a buck sergeant within three years, I was promised. But I turned down this offer. My library work among educated GIs, my association with university students, my high school studies – all served to give me confidence that I could seek a higher level of education. I wanted to get out of the army and into college.

1948-1953

On September 10th, 1948, exactly 18 months after I had enlisted, I was discharged from the U.S. Army as a PFC, private first class. Five days later I received my High School Equivalency Diploma, just in time to begin fall classes at George Washington University under the full benefits of the GI Bill.

College classes, I discovered, were challenging and enjoyable, and the open life style of large city university agreeable. I looked forward to studying and attending my classes. In my spare time I tried out some of the school's clubs and social activities. Soon I was part of a small group of friends with similar interests, and three of us became close.

One friend got me a bid to his national fraternity, Kappa Alpha, that allowed neither Jews nor Negroes among its members. I could not duck away from experiencing deep humiliation when I learned of their policy, but such humiliations had long been a fact of my survival. I became a pledge, only to drop out soon afterwards, not consciously because of policies of discrimination, but, as I told my fraternity friends, because I had learned how high the dues were. Fraternity life was not for students like me, nor could I accept the racist attitudes, remarks, and policies that wove through our daily lives like a game or a threat, depending on who the player was.

Between classes I spent most of my spare time playing bridge in the student union lounge with my two new friends, Jim Pearce, a Floridian, and Budge Beckman, an upstate New Yorker. That year the three of us went to Budge's home in Westfield, New York, for Thanksgiving, and to Jim's home in St. Petersburg, Florida, for Christmas. Both families welcomed me warmly and treated me as openly and casually as if I were another son. From then on, I was assured of a home to go to during school vacations.

I became an avid student of American history and government. An excellent professor taught me about the key figures who helped to found this nation, about the acts and documents that created almost two hundred years of government policy. I eagerly studied the functions and responsibilities of the three branches of the Federal government, and decided that American participatory government was far more effective than the parliamentary Social Democracy of my earlier political training.

Often I would seek out my professor after class because he always answered, in detail, the many questions I posed to him, I finally asked his advice about how I might get started in architectural training and he told me I was heading in the right direction by taking undergraduate classes in general studies, but that I should soon enroll in an architectural school. Stick with it, he told me, even knowing you will have to work most of your way through. As to where I should settle down, he emphasized that if I wanted to understand the many-faceted character of the United States, I should get away from the Eastern seaboard. He believed that the East was too dominated by European thought to understand the strong influence of other vast regions of the country. Far too many immigrants, he thought, stagnated in New York and other large Eastern cities, because they were afraid to break their ties with Europe. Like Horace Greeley, he advised me to go West. There, he said, I would find not only an opportunity to develop myself, but to help influence the direction of this still growing country.

George Washington University offered no architecture courses other than a survey history course in the fine arts department, which I took in my first term. I covered the curriculum offered and supplemented my studies by joining the art club, soon becoming its president. After the Christmas recess I continued a full schedule of classes at GWU, but I also enrolled in a class in residential design at an adult night school. Our instructor was a young *Washington* architect named Nick Satterlee, who struggled to teach a class of do-it-yourself house builders some of the elementary points of architecture, and Nick seemed glad to have me there. He offered me babysitting work at his Georgetown home, which he had recently remodeled, encouraging me to browse through his extensive architectural library whenever I cared for his two little girls. By spring I asked Nick what he thought of my attending architectural school full time.

He not only encouraged me, but used his influence with an old friend who became the dean of a new architectural department at North Carolina State College who accepted me for the fall 1949 term. He also recommended me for a summer job with an up-and-coming *Washington* architect named Vernon deMars. Vernon – who later developed an outstanding practice in Northern California – taught me the rudiments of drafting, including some valuable lessons in achieving various line qualities just by the way you hold a drafting pencil.

At North Carolina State College in *Raleigh*, I immersed myself in architecture, working often more than 15 hours a day at classwork and design problems. I studied eagerly under excellent instructors. My favorite design teacher was Mrs. Nowicki, a Polish architect married to Matthew Nowicki, another Polish architect, who, at that time had been one of the collaborators with Le Corbusier on the United Nations headquarters building in *New York City*. Mr. Nowicki would teach us when his wife was unable to do so. Frank Lloyd Wright, Buckminster Fuller and many others came to *Raleigh* to lead annual seminars. I managed to hear Mr. Wright during my first year when I joined a group of freshman architectural students who crashed a Wright party the dean and his wife were giving for the senior students. We were permitted to stay only by the intervention of the great man himself. I also had first-rate instruction from teachers near my own age, such as George Matsumoto who became a distinguished Northern California architect.

Budge Beckman's father, who was a general contractor in *Westfield*, New York, invited me to come to work for him during the summer of 1950. I worked as a laborer on some tank buildings and was even permitted to help design a house for a client of his. The Beckmans and their two grown sons allowed me to live and take my meals with them, and to hang on to all the wages I had earned during the summer with them. The Beckmans knew that I had used up two of my GI Bill years and that less than a year of college support was left.

I needed every penny of the money they had let me save when I returned to *Raleigh* in the fall. I rented a small basement room not far from school, lived frugally, and devoted myself full time to my studies. My secondhand radio was my constant companion. Stuck for an idea one day, I took inspiration from listening to a Stan Kenton jazz concert on Saturday night and turned in a design project of which I was proud; it received second place for that assignment. I also discovered the Saturday afternoon Metropolitan Opera series, which took me home to the radio fare of my childhood. I listened intently every week during the season from that time forward, memorizing the music of the more familiar operas, learning the parts and singing along with them, identifying the voices of many of the stars.

Within a few months my GI Bill support ran out and I took a part-time job in downtown *Raleigh* as a five-day-a-week draftsman in an engineer's office. I had brought an old car to take me from the campus to work, but my grades began to fall as study hours were forfeited to working hours. I applied for scholarship aid but the dean of the architectural school told me that my grades were not where they should be and furthermore, he continued, the fact that I operated a car worked against me. If I could afford to drive a car, he told me, I could afford the cost of attending school. I pointed out to him I was by myself in the United States, had no one to turn to, and needed help. As a final send-off he told me he didn't think I would ever be a good architect and was sorry he had accepted me to begin with. I was awarded a scholarship of $100.00. Corresponding with the Clarks, I had obtained Jesse Miles's address in the States. I called him to borrow a small sum to get me through the semester, and he soon sent it to me. I finished up the year still working and with lower grades.

The Clarks and I had kept in touch; Jean Clark wrote me occasional letters containing news of acquaintances and happenings in *Buffalo*. She had written me in the spring of 1948 about the birth of a third daughter, Peggy. From time to time she sent me pictures of the growing Clark daughters. She sent me a clipping and a note when Arthur assumed command of a Reserve National Guard Regiment in upstate New York and notes about his management duties in the family chemical plant. I wrote them about my activities, first as a soldier, then as a student. However, I did not return to *Buffalo*. It was not dislike that held me back from going to *Buffalo*, but pride. I wanted to live up to the confidence that both Clarks had shown in me when Arthur sponsored my coming to the U.S.A. I wanted them to see me as an immigrant-turned-American- citizen who had succeeded in carrying out his dream. They would be proud of me again, and justified in their decision to bring me here.

I had little else to do but try. I was beginning to understand that there was no replacing a family, and that forgetting one's own family was more isolating than helpful. A family could give a man a starting point, a sounding board for ideas, inspiration for achievement, a refuge in times of need. One had to be deprived of one's own family to understand what being alone meant. I had to care about what I was doing. Who else would? By myself, I had to try to give meaning to my survival. Secretly I worked for my father's and mother's approval, realizing fully well that I was holding on to a fantasy. My parents had been reduced to ashes in *KZ Sobibor*.

The Clarks had tried to help. Jim Pearce's family and the Beckman family had invited me often to their homes during school holidays. Others had invited me into their homes as well. But when the holidays were over, family members parted from one another and remained attached by invisible strings that would last them all their lives. I was left by myself, unattached. I found my own way and kept my own counsel. Often I lost my direction. Often I started over again.

Gradually I became a part-time college student, part-time wage earner. I spent the early weeks of the summer of 1951 in *Raleigh* working for an ice show that came through town. I sold programs and flirted with the female ice performers. By the 4th of July, I was back in *Washington*, D.C. taking pictures of President Harry S. Truman and members of his cabinet reviewing a traditional parade in honor of America's independence. I landed a job as a draftsman with the Rural Electrification Administration (REA), a Division of the U.S. Department of Agriculture, and through the fall I continued taking a class at George Washington University in elementary German. I was still thinking of using my translating and interpreting abilities and wanted to improve my German grammar.

To relieve my loneliness and to attach myself to a group with whom I could find at least intellectual affinity, I occasionally attended services at the Unitarian Church and chatted with various members for companionship. I stayed away from synagogues and their congregations. And yet my mind, at times, was punctured with yearnings I wanted to stifle. Nevertheless, it soon happened while I was working at the REA in *Washington* that I was seized with a strong impulse to attend Jewish New Year services. On the High Holy Days I joined a large Jewish throng in Constitution Hall, which served as a synagogue of adequate dimensions for the New Year congregation. The size of the crowd of worshippers frightened me, and the unfamiliar structure of the service disappointed me. I walked away that day still very much alone and still afraid to join a large Jewish herd. Even in *Washington* my survival instincts had been aroused. Did I not know how readily such herds could be herded?

I continued to work days and study nights. When I had saved enough money, I returned to NC State for another go at my architectural education. During spring semester, I received a notice from *Washington*, my stated permanent address, that I was to report to the Federal Courthouse to be examined for citizenship eligibility. I drove my jalopy up to *Washington* and called on two good friends, Nick Satterlee and my former American history professor at GWU, to request their appearance as my witnesses at the Courthouse the next morning. Then I called a girl I knew and picked her up that evening as my date. My mood was ebullient, for tomorrow I would be a citizen. In the years since my arrival in the United States – months of confusion and homesickness, months of learning to stand on my own two feet – I had acquired American habits. I now had the freedom to become whatever I wanted to be, to seize or reject opportunities. Truly, I did not yet know what I would or could become, but I very much looked forward to assuming the privileges and responsibilities of American citizenship.

My elation, as I drove to pick up my date that evening, outweighed my new sense of responsibility. The wail of a siren notified me that a motorcycle cop wanted me to pull over for speeding. I could not believe that I let myself be caught speeding the evening before my citizenship examination.

"Officer," I pleaded, as he started to write me a ticket, "if you give me that ticket I will not be able to be sworn in as a citizen tomorrow, and I am in *Washington* for that reason."

"What are you trying to tell me, buddy?" snarled the cop. I explained that even one arrest on any count during the past year would automatically disqualify me from eligibility of becoming a new citizen. The cop accused me of being a con artist, good at ingenious excuses, but enough doubt crossed his mind that he put his ticket book away and ordered me to follow him to a police station. There the police put their heads together to read ordinances and debate my point. They had not heard of such a law. A phone call to an attorney of the Department of Justice confirmed what I had told them. A misdemeanor arrest disqualified an applicant for citizenship. The cop tore up the citation.

"It's my gift," he said, for becoming a citizen, but if I catch you speeding tomorrow evening, you're going to be one sorry citizen." Of course I had to explain all this to my date who thought I had stood her up. She could not stop laughing and we talked about it for most of the evening.

The next day my friends met me at the courthouse, as promised. They laughed over the story of my close call and kidded me that they did not believe my jalopy could run fast enough to get me into such trouble. Inside, an interrogator questioned me on points of American history. My witnesses signed affidavits in my behalf. On April 8th, 1952, I joined a number of other immigrant petitioners in a courtroom to be sworn in as an American citizen. Right after the ceremony I called the Clarks in *Buffalo* to tell them that I had become a citizen that morning and to thank them for bearing the long-term responsibility of sponsoring me in this country.

"How does it feel to be an American?" Arthur asked.

"I don't really feel much different except that now I'm able to do one thing I could not do before," said I in a mood to josh with him.

"What's that, Max?"

"When I get back to *Raleigh* I'm going to write my congressman to demand that the Marshall Plan aid be stopped and immigration curtailed. Let those damned foreigners take care of themselves!"

We both laughed. I thanked my witnesses for standing with me and each of us went his way. That afternoon I returned to NC State. When the ice show came through town again, in early summer, I worked it once more until it closed. One of the girl skaters who lived in *Chicago* suggested that I could probably easily find a drafting job there. Why not try *Chicago*, I thought. I could not earn enough in *Raleigh* to get me through another semester of schooling and *Chicago* might be an interesting alternative to *Washington*.

I drove the girl to her home in *Chicago* and within a few days found a job with Rand McNally, the map maker. But cartography did not interest me, I soon discovered. The tracing and drafting work assigned me were without creative challenge. I quit and soon found a job with a large architectural firm on Michigan Avenue, called Fugard, Burt, Wilkinson, and Orth. Among the junior draftsmen in their employ I was on the bottom rung but I was pleased with the experience I gained there as we worked on drawings for a large hospital. One of the draftsmen invited me to his home for Thanksgiving, just as someone had invited me nearly every previous Thanksgiving. The easy hospitality of American families to outsiders always amazed and disarmed me.

Chicago was a dirty, unappealing city, but in the summer of 1952 it became an exciting place for me to be when I managed to attend both the Democratic and Republican nominating conventions there. Learning that the Democratic convention would be headquartered at the *Chicago* Hilton Hotel I had gone there the weekend before the convention was scheduled to open. On Michigan Avenue, near the Hilton, I ran into Bobby Baker who had been a pledge with me at Kappa Alpha at GWU and he asked me what I was doing in *Chicago*. I told him I lived here. In turn I asked him what was he doing here and he told me that he was in charge of organizing the Democratic nominating convention. I then asked him if he could get me tickets to attend the convention. I knew he had been a page in the Senate, that he was a South Carolinian and that he was very close to the Majority Leader in the Senate, Senator Lyndon B. Johnson, of Texas, but I had not known that he had risen that high in the Democratic Party's hierarchy. He obliged me with a South Carolina Press Pass and told me with that pass I would be able to go everywhere in the convention hall at the *Chicago* Stockyards. Suddenly I had become a member of the press corps! He also gave me a parking pass for my car.

The following Monday I went to see my boss, a member of the firm, and requested permission to quit work at 3:00 P.M. in order to attend the convention meeting. My boss was taken aback, as were my fellow co-workers, all of them born Chicagoans, that I had been able to gain entrance to the convention while they had been unable to get even a single ticket but then, I thought, they had never been trained in "*Organisierung.*"

As an accepted – if bogus – member of the press corps, I had driven my old car in a line of press cars behind a police escort right up to the convention entrance. Inside I had roamed the floor, studying the former governor of Illinois, now presidential candidate Adlai E. Stevenson, Democratic Party leaders and congressmen, observing the maneuvers of their political process.

Later on, as the date for the Republican nominating convention rolled around, I snooped about for a way to get into that one too; joining the Young Republicans was my key. By volunteering I observed firsthand the nominating process of General Dwight D. Eisenhower and Richard M. Nixon, just as I had earlier observed the Democratic nominating convention. I was very impressed with General Eisenhower, who had been in charge of defeating Nazi Germany and to whom I felt a personal vote of thanks.

Having had the opportunity to look at both nominating conventions firsthand I now looked at both parties to determine which was most likely to maintain the balance of the legislative, executive and judicial branches of our government. Such a balance, I believed, was the key to America's strength as a democratic nation. Thus I prepared myself to cast my first vote as an American citizen in the upcoming November election, a responsibility I took extremely seriously.

I never did get back to school. I voted and finished out a year's work in *Chicago*, and then drove to Florida when summer came, hoping to establish residency with Jim Pearce's family and to finish my architectural education at a Florida state school. Jim's family was in no position to take me on as a long-term resident, however, and so I took a cabin on a beach outside St. Petersburg and worked as a draftsman for a small-office architect there. The summer's heat and humidity drained me – there was no air-conditioning then – and the drafting work was not very stimulating. I became discouraged. I called my old friend Jesse Miles, who by now had become a colonel and was living in Bloomington, Indiana, and asked him for advice. When he invited me up for a visit, I packed my jalopy and left Florida as abruptly as I had arrived.

Once again I found myself crossing the country, from South to North this time. As usual I drove very fast, and with assurance, tailing slower cars, awaiting that moment when I could pass. My reflexes were good as I worked at out-thinking and out-maneuvering other motorists. I drove through vast farmlands, small towns, over mountains and plains. I saw a country that consisted of many cultures and very different communities. Yet, no matter how far I drove, I talked with people in one language only, even though we spoke to one another in a variety of accents. There seemed to be a thread of understanding that tied them all together. On the car radio I listened to our new president, Eisenhower, speak about sharing nuclear isotopes for peaceful purposes with all peoples of the world.

Colonel Miles was in charge of the ROTC program at Indiana University. He had married Ruth, a native of *Berlin*, whom he had met in Bavaria, and whom I remembered very well. I badly needed to talk to this old friend and his wife. They knew who I was, where

I had come from. During my years in the States I had experienced many highs and lows, sometimes feeling that nothing could hold me back from becoming an architect and contributing useful and harmonious buildings but just as often feeling alone and unwanted, certain I would never design anything that would be built, and barely able to get through a day. At the time I visited Jesse and Ruth I was in one of my low moods. I was almost 30 years old. The money I had earned had never been enough to allow me a year of schooling at a time. I felt tired and very much alone. I told Jesse I had decided to give up on architecture and to re-enter the army as a career soldier. I could put in my 20 years, be pensioned off at 49, and spend my old age sunning myself.

Jesse and Ruth were sympathetic and did not discourage my new resolve. Jesse, a West Pointer, had always taken pride in his career of service to his country. If I had bitten off more than I could chew he was able to vouch for the satisfactions of an Army career. The Korean War was in full swing, and having the option to take a year of military schooling before assignment to two years of active duty, I applied for and was admitted to Russian language studies at the Presidio of *Monterey*, California.

1953-1954

I took the train from *Chicago*, Illinois to *Oakland*, California, dozing and dreaming as the train rolled through long, flat stretches of rich farmland. The train crossed dry prairie lands, such as I had never seen, then began a slow upward climb into rugged mountain country that was both exciting and frightening to look upon. The train snaked its way down from the mountains to arrive in *Oakland* on the *San Francisco* Bay almost three days after departing from *Chicago*. The length of the country from *Chicago* on Lake Michigan to the West Coast stunned me.

I took a morning ferry to *San Francisco* where I was to connect with a train to *Monterey*. Crossing the Bay toward *San Francisco* in fog, I could not see her modest downtown skyline or her beckoning hills and white residences. The fog persisted throughout the day and since the train for *Monterey* would not leave until late afternoon I had plenty of time to fill. I walked through the center of town and then took a bus tour of the city. What I could see of *San Francisco* enchanted me. I was in a European city again. Knowing that *Monterey* was no great distance from *San Francisco*, I resolved to come back often on my weekends off.

Five years had gone by since my discharge from the U.S. Army, and by 1953, when I re-enlisted; basic training was required of me all over again. I entered training camp at *Fort Ord*, California, near *Monterey*. There I maneuvered according to past experiences to avoid the more rigorous routines, and sold candy bars in the barracks to hustle a little extra money.

Basic training completed, I began Russian language study at the Presidio of *Monterey's* Army Language School. My classmates were a fairly intellectual group, above-average college boys who like myself, preferred intensive language training in order to qualify for special assignment during the Korean War years. Vocabulary building, phraseology and pronunciation were stressed. Our goal was to speak and understand more than passable daily Russian within 11 months. I studied hard to keep pace with my bright classmates, but the migraine headaches, which still plagued me from time to time, returned with a vengeance during that period. I went to the infirmary to seek relief. The various drugs the doctors prescribed relieved my pains, but also knocked me out. I began to miss classes.

One day I went to the infirmary to request a refill of the medicine prescribed for me and was ordered to a mental health clinic at *Fort Ord*. At the clinic I was admitted by appointment to see a psychiatrist who began to look at my records while sitting at his desk. He then began to question me about the nature of my bouts of pain and disability. He wanted to know if I was having difficulties coping with the school. I replied that I did not believe school was the problem except for the constant interference of migraine attacks. He wanted to know why I had quit architecture. I searched my mind: money problems, discouragement, I offered; I added that I reasoned that I might be better off in the service because I was familiar with army life and wanted to make myself useful as a translator/interpreter in exchange for obvious benefits of security. Apparently having noticed references in my papers to concentration camp survival, the doctor quickly pinned me down as a Jew. He asked me leading questions about my Jewish background. I tried to deny that I was a Jew but found myself becoming quite agitated. The interview ended unsatisfactorily. The psychiatrist was not pleased with my attitude but he did renew my prescription and sent me back to duty.

I got along fine with my classmates, who filled our barracks with classical music instead of hillbilly tunes, preferring games of chess or bridge to the reading of comic books. Yet I remained an outsider among these boys from solidly middle-class families, many of whom had lived in one town all their lives. Some of them were Jewish and sensed that I was a Jew. They would invite me to Friday night services and they would kid me when I insisted that I was a Protestant, as my dog tag showed. They asked me why I had a concentration camp number on my arm. I answered that I had been imprisoned as a member of he Dutch underground, a story they refused to accept.

My migraines grew steadily worse. The intensity of our daily Russian sessions drained my mental and physical strength. My once ace-in-the-hole was my weekend enjoyment of the California coast and the towns of *Monterey, Carmel* and, of course, *San Francisco.*

I had not succeeded in forgetting about my architectural training. In fact I missed it immensely. I found the *Monterey* public library and on weekends often spent afternoons there reading architectural magazines and art history books. One of the librarians, noticing my interest, told me that her husband was an architect. After that we often talked and one day she invited me to meet her husband and to see their home he had designed. I was impressed with the architect's use of space in their low-budget, rustic home, and delighted to be able to exchange ideas and philosophies with this couple. Together we looked at examples of contemporary California architecture in *Carmel* and *Monterey.*

Through my new friends I met architects who practiced in the area and I was invited to attend a charter dinner meeting establishing a new chapter of the American Institute of Architects on the *Monterey Peninsula*. Frank Lloyd Wright, who had come to town for that occasion, had accepted an invitation to speak at that dinner, and also to inspect and supervise a major house he was building on the edge of *Carmel* overlooking the ocean. I sat content among these architects and listened intently to what Mr. Wright had to say. After the dinner and Mr. Wright's talk many of us pressed around him to ask questions and listen to his answers. More to remind myself than him that I once had been an architectural student, I blurted out that I had met him when, as a student at NC State, I, and others, had crashed an upperclassmen's party in his honor at the dean's house. Looking at me sharply, he asked me what I was doing in the army, but did not seem to comprehend my answer that I had joined the service in order to raise money to finish my education.

Many a weekend I took a bus the few miles to *Carmel-by-the-Sea*, which was then a quaint and sleepy town that would come alive once a year for the Bing Crosby golf tournament. It was inexpensive enough to attract writers, artists, and professional people in retirement. I even took a moonlighting job there for a couple of months as a weekend bus boy in the dining room of the La Playa Hotel.

One Friday, when I heard some of my classmates were driving to *San Francisco* for the weekend, I jumped at the chance when they invited me to join them. That night we toured the town after we had secured rooms at the local YMCA. I awoke to a sunny Saturday morning and set off by myself to see as much as I could of a *San Francisco* that I had only glimpsed during my bus tour when I first arrived. I fell under the spell of a sparkling white harbor city built into, its many hills. The climate, the size, the shipping activity on the water, the liberal spirit afloat, reminded me of *Amsterdam*. I heard many languages spoken as I walked through the several neighborhoods. I saw Italians, Chinese, and Japanese, Mexicans, Filipinos and Indians living and working without strife alongside Russians, Irishmen, Germans and black Americans. I discovered the opera house during the fall opera season. Thereafter, since servicemen were allowed in free, I became a weekend commuter to *San*

Francisco and a volunteer usher at the opera house, in order to see as many operas as possible.

I had become a regular at the YMCA on Turk Street and began attending the Unitarian Church on Sunday morning. There I met and talked with a woman, Anne Chamberlain, who invited me to her apartment on Gough Street for Sunday supper and introduced me to her sister, Mary. The sisters belonged to a large family who were long-time residents of *Berkeley*. One weekend I was invited to come to *Berkeley* where I was introduced to the entire Chamberlain family at their parents' handsome turn-of-the-century home. The parents and a number of their children were teachers and musicians. One son was a practicing architect. They were a warm and interesting group and I enjoyed being included as a guest within their circle of friends. To my surprise I met there an old friend from my GWU days who at that time was stationed at Fort Baker as an adjutant to the Post Commander.

During the ninth month of my schooling at *Monterey* I suffered a nervous breakdown. I had been given very strong medication for severe migraine attack and was lying semiconscious on my cot when my bunkmates began a routine "GI Party," that is, a vigorous housecleaning of the barrack prior to an inspection and the issue of weekend passes. Awakened by the noise around me, I flew into a rage, jumped up and began overturning furniture, throwing objects around, and tearing up anything I could destroy. With enormous strength I fought and screamed as some of the GIs tried to pin me down. Eventually I was subdued. Some orderlies wrestled me into a strait jacket and onto a stretcher. They took me by ambulance to the "psycho ward" at the Fort Ord hospital. There I rested in bed for a couple of weeks and was visited daily by a young psychiatrist assigned to help me.

The psychiatrist asked me for a complete history of my life, exploring details of my life I had almost forgotten. My youth and the details of why I ended up in a concentration camp were of great concern to him. I tried telling him that my parents had died in bombing raids and that I had been caught and imprisoned by the Nazis while working with the Dutch underground, a story I thought I had been getting by with quite successfully. The psychiatrist asked me if I had been raised a Jew and I denied it. He was tenacious. At one session he told me that he knew that *Amsterdam* had never been bombed. At another session I learned that the psychiatrist who had seen me in the mental health clinic had filed a report alerting my commanding officer to expect my breakdown at any time because of unresolved inner conflicts relating to my identity.

I soon realized that I was not going to be allowed out of the psychiatric ward until I opened up to my psychiatrist who, after all, was a sincere and likeable fellow. With nothing to do but lie around and await his visits, I began to relax and decided to cooperate with him. I told him about my early life and background. I told him about my concentration camp experiences from those of a starving forced slave laborer to my pneumonia, my operations and hospital convalescence, to privileged member of the *Paketstelle*, to subhuman forced slave laborer again. I talked with him about my reasons for having rejected my Jewish heritage and my hopes for the future, which included more talk about architecture than a career in the service. Proudly I pointed out to him all that I had done by myself in the United States. A European working class boy obtaining a partial college education and almost completing architectural studies was an accomplishment that I was not sure the psychiatrist could appreciate. I was beginning to describe the army once more as a way-station, and probably a mistake, but at least it was a way for me to earn and save money, and I emphasized that I was continuing my education, even here, increasing my language skills.

By the time I was admitted to the general ward and permitted to walk to the psychiatrist's office for our frequent mental health sessions he began to encourage me to get out of the service as a first step toward mental recovery. I was frightened by his advice because I thought he intended to get me discharged on a "Section 8", or "psycho" discharge, which could jeopardize my future by severely limiting my chances at worthwhile employment. The psychiatrist explained that I could separate from the service with a General Discharge because of medical findings, and that it would carry no psychiatric or other liabilities into the civilian world. However, I would no longer be eligible for service in the armed forces. He advised me to seek further psychiatric help after discharge and for me to return to school and complete my architectural studies.

I promised him I would see a psychiatrist when I left the service, but I confessed I felt too old to return to school and I relied on the words of one of my professors at NC State who had advised beginning students that those who could get through the first two years of an architectural education could probably get through the rest on their own. If a student could master the basics of the first two years, he continued, he would probably have little trouble getting through the next three years extending that basic knowledge. I reasoned that it could probably be learned by working in architects' offices. I made up my mind that I would settle in *San Francisco*, work in architects' offices and take courses at night until I gained the additional knowledge and experience necessary to take the California State licensing examinations.

In short order I mustered out of the army. By terms of the General Discharge I was asked to turn in my army uniform and was issued a civilian suit in my size, and other garments, along with my mustering-out pay. Carrying with me a Certificate of General Discharge from the army under honorable conditions and a referral to the outpatient psychiatric clinic at Mount Zion Hospital, I arrived by bus in *San Francisco* in July 1954.

My San Franciscan friend, Anne, helped me find a small, first-floor studio apartment in a Taylor Street building on top of Nob Hill. A Murphy bed was the only furniture in the place besides some ancient kitchen appliances, but I was pleased with the hilltop location, and that evening I went out to explore my new neighborhood.

Night had fallen as I walked back to my apartment past little Huntington Park in the next block. Suddenly I was stopped in midstep as a man jumped from behind a bush and threatened me with a knife. His eyes were bloodshot and he appeared drunk but determined as he demanded my money. In my pocket was my mustering-out pay and my small savings, the only money I had. I looked at the man for no more than a moment, and then sprinted off as fast as my legs could carry me to my apartment. I fumbled, sweating, to unlock the front door with my key and, as it turned in the lock, I glanced back. The man was nowhere in sight. I guessed he had been too startled by my reaction to chase me. Back in my apartment, however, I lay on my bed shaking for a long time before I calmed down enough to fall asleep.

The next morning I began my rounds of architects' offices. Before the week was out I had found myself a job as a draftsman.

Two nervous young people, Pat and Max, standing in front of the door leading to the Judge's Chambers where they are to be married.

PART 6

Taking Root

$\big|$

D ecades have passed since Arthur and Jean Clark sponsored my coming to the United States. The opportunity their generous act gave me was the first step in a long climb toward a better life that millions of immigrants like myself have taken. The American dream, I was to learn, is as varied as the people who seek it, and as valuable as the effort put into realizing it. When I first arrived in the United States I very much believed America owed me a living because of the injustices and suffering I had been through. My head had been full of misguided ideas. America, after World War II, was exploding with prosperity, creative vitality, and social revolution. At the time when I was wandering the country seeking my identity and my fortune, the GIs of that war were raising what was probably the most privileged generation of young adults to have yet been born. They were the beneficiaries of their parents' dream.

Taking prosperity for granted, postwar generations have come down hard on America's shortcomings, but they have also helped bring about some significant social changes, such as the advancement of civil and human rights, since the time I arrived in the United States. During these years all of us have been profoundly affected by continuing domestic and international ferment, by political murders and scandals. America's failures have been identified and damned throughout the world, thanks to our habit of open self-criticism and our free press. We have debated and fought over various emerging issues, always working to make our system more justly responsive to our varying needs.

I cannot stand on the side of our country's detractors. From what I have observed and experienced, Americans possess a high degree of goodwill and balance, a balance that makes it possible for all to achieve what they set out to do, to be in charge of their own destiny and not necessarily to be interested in obtaining power. Americans will always work toward change and reform, but because they prefer their individual and collective freedoms to power building, they will probably continue to swing away from radical manipulations. Perhaps because of their immigrant backgrounds and their common experiences with becoming self-reliant, Americans are quick to help others to stand on their own two feet. They will help immigrants, disaster victims anywhere in the world, the poor, and the handicapped, but after they have provided a minimum standard of security, they will back off. Each needy one is expected to try to master his or her own destiny rather than to be mastered by the rescuers.

What America gave me, and all of us who came to this land, was an opportunity to shape our own lives. What we have done with that opportunity has been up to each of us. In one sense, each of us immigrants has become a pioneer in the same style as the American forefathers. They staged a revolution in the name of life, liberty and the pursuit of happiness. Thanks to my American liberators, when I came to this country I had life (knock on wood). I had liberty (and it was scary). Happiness I could not start chasing fast enough. Opportunity was one thing. Finding my way was another. Years of trial-and-error effort and loneliness lay ahead. Today I have to thank the Clarks for allowing me my own crack at the American scene. My dream had grown in scope from what it was when I arrived. It includes love of family, love of my tribe and heritage, love of this country that allows her varied millions to live and work peacefully in an ever changing but ever opening society; it includes the satisfaction of learning my capabilities, and that they can be expanded infinitely.

||

At 30, in *San Francisco*, I began to come to terms with myself. In 1954, I signed on as a draftsman in whatever architectural office needed a hand. The end of a project often meant the end of a job for me, and I would move on to another office. After some months of drifting about, I settled into the office of Mr. Harry A. Thomsen, Jr., who was in the last years of his practice before retiring. He had designed a number of *San Francisco's* post-earthquake, downtown buildings before the influx of new architects after World War II. Mr.

Thomsen gave me my first projects to see through in their entirety, from planning and design stages to working drawings and supervision of the construction. He also granted me time off for weekly sessions with a psychiatrist, which continued for almost a year. I consulted with a doctor from the Mt. Zion psychiatrist clinic, who was not only in possession of my Fort Ord records, but was Jewish himself. We faced each other over my problems, which to me meant migraines. My breakdown was behind me and I was heading once more in a direction I liked. To the psychiatrist my problems were viewed as somewhat more complex, apparently, because he tried to steer me toward the dangerous territory of my rejected Judaism. This was upsetting. I pointed out that I had always had migraines, even as a child, and that my mother, and other relatives on her side, had suffered them as well. Nevertheless, he felt there was a link between the present intensity and frequency of my migraines and some inner conflicts I wanted to suppress.

In one session the psychiatrist brought up anti-Semitism, and I was shocked that he might see my turning from Judaism as anti-Semitic. No, doctor, I was not anti-Semitic. Almost crying with frustration, I groped for reasonable words of explanation. The problem, doctor, was fear, fear of anti-Semitism, and fear for good reason. Why should I subject myself, and children I hoped to have one day, to such agonies as I had already experienced as a Jew. The religion did not mean so much to me that I must be prepared, at all times, to martyr myself over it. I had the same privilege of choice as everyone else and I made that choice. To think upon the history of the Jews was to remember long Sephardic laments that used to resound through our Portuguese Sephardic Synagogue in *Amsterdam*, recalling the sorrows and losses because of centuries of anti-Semitism in Europe. I did not understand why people hated Jews, but I had no reason to doubt that they did, and I, for one, wanted out of that exhausting identity. And so we talked about this and all manner of things.

In my apartment, now slowly being outfitted with furniture, I experimented with Buckminster Fuller's concept of space-framing, using colored plastic toothpicks as struts, then turning out a three-dimensional Christmas tree that, to my surprise, won some design publicity in a national magazine. "Manual Therapy," my friends called my puttering.

One morning I awoke with chills and fever and could not get out of bed. The doctor I called in to examine me diagnosed my illness as a severe flu. Since I had no one to shop for me or help me, the doctor arranged for me to enter Mt. Zion Hospital where he was on staff. I recuperated for a number of days in a primarily Jewish institution. Doctors and nurses talked and joked with me as one Jew to another. The other patients I met on the floor were mostly Jews and they treated one another sympathetically and familiarly. Some of them ordered kosher meals. The hospital seemed like home and I was overcome with the realization of how homesick I had been. The day the doctor discharged me, I cried, and a nurse squeezed my hand and told me to visit the hospital staff any time I wished.

At my apartment I cried some more. Gradually, my tears of frustration became tears of relief. It had been a long time since I had cried over anything at all. My uncontrolled emotions surprised me. I wanted, needed, to live openly as a Jew again. My desire to hide had dropped away. A great weight, that had exhausted me ever since my liberation, now had lifted. Now I wanted to proclaim to the world that I was a Jew. I started the process by visiting Anne Chamberlain and confessing to her that her Unitarian friend, Max, was actually a Jew who wanted to live as a Jew from that day forward. I told her about my Jewish upbringing as the true reason I had been sent to the concentration camps. I described how I had resolved, when I came to the United States, to shed my Jewish past, but how I had suffered and had become isolated as a result. Anne listened sympathetically and suggested I call a rabbi. When I did, the rabbi said, in effect, welcome back and don't feel so badly. Come to temple on Saturday to reacquaint yourself with your people.

I began attending a conservative temple regularly each week, and at some point during this period of return and rebirth I stopped seeing a psychiatrist. My headaches had continued intermittently, and the psychiatrist had told me that, more than likely, I would have to learn to live with them.

I was attracted to a girl I met at services, and began to visit her often at her apartment, where she lived with her mother. Within a few months I became engaged to her, then, disastrously, realized that I did not love her or share much in common with her. I was also becoming aware that attending temple every week was becoming a chore, and it was no ready cure for past mistakes and present pains. With a sense of guilt and failure that made me physically ill once more, I broke the engagement, and at the same time began to slip in temple attendance.

Nevertheless, I was a Jew and no longer inclined to hide it. I had failed to lose myself in weekly ritual, but that did not change my Jewishness. My parents had not been devout, but they had lived as Jews and had been murdered as Jews. They had never experienced the shame, the self-disgust, that denying one's heritage can bring.

Behind me were years of bleak loneliness in America. Some stretches had been so awful I had almost wished I had not survived. I had lived a lie and been isolated by it. The defeated Nazis had continued to triumph over me and keep me little more than a terrified survivor in spite of my efforts at accomplishment. Finally, I could respect myself once more. My destiny was that of a Jew. I embraced it. I looked forward to it. I could admit to myself my pride in the accomplishment of my people, and my love for them.

Down the ages of history Jews had often been persecuted mercilessly for their religious non-conformance. With depressing regularity, in one place or another, they have been deprived of their livelihoods, their property, and their lives. No matter where they were driven, these same people managed to retain their identity. Centuries of persecution have made the average Jew acutely interested in legal rights and humanitarian policies. Individually, and as a group, the Jews have directed great energy and intelligence toward human welfare. Some work for the downtrodden. Some elevate the arts. Some sharpen the sciences. Many sell and trade, thereby creating jobs and spreading prosperity. Others teach, or entertain, or practice law, work in government, ponder philosophy or run a variety of businesses. Very few are scoundrels. Most seek a better life for their families and their communities. How could I not be proud of my fellow Jews?

In 1954, I also discovered an inviting delicatessen and an outstanding Jewish bakery, the Ukrainian bakery, on McAllister Street, in the heart of what was left of an old Jewish ghetto (all since torn down and redeveloped for subsidized housing). Each week I was drawn to McAllister Street as by a magnet. The odors and the sight of the foods displayed in the shops overwhelmed me as I mingled with Jews and gentiles who shopped and window-shopped alongside me. I stuffed my tiny refrigerator with salamis, lox, chickens, and kosher dills I had brought, much of which had to be thrown away before I could get around to eating them. The dietary laws were not the reason for my enthusiasm, for I relished all kinds of foods, but I had a particular appetite for Jewish foods, even those that we Dutch Jews had never tasted.

At the office, and among friends, I told Jewish anecdotes and jokes to anyone willing to listen. My joking sometimes angered intellectual friends who were offended by ethnic jokes, and whose educated strivings stood in the way of their laughing at the human condition. I was no longer afraid of prejudice. It existed in America as it did in Europe. I accepted its existence but now felt free to express myself as a Jew.

I wrote to the Portuguese-Sephardic Synagogue in *Amsterdam* to inquire if any of my relatives had returned. Eventually I learned that five cousins lived: brothers Flip and Appie Cohen de Lara and Hans Rubens lived in *Amsterdam* with their wives; Floortje Melkman had remarried (her first husband, Ies, had been gassed in the Holocaust) and she and her postwar husband had emigrated to *Milwaukee*, Wisconsin. I assumed that Meijer Hekster still lived – the older cousin who had left for South Africa in the early thirties – but I did not know how to get in touch with him. These five cousins, were children of four of my mother's sisters: Klaartje, Grietje, Duifje and Jetje.

Having learned Floortje's last name I traced her through the *Milwaukee* telephone system and called her in a state of high excitement. She was shocked to hear from a cousin whom everyone believed to have disappeared during the Holocaust. She would not believe that I was the one I claimed to be and thought a cruel joke was being played on her. She asked me all sorts of questions to make sure I was not an impostor, questions that only family members would have the answers to. At last she believed me and now her tears began to pour. With the ice broken, we were soon talking joyfully with each other. Impulsively, I told her I would fly out that weekend for a visit. I knew I did not have the money for that trip. Credit cards did not exist then and I rarely managed to save anything, but lived from paycheck to paycheck. Anne, my friend, admitted to having a little extra cash, however, and she lent me the airfare. I flew to *Milwaukee* for a very emotional reunion at the apartment of Floortje, her Dutch husband, Joep Hony, and their daughter Anneke.

Floortje I remembered as a happy girl growing into a carefree teenager as the war began. She had matured into a pretty but anxiety-ridden woman. For two days the three of us, Floortje, Joep and myself, flooded their apartment with tears about our families, and what we, ourselves, had experienced. Floortje described her lonely life in hiding during the war. Her grief over the loss of her family and her first husband was such that their deaths might have happened the week before. Time, for her, had erased nothing. We exchanged stories and shared remembrances. We vented our bitterness over the families we had lost and our helplessness to bring any of them back. But talking together, one person to another who had suffered the same wounds, was a balm of sorts. I left *Milwaukee* a relieved man who had been able to talk about relatives and friends to a living cousin who shared my ties with them.

I wrote my cousins in *Amsterdam*. We, too, exchanged pictures and news about what had happened to each one of us. Flip and I corresponded most frequently because we had once been the closest in companionship among my living cousins. I, alone, was unmarried.

As soon as I could I paid Anne back the money she had lent me to make the trip. I told her all that had transpired and she was delighted to hear that things had gone so well. I continued to live as I always had, making friends by intuition and common interests.

I found many Jewish friends, but I did not seek out a solely Jewish community. Indeed, I was pleased that *San Franciscan* Jews lived like Jews had in *Amsterdam* as I remembered it, well-integrated citizens of the town.

In 1956, I married a Protestant girl, Priscilla Alden Thwaits, called Pat because of her initials. I met Pat on the rooftop of the Nob Hill apartment building in which we both lived, she on the top floor, I on the bottom. She was sunning herself and enjoying the view on a clear spring day. I was hanging up my socks to dry. Before the afternoon was over I lent her my volume of Andre Malraux's *The Voice of Silence.* A few years after her graduation from Middlebury College in Vermont, she had left her *Plandome*, Long Island, home and her public relations job in *New York* with Newsweek to live and work in the West. She had spent two years in New Mexico, and lived and worked in *San Francisco* almost a year before I met her. Living in the same building, I visited her often, enjoying her company and many of her interests. I invited her on excursions to see art museums and galleries, and to look over examples of Bay Area architecture. She divided her free time between me and a few tennis-playing friends of hers who shared her enthusiasm for that sport.

We spent many hours talking, and she questioned me, uncomprehending at first, about my history. She was pleased to hear me tell of finding my way back to Judaism, but, later, when I talked of marriage, she refused the idea of conversion in order to marry. She knew little about Judaism, she reminded me, and she believed that sharing a common religion was insufficient reason for marriage. Recalling my broken engagement, I did not push the point. We were married by a San Franciscan judge in a civil ceremony. Our honeymoon was spent visiting first her family and friends on Long Island, then my surprised "family": Arthur and Jean Clark in *Buffalo*, and Floortje and Joep Hony in *Milwaukee*.

In *San Francisco*, Pat accompanied me to services whenever I attended them, and began familiarizing herself with Judaism through reading, observing, and asking questions. She also met my Jewish friends. From the time our first child, a son, was born, she wanted him to be raised a Jew. After all three of our children were born, she studied with a rabbi of the reform congregation we had joined, and converted to Judaism. Pat came to Judaism of her own volition. Even if by heritage she could not be Jewish, or, by nature, reject her own heritage, she hoped her family would want to live as Jews and to stand in the places of some of those Jews lost to fascism's "final solution."

We had few possessions when we married, but from the day we took our vows we felt wealthy. Life was a celebration. We bought paintings, ceramics, and plants before we bought washing machines and dishwashers. We bought books, and I set up a drafting and study room in a large walk-in closet of the first apartment we rented. I filled our three rooms with flowers and brought my wife candy and pastries on weekends, just as my father had brought to my mother whenever he could afford it.

By the time our first child, David Alden Rodriquez Garcia, was born in 1957, 10 months after we were married, I was spending long evening hours hunched over my books or in classes, preparing for my state boards in architecture. Shortly after the birth of our second child, Tania Sippora Alden Rodreguez Garcia, in 1960, I received my California license. My wife called me at the office where I was working to read me my license number. I told her that I could die on the spot a satisfied man that I had achieved my childhood goal. She laughed and remarked that my childhood dream might be fulfilled, but my life's work had just begun.

Several months later I applied to the Hebrew Free Loan Association, about which a friend had told me, for their small maximum loan in order to start a business. Hebrew Free Loan officials informed me that they had not lent money to anyone before for the purpose of starting an architectural practice, and they considered me a risk. However, They accepted my application and the signatures of four underwriters as collateral, and lent me $2000.00, interest free. I had lined up some kitchen remodelings, room additions, and a house for a family of six in the hills of Marin County. One room of the Jackson Street Victorian flat we had moved to became my office-drafting room. Pat took on my secretarial work. We earned enough to pay the rent, increments on our loan, and save a little. In the following spring on 1961, our third child, Michelle Rozetta Helen Alden Rodriquez Garcia, was born. Our flat was looking more like a nursery than an architect's office. I rented office space in a building on Mission Street, and moved my practice downtown.

I had about seven years of work in architectural offices behind me when I opened my own office in 1960. I thought I knew how to run an architectural practice, and, indeed, I had gained good experience in almost every phase except one important one: selling my service to clients. No sooner was I licensed than I started to practice. Looking back, I have to laugh at my audacity. But I was 36 years old, and a man who had fought hard for the privilege of life. The risk of starting a practice had not seemed all that great. We had children. We had no savings in the bank and no backlog of wealthy friends waiting to engage my services for building projects. To be sure, Pat's family helped in the early years. Aunts and uncles and sister and brother-in-law commissioned variously a home-remodeling, a house, an office design. Pat's parents lent us another couple of thousand dollars when a client was slow in paying, and I could not otherwise pay my draftsman. Locally, I followed up every remodeling, building, or planning possibility that I heard of. I believed I could sell my services and, somehow, I did. No project was too small for me to undertake. I relished the challenge of learning to design for small budgets, and of learning the necessity of carefully detailed working drawings and specifications.

The first years of practice were difficult. I brought in a miscellany of small budget jobs, but no matter how much time I gave my clients or how well a project turned out, the prestigious work always went to better known architects. Some nights my wife and I hardly slept wondering how we would get through the next month. If I became discouraged and talked of teaching or going back to work for someone else, Pat encouraged me to continue, reminding me of the pride I took in seeing each project through. Sometimes the shoe was on the other foot, and I would have to convince my wife that the practice could yield a decent living to take care of the needs of our growing family. Luckily, neither of us was ever of a mind to quit at the same time. Often on weekends, however, we would put our cares aside, entertain our friends, and laugh. We liked what we were doing and we felt good about life.

For its population, *San Francisco* attracts a disproportionately large number of architects. I competed for commissions with established firms and a mushrooming number of new practices. For the first five years, I worked on residential and small commercial remodelings, additions, and new buildings. I designed individual homes for middle-class families in the early sixties when such homes were feasible. Gradually, I developed a clientele in commercial and corporate work, and some luxury custom homes. The size and number of the projects grew. There were many satisfactions. There were also some tough lessons that were blessings in disguise. The more I learned about the business of architecture, the better I could handle the bigger and more complex projects that came with time.

From the start I took great satisfaction in being able to support my family by doing work that I had always wanted to do. At first, draftsmen were hired only intermittently. Later, I learned the responsibilities of employing a steadily-expanding, full-time staff. In time, key staff people emerged who helped develop an efficient team operation. I continued to put in many hours of effort seven days a week, but I rarely looked upon the practice as work. In truth, I was delighted to be paid for spending my time so agreeably.

Our son David and our daughters Tania and Michelle transformed our lives, making each day meaningful, giving us strength we did not know we had. We were pleased to become parents, to love and interact with our children, to help and be helped by them. We disciplined and taught them according to what each of us had learned, and, at times, ours must have been conflicting messages. In no time at all, the children began teaching us, bringing us in touch with their generations of the American young. We worked to give them security and opportunities to develop themselves. They rewarded us with astonishing growth and a variety of abilities. Our home filled up over the years with their friends, hobbies, pets, musical instruments, and sporting equipment for every season. As each child reached school age, he or she began public school on the weekdays and religious school on weekends. David celebrated his

Bar Mitzvah at the age of 13. One by one, all three children were confirmed at our temple.

Nine years after I opened an office, Pat and I bought a comfortable Edwardian house for our family. As American houses go, it is old, but even after building or remodeling various luxury homes for clients, buying a spacious older home for my family's use seemed foolhardy. How could I be sure that my practice would not falter? Once my debts of earlier years had been repaid, I had vowed never to borrow money again, and I had not. Buying a home meant a mortgage and taxes in addition to office overhead. For me, home ownership was uncharted territory, a luxury beyond our needs. For Pat, it was a way of life. She was used to property and a surplus of seldom-used rooms. She thought the children would thrive in a home of their own. I thought they were thriving anyway. We had our first bitter quarrel over the need for a house. Pat argued that the practice was well-established and that regardless of ups and downs in the economy, home ownership would prove cheaper and more beneficial than rental. I looked at the scale of interest rates and was not convinced. My wife won that one, and I have never regretted her talking me into buying our house.

We corresponded with the Clarks every year, until they passed on, but because we were at opposite ends of the country, we saw relatively little of each other. In 1968, however, Arthur and Jean brought Barbara and Peggy, then college girls, through *San Francisco* on a touring trip. They joined us for drinks at our Jackson Street flat, then dinner in Chinatown. Our three young children accompanied us and met the Clark family for the first time. The Clarks had recently taken a Florida home, where they had begun to spend their winter months, far from the frigid winds and snows of *Buffalo*.

Arthur and I reminisced about the early days of our meeting at the end of the war. Neither Arthur nor I knew much about former associates. We no longer knew where Colonel Jesse Miles was. A few years previously we had both been invited to a reunion of a few members of the 319th Infantry Regiment whom former Captain Salomone had somehow tracked down. Salomone had sponsored the reunion at the Plaza Hotel in *New York*, of which he was then manager. Clark had not been able to attend, and I had not been able to afford the trip. Years later I managed to find Jesse Miles, and to reminisce with him by phone about the course of our lives since we had seen one another last in 1953. I was surprised to hear that he, Salomone, and a few other members of the 319th still got together from time to time. Jesse and his wife Ruth had also retired to Florida, but were unaware that the Clarks had a home there too.

We have visited the members of my wife's large and far-flung family on a number of occasions, or they have visited us. We kept in touch with Floortje Hony and Appie and Hans de Lara. Jim Pearce, my University of Washington friend, settled in *San Francisco* soon after Tania was born. He remained a close family friend and a much-needed "uncle" to our children through their growing years.

At about the time of my marriage, Anne Chamberlain's sister, Mary, had also married; and she and her husband left soon there-after on a European trip. As a favor to me, they called on Flip and Appie de Lara and their wives in *Amsterdam.* Not long after their visit, I was shocked to receive two letters within a two-year period informing me that first Flip, then Hans Rubens, had been killed in separate automobile accidents. My *Amsterdam* relatives were nar-rowed to Appie de Lara and his wife, Hans. Today, Hans remains my sole surviving relative.

III

From time to time Pat would ask me about the things I remem-bered about *Amsterdam* and if I ever missed my native country. She was disappointed that I did not teach our children Dutch, not even a few phrases, not a Dutch song. Occasionally, I had told her a little about my childhood in *Amsterdam*, but I maintained that I disliked any thoughts of Holland. There were too many painful memories. Dutch was a language I had given up when I emigrated, and I did not intend to teach it to my children. The children were Americans. I tried to forget my native language and spoke it only when I talked by telephone to Floortje who spoke to me in Dutch during long, intimate conversations that were weighted with her unalleviated grief.

With the passage of time, however, I found myself secretly yearning to walk the streets of *Amsterdam* again. At times I had awakened from sleep recalling a dream of some remembered childhood scene or experience. Sometimes I awoke still a prisoner in the camps and convinced that everything that had happened to me since had been a dream. I could not relate this to my family, but one day I surprised them with an announcement that we were all going to Europe where we would buy a car and tour many countries, including my country and my hometown.

In 1971, twenty-five years after my arrival in the United States I took my family back to Europe. I drove them to *Amsterdam* and *Antwerp* to show them the places where I had lived. We drove down familiar streets of my childhood where I easily found my old neighborhoods. I showed my family the apartment blocks in which I had grown up. The children caught my mood of joy and relief at finding the buildings still standing. I would have doubted everything I remembered had these structures disappeared. To my delight, my children were able to understand my need to find again the world of my childhood, and they encouraged me to show them every piece of evidence I could find of my living boyhood. One of the children remarked that I had lived in some very nice neighborhoods. I was proud that the neighborhoods I had once roamed, in two different cities, *Amsterdam* and *Antwerp*, were "nice" even now. The tidy blocks of low brick apartment structures pleased me anew in their discreet detailing, in their unity and scale. We toured the old working and shopping neighborhoods, and looked at the old Asscher Diamond Factory. The Graaf Floris School had been changed into an administration building. In *Antwerp* the middle school was still there, along with its awful memories of the school dentist.

Back in *Amsterdam*, I walked joyfully through the streets, showing my family what must have been for them a bewildering number of points of interest. I spoke Dutch eagerly with the Mokummers, sharpening my ability with each passing day. I introduced my children to the delights of eating smoked eel and swallowing fresh herring with chopped onions at open street stalls.

One luxury I had not been able to resist for my family was to treat them to two nights as guests at the Amstel Hotel. In my childhood, as now, the Amstel, at *Sarphatiestraat* and the *Weesperzijde*, facing the Amstel River, was one of the finest hotels in town and was always used to house royalty when they were in the country. As a boy I used to pass by there on my way to the *Jodenbreestraat*, and watch the well-dressed guests come and go. On many an occasion I had run up the steps to peer through the doorway, only to be chased back down those steps by an indignant doorman. It gave me great pleasure, therefore, to spend our last two nights in *Amsterdam* enjoying the comforts of the Amstel Hotel.

After touring much of Holland that I had never seen, we headed for Germany and followed my route through postwar Europe as a volunteer aide to three units of the American army. We retraced my travel through Bavaria, Czechoslovakia, and Austria, ending that part of the trip in *Ebensee*.

To get to the camp I had turned our car up a mountain road and through an arched gate that for me alone were familiar landmarks. Had it not been for the road and the gate, even I would have been lost. The cobble stones on the road were still in place. Most of the area on which the camp had stood and on which so many of my fellow prisoners had bled to death after severe beatings by the *SS*, was now covered with new homes, lawns, and gardens. Children played as if nothing had ever happened there and they did not know, because no one ever told them, that the area on which they were playing had once been a murderers' killing field.

To the left of the gate was a small memorial graveyard consisting of four areas that held the remains of thousands of fellow prisoners whose identities were unknown. Memorials to citizens of many nations who had been murdered here lined a memorial wall. Among them we found plaques to Catholic priests, political dissenters and a great number of Jews. Behind the memorial wall a crematorium firechamber and chimney were still standing.

We stayed at the POST Hotel in *Ebensee*, the inn that back in

1945 had served as the Command Post of "F" Company of the 3rd Cavalry Reconnaissance Squadron (Mech.), whose Commanding Officer was Captain Timothy C. Brennan, Jr. They had remained there for a little more than two weeks when they were ordered to proceed to *Trieste*, Italy, where Tito was creating problems about annexing *Trieste* to Yugoslavia. The POST Hotel had been extensively remodeled, and I recalled for the startled innkeeper details of how the place looked when I first saw it. I told her who I was and asked her how parts of the old concentration camp grounds could have become a graveyard inasmuch as I had witnessed the mass burials of the dead prisoners along the road to *Bad Ischl*. General George S. Patton, Jr. had ordered those roadside burials "...so that the people of *Ebensee* will always remember what happened here." She told me that the bones had been moved up to the memorial graveyard when the place had been dedicated after the U. S. Army had left Austria and restored Austria's freedom.

We walked about, and marveled at the breathtaking blue lake, Traun Lake, surrounded by emerald mountains. It would appear to the innocent traveler passing through that this resort did not have any dark secrets.

Wherever we drove, as we retraced parts of my journey 25 years before, I talked with people about what I remembered. They discussed the occupation years with me with more introspective interest than reluctance to talk. At *Aschaffenburg*, where the 80th Infantry division was processed for return to the United States, a middle-aged woman innkeeper told me the story of how the Americans, when they invaded her area, had shelled the town from across the river, and how she had managed to save her inn from the path of the shells. Scheinfeld Castle, where I had been stationed with the 18th Regiment, 1st Infantry Division, had been converted to a private girls' school. The headmaster invited my family to his house, where we talked for an hour. His daughter was married to an intern who had taken much of his medical training in the United States, and they planned to settle in Colorado.

I talked with Germans and they talked with me. As a Jewish survivor of mass murders by the Nazi-German State, I no longer felt qualms about presenting myself, and my views, to Germans. They had to deal with me as a Jew. I was back among them. I did not accuse them, but I recalled with them some of the things that were probably not comfortable for them to remember. If I had refused all intercourse with Germans, if I did not set foot in their country, I would be their victim still. I would be shriveled with my hatred. Some words of advice my father used to give his family have never left my memory. Forgive, my father advised us, but do not forget. I used to wonder about the how's and why's of those words. In the long run, his advice has served me well. I bear no hatred for all Germans such as they once demonstrated toward Jews.

After retracing my European journey, we traveled through many cities and countries in a high mood. I had warned my family as we were flying to Europe that they would find that continent old-fashioned and slow paced compared with what they were used to. I was the one to be surprised. The western European countries were booming, working at a frantic pace to produce and consume on an American scale. Networks of highways had been built to accommodate the Europeans' new cars. Imaginative contemporary buildings mingled freely with ancient, traditional ones. The interiors of some of these classic buildings had been transformed to ultra modern spaces. Shops and restaurants had multiplied. Self-service and self-expression were the new order of the day. The cities – each with its distinctive style and traditional flavor – bustled with new life. The regional foods were still delicious; the rolling, fertile countryside a feast for the eye.

Czechoslovakia, on the other hand, had deteriorated since the end of the war. Cities, towns, and farms were run down. I had missed seeing *Prague* in 1954 because the Americans would not risk my being picked up by the Soviets while there. I obtained visas for all of us to go there in 1971. Getting into Czechoslovakia at the border crossing between Germany and Czechoslovakia, east of *Bayreuth*, was a fearful experience. Soldiers with machine guns hung across their chests stood guard and one had to drive through a set of obstacles at about five miles per hour. We waited a long time before we were allowed to pass while Michelle kept pleading with me to turn around. Once our visas were checked and found to be okay we were allowed in. At the time of the visa applications, the Czechs had stipulated that we would be required to purchase a certain amount of their currency based on each person in our party. That sum, in U.S. dollars, had to be included with the application.

We stopped at *Marienbad* (*Marianske Lazne*) and *Karlsbad* (*Karlovy Vary*) on the way. Quiet, sullen men and women took the waters in shabby surroundings that had once been beautifully maintained. The waiters in the hotel we stayed in were covered with grease as was the tablecloth on our table. Pat and I felt sorry for these people who had been made prisoners in their own country by the Comintern, the international communist/fascist system. The restoration of *Prague's* elegant but crumbling old buildings was just beginning, and that was 25 years after the end of the war. It was moving forward at a snail's pace as laborers worked with muscle power and wheelbarrows more often than with machinery and trucks. Had they been forced to wear striped uniforms, as we had in the concentration camps, their nation would have looked like one big concentration camp.

Pat and I were appalled by the fascist style of their new architecture. People lived in walk-up apartments stacked like shoeboxes. It was evident that human proportion and style had never been a consideration, nor were the amenities of living. The buildings were drab blocks, poorly landscaped, their dullness relieved only by the festive red of the ever present communist flags draped from their sides. The red flags of the communists lacked swastikas; otherwise, they reminded me of flag-draped buildings of the era of the Third Reich.

Seeing that we were Americans, first a woman, then a man, stopped us on the streets to complain to us in English or German about the conditions of their lives. They were bitterly opposed to their Soviet masters, but felt helpless. Our children, who had enjoyed Western Europe thoroughly, now were anxious to leave Czechoslovakia, her unappetizing restaurants and empty shops, her endless restrictions, and machine-gun-toting border guards.

An important mission of the trip was to meet Appie Cohen de

Lara and his wife Hans, now my closest living relatives in *Amsterdam*. The two of them met me for the first time as an adult and, at the same time, began a cordial relationship with my family. Appie had picked up the shambles of his father's hides and feather business and decided to forgo the hides part in order to concentrate solely on feathers. By the time we saw them during our first visit to *Amsterdam* since my emigration to the United States he and Hans had built the business into a substantial trading firm. Hans and Appie had two grown and married children and four grandchildren. Their son Michael, the youngest of the two, was a partner in his father's business. Their daughter, Philike took up medical studies while raising two young sons, and she was to become a physician by 1976.

Even though my cousin is almost 15 years older than I, the two of us easily fell into a brotherly relationship. Our families remarked in amazement about our resemblance to one another. Hans seemed like my sister. Not only as Appie's wife, but as a fellow Mokummer and a survivor of concentration camps *Ravensbruck* and *Bergen-Belsen*, she and I had much in common. We began a long dialogue about survival that showed us very clearly how preoccupied we had become with that subject. In our subsequent visits to *Amsterdam*, or their one time visit to *San Francisco*, the dialogue has continued and been joined by her children. Hans, who had repressed her memories of the concentration camps, found the ability to talk with me about her experiences and mine, and then with her whole family. She showed me a book about concentration camp *Ravensbruck*, written by a former prisoner, in which she was mentioned for particular compassionate acts. But why, we asked ourselves, did we few survive all our dead?

We did not dwell always on grim subjects. More often, we paid tribute to our departed loved ones by laughing affectionately over remembered episodes in our lives with them. As we talked, we repopulated the streets of old *Amsterdam* with relatives and friends bustling about their daily chores. We pored through the illustrated books of *Amsterdam* that Appie and Hans had on their shelves to verify details of our remembrances.

Appie, like Mrs. Klaverstijn, had been spared by the Nazis during the occupation because he had married a gentile. Hans had been born of a Jewish father, gentile mother, and had been raised a gentile. Ironically, it was Hans who had landed in a concentration camp, not as a Jew who had converted, but as a participant in the underground who had been caught at her work of placing orphaned Jewish children into hiding. Since the war, Appie and Hans have raised their children Jewish and their children, after having married themselves, raised their children Jewish, thus maintaining their Jewish heritage.

Before we left the United States I had arranged to attend Saturday services at the Portuguese Synagogue to say Kaddish for my parents and sister. To my amazement we met a second cousin there, Appie Garcia, whom I had known in a very limited way when we were both very young. He was an officer in the Synagogue and had sworn to God that if he survived the war (he had been placed in hiding) he would devote his life to God and become very devout. This he had done.

Appie's father and my father had been cousins. Appie's grandfather and my grandfather had been brothers. He and his wife Mimi invited our family to join them for dessert that evening. They invited his mother as well. I remembered her far better than I did Appie, who is quite a few years younger than I. Appie's father, like mine, had paid very little attention to religious observance. His own mother admitted, in our presence, that she was not devout. I was surprised that Appie and Mimi kept a kosher household and attended the Portuguese Synagogue regularly. Appie explained to us how he had encouraged his family to become devout after he had begun to consider deeply what being Jewish meant. He had consulted the rabbi of the Portuguese Sephardic congregation to help him understand the significance, to a contemporary Jew, of what is written in the Torah, the body of cultural, philosophic, and moral teachings that guided Jews through the ages of their history. The six-day war of 1967, in which Israel triumphed over her Arab attackers, served to confirm to the Appie Garcia family the importance of continuing the struggle to keep Judaism and a Jewish homeland alive.

AUSCHWITZ, AUSCHWITZ... I CANNOT FORGET YOU

The Garcias, the Rodrigues Garcias, are one of a handful of families making up the active Portuguese-Sephardic congregation today. Appie gave me a copy of our family tree that traced our Sephardic ancestry back to South America and before that to the Iberian Peninsula, where they had lived until the Spanish Inquisition forced them out.

Appie's mother, Appie and Mimi Rodrigues Garcia, and others of my family and some friends, owed their survival to individual Dutch citizens who took it upon themselves to hide their countrymen who happened to be of the Jewish faith just as I had been hidden. A number of Dutch citizens, I was proud to have verified, had assumed great personal risks to help their Jewish compatriots. Appie's mother's case was unusual in that she remained hidden in the attic of their home after Appie's father had been sent to the gas chamber in *KZ Sobibor* and the new occupants, who had been especially selected for that house, had agreed to assist her in her hiding place. She spent the entire war years in her own home in her own attic with the help of others.

I tried to look up Mevrouw van der Roest, my primary school teacher, at her house, which is still standing. She was no longer there, nor could her name be found in the telephone book. I would have liked to have seen her again and to have talked to her about what she remembered as our teacher in a classroom of Jewish and gentile children, many of whom disappeared in the Holocaust.

During our travels, one of the cities in which our family stopped was *Zurich*, Switzerland, where the brother of a *San Franciscan* friend of ours lived. I called Ralph to bring him greetings from Kurt and Hans, his younger brothers. All of them had fled Germany to *Shanghai*, had survived the war except for their father who died on the journey to China. Ralph and his wife invited us to their house that evening for coffee and dessert, mentioning that they had a houseguest. We were welcomed into their home in the hills above Zurich Lake and introduced to their houseguest, an older man from *Johannesburg*, South Africa.

"Silly of me to ask," I began as we shook hands with the *Johannesburger*, "but would you by chance know a man named Meijer

Hekster? I believe he may live in or near *Johannesburg.*"

"Meijer Hekster? If we are talking about the same man, we are talking about one of my best friends."

"Meijer Hekster?" it was my turn to question the name in astonishment. Together we established that we were, indeed, talking about the same Meijer, a man who had come from *Amsterdam* in the early thirties and established himself in the South African diamond industry. He was then nearing his seventieth birthday, I learned, and I obtained his address from his friend. Our little group who had barely met, and had just become acquainted, marveled that two of us from widely separated parts of the world would know someone in common. Their guest's friend was my cousin. Shortly after our return to *San Francisco*, I began exchanging news with Meijer and his wife Eva, who lived in *Cape Town.* Their son Ralph was married, the father of three children, and a practicing dentist in *Cape Town.* Some years later we received news that the entire family had left South Africa to return to *Amsterdam* because of the "Apartheid" situation in South Africa.

On subsequent European trips, Pat and I have visited with the senior Klaverstijns - the parents of my childhood friend, Appie - who still lived in a tiny but pretty apartment on *Saffierstraat.* It was Mrs. Klaverstijn who was able to tell me details I did not know of my mother's interest in attending operettas and her unfulfilled passion for fine clothes. Mrs. Klaverstijn and Eva Hekster had all worked in the same garment factory on the *Jodenbreestraat* when they were teenagers and young women. Mr. Klaverstijn reminisced with me about the days in the thirties when he, my father, and other Social Democrats had fought with Communists in the streets of *Amsterdam* during election campaigns. Laughing modestly, he told me my father was the more active combatant in such encounters. In socialized Holland Mr. Klaverstijn is still a Social Democrat, but he is proud of the accomplishment of Appie, their son, in Australia, and they enjoy their visits back and forth. He showed us an album of pictures of Appie's family and home in Australia.

Like our American senior citizens, the senior Klaverstijns worried about increasing crime, the number and speed of passing cars, dirty streets , and the heedless pace of modern life. Their hospitality was shown us in the gracious style of another day. As we chatted, they offered us tea with cheeses, sausages, cakes, cookies, candies and nuts.

Appie Klaverstijn had moved to Australia soon after I saw him last when I visited *Amsterdam* during my stint with the C.I.C. in *Nurnberg*, Germany. We corresponded steadily and shared our remembrances of boyhood antics and former classmates at Graaf Floris Grammar School. It was news to me that Appie, too, had an eye out for the delicate blonde who occupied a rear seat in the row next to ours. We congratulated each other on how well we have raised families and prospered in the societies in which we lived. We commented ruefully on the evidence of aging our latest photographs reveal to one another; yet we can still recognize the skinny, light-hearted buddies who were born a few days apart, and who sat near one another for six years in Mevrouw van der Roest's classroom.

We discussed our concerns over the struggle between communist and democratic blocs of nations, for we both see communism and fascism as essentially the same wolf under different skins. A reunion of our grammar school classmates would be small indeed, and we do not forget why. We have reason to be wary of the wolf.

Since our trip to Europe in 1971, those visits and the letters exchanged between relatives and boyhood friends have been the keys to the box in which I had locked away the memory of my heritage in order to survive. I no longer watch with envy Pat's intimacy with members of her family. As I grow closer to my own family, I also draw closer to hers. We all have much in common, we family people.

Whenever we visit the Cohen de Laras in *Amsterdam*, Hans is delighted that I not only remember, but hanker after her Dutch cooking. After a day's work, Hans does not begrudge shopping and cooking for her American cousins. With great enthusiasm we sit down to eat her bountiful dinners, starting with a good soup, and ending, after many courses, with pastries fresh from a local patisserie. Hours later we munch candies, nuts, and fresh fruits. We talk endlessly and are comfortable with each other. I try to remember to interpret for Pat because the conversation is in fluent, fast Dutch since Hans only knows a few words in English. Sometimes Appie and I shout at each other, his Dutch point of view at angry odds with my American one. The storm passes. We laugh and we joke and we needle one another. We do not stop talking. Before we know it, it is 2:00 A.M. My cousins plan to be in their office on the Oude Schans by 7:30 in the morning.

IV

As I said a few pages back, my father used to say, forgive but do not forget. I have forgiven the German people. Toward which ones would I direct my vengeful anger, and to what end, if I dare hope that our children will live in a free society? The perpetrators of incredible crimes against Jews have died or changed or have slipped through the fingers of pursuers.

The victims and the survivors themselves stand accused, in some widely read scholarly studies, of cooperating in their own destruction and not resisting enough. As these criticisms pertain to Nazi-occupied Holland and to conditions of survival in the camps, I have found some basic misconceptions and inaccuracies. On these pages I have tried to set forth, honestly, my own experiences, reactions, and learning processes for the reader to evaluate. I came by my information firsthand. I lived through all the experiences I have described. Thus, it is difficult for me to read or listen to the opinions of scholars who were able to escape the eye of the storm about individual or collective guilt of victims or survivors. The aim, I suppose, is to strengthen Jews to believe that such a catastrophe need never happen again, but from my point of view their lofty statements are made at the expense of victims and survivors.

Their reasoning seems wishful. We should have been ideal Jews, unified religiously with our entire people, realizing as a group that resistance would lead to many deaths but would also bring an end to persecution. Though holding to unique ties of religion and tradition, Jews are not above, or beneath, general human experience. Many are learned, but some are ignorant. Some are pious, some are not. Some are selfless in the service of God and mankind. Some prefer secular or selfish interests. Some are rich, some poor.

I can speak for the poor at the time of the Holocaust, such as my family. The story I have told is typical, I believe, of Jews who were caught in Europe without resources. In spite of postwar conjecture, all Jews did not know what was in store for them at the hands of the Nazis. Many would not believe such evil intention toward them; and if they did, there was no place for them to go unless they saw the light very early on. Many Jews were bound by poverty and by family ties. Once they were netted and sent to the camps, they lived, if they were lucky, by their own will and by hope. Most camp victims were alone, and there was no beating the system. An uprising of the few meant death for many. Most of the prisoners were of poor enough stuff not to seek out martyrdom or the brief glory of the hero. So we bear the brunt of some accusations.

I, too, would like to hope that the lessons of the Holocaust have helped prevent the igniting of similar infernos, but our news sources tell us otherwise. Even today in many countries of the world bloodbaths continue, and torture and imprisonment of "undesirable" citizens are taking place. As for my survival, I refuse to bear guilt for having survived, or for anything I had to do in the camps in order to survive. According to the will and conscience of the boy I was then, I did the best that was in me.

I have forgiven much, and in doing so I have gained a great deal. It is also true that I do not forget. I am at one with myself as a Jew, content to be a husband, father and family member. I enjoy the practice of my profession and all the benefits of life in America, including the beauty of the city I live in, to which I contribute my efforts. Still, I have not forgotten, even for a day, my uprooting in early life and my experiences in Nazi concentration camps. A remark, an incident, a dream – any of these things – can bring the camps sharply back into focus at any time. After seeing *Ebensee*, I begged Pat to go with me to Poland to see *KZ Auschwitz*. Pat resisted at first. *KZ Ebensee* had been enough, she said, and the recollections I had shared with her had supplied her with clear and believable insights into what life had been like in the camps. She asked me what would be served by seeing *KZ Auschwitz* again, and I could not answer.

But by 1975, Pat was ready and we made the necessary pilgrimage together to *KZ Auschwitz*, a trip made no easier by travel conditions over the peasant-dominated roads of "modern" Poland. Our car inched slowly over two-lane roads behind peasants walking or driving horse carts, or riding bicycles or motorcycles. Supply trucks dominated the sparse motor traffic. We crawled through strings of their villages. Road signs to *Krakow* were not to be found. We carefully followed our map. Travel conditions were much slower than anticipated, and despite warnings against night travel, we arrived in *Krakow* after dark. A room at a good hotel for unexpected and unescorted visitors from America was coldly granted. Our passports were held at the desk until our departure after breakfast the next day. We set out for *KZ Auschwitz* in a fine rain and arrived there by late morning.

The camp had been converted into a museum, and the museum-like quality of the preserved buildings all but obliterated my memory of the gaunt hordes of prisoners who once filled them. Knots of adults, most of whom were military personnel from communist countries who were there to see the cruelties of Nazism, and lots of Polish school-children – most of them brought in by bus – swarmed through the camp in small groups led by tour leaders. I got my bearings and led Pat on a tour of our own through the buildings and the grounds.

The buildings were smaller and closer together than I remembered them. Grass-covered courtyards and tall poplars lining the avenues of barracks were added amenities. Some of the blocks had been preserved in their original forms: the brick of the walls, the tiers of wooden bunks filled with straw, the room where the *Blockälteste* had lived, the hospital blocks. There were torture rooms, solitary dungeons, rooms I had not seen as a prisoner. A number of the buildings had been converted into memorial museums to commemorate various national groups who had been murdered there. The Jews, too, were given museum space. We were moved by the Jewish memorial display of symbolic and traditional designs worked into glazed tile walls and highlighted by spotlights in a darkened room.

More than any other element, however, the use of photographs brought the camp back to life. Blow-up shots of skeletal prisoners, taken when the camp was operative, were used effectively on the walls. The block's hallways were lined with smaller identification photographs of shorn-headed victims. Their names, place of birth, and dates of death were recorded beneath their pictures.

We entered a small bookstore that had been erected outside the main gate. Many books about the camp, Nazism, and related subjects, were offered for sale. Most of the books were in Polish, but a number were offered with Russian, German, French and English translations. The bookseller, a Polish man in a short-sleeved shirt, bore a tattooed *KZ Auschwitz* number on his left forearm; his number was considerably lower (older) than mine. He was talking in German to a small group of students who were inquiring about his books. When he finished I introduced myself in German, as a former member of the camp, and asked him if many other former prisoners came back to see the place. His face broke into a grin as he told me that many prisoners used to visit but fewer come back each year. So it isn't true that we who survived *KZ Auschwitz* will never die again, I remarked: but I am not sure the bookseller understood my reference to that song we prisoners had once sung.

We bought some books and asked him where we could find records of the precise arrival and departure dates of my transports into and out of the camp. He directed us to a converted barracks building which he said housed the camp's archives. We found the archives, but to our great disappointment we were turned away without explanation by the people working inside. Nearby, we listened to Polish school children exclaim in shock over their discoveries at the museum. I wondered how much they knew about the Soviet gulag or the writings of men like Aleksandr Solzhenitsyn.

The *"Paketstelle"* was closed to the public, as was one of the infirmaries in which I had stayed. I showed Pat the kitchen building in front of which they had erected a gallows and forced us prisoners to watch many cruel hangings of poor souls who tried to escape. The iron entry gate, the main gate, still had over it the wrought iron legend, *Arbeit Macht Frei,* under which we passed at least twice a day. The bordello to the left of the main gate was still there, the place, you'll recall, where Lex had rehearsal sessions with his jazz combos. My last impression of the camp was also my first impression as we entered it: how much smaller in scale everything was than I remembered.

We did not stay for a guided tour or to see confiscated Nazi films about the efficient operations of the death camp. We did not follow the crowd to view rooms filled with victim's hair, clothing, glasses, shoes, and such. I did not need that kind of reminder. Touching back to this bitter ground, seeing that it did indeed exist, that the buildings, even if moderated, were still there – this evidence was enough for me. We did not stay long in *KZ Auschwitz.*

We paid our parking fee to a young boy dressed as a Polish Boy Scout, then could not resist buying from his mother's souvenir booth a small, plastic-covered *KZ Auschwitz* pennant before we headed down the cluttered road to Czechoslovakia, planning to reach *Vienna* by nightfall. Pat and I hardly spoke to each other on the early part of that drive. Both of us were overcome by the experience, she by what she had seen, I in remembering.

The rain continued to fall.

N.B. The original book as published in 1979 (though much extended here) ends with this chapter. I have written, longing for her guidance, the two chapters that follow.

Capt. Timothy Brannan, "F Company's" Commanding Officer and his two tank sergeants who took possession of KZ Ebensee after the noon hour on Sunday, May 6, 1945. L to R: Sgt. Dick Pomante, survivor Max Garcia, Capt. Timothy Brannan, and Sgt. Bob Persinger. Photo taken May 5, 1995 at the *50th Anniversary of Liberation of Ebensee Camp,* Prince Eiger Hotel in Vienna.

PART 7

The Liberators

|

Early in 1985 I felt myself drawn back to *KZ Ebensee*. I did not know why, but as I said to Pat, it might be because it had been 40 years since the camp had been liberated. Pat immediately agreed that I should return to *KZ Ebensee*, and added that she would go with me. When he heard about our plan, our son David asked if he could come along and we were pleased at his interest.

I then asked David Wagner, my younger associate, to take over the office while I was gone; I gave him the authority to write checks and attend to other fiduciary responsibilities along with overseeing the work of my staff. I made the necessary flight and lodging reservations and reserved a rental car for our arrival at the *Amsterdam* airport to use in Holland and drive to *Munich*. There we would pick up the 500 Series BMW I had bought, both to save the cost of renting a car for our travels in Europe, and to use on our return to the U.S.A as David Wagner's company car.

I also requested that the Holocaust Center of Northern California make the negatives of *KZ Ebensee* available to me so I could select five of them and have them enlarged and mounted. Finally I bought a three-by-five-foot United States flag to hang within *KZ Ebensee* as part of the exhibit I was planning to mount there.

Once we arrived in *Amsterdam* we visited Hans Cohen de Lara, my cousin by marriage who had also been in the camps for two years, as well as *"Het Keukenhof,"* the incredible flower gardens maintained by the various Dutch bulb growers and many other such attractions. We also visited Nico Wijnen, a fellow survivor, in The Hague, who had been in *KZ Ebensee* and had the designation of *"Nacht und Nebel"* (Night and Fog) imposed on him by the Nazis. Those who had that designation in their files, in the *SS* Political Department, were meant never to leave the camps alive.

Nico told me that he had given my name to a young Austrian historian. I was to introduce myself to him because he was in the process of doing his doctoral thesis on the origins of *KZ Ebensee* and wanted to interview me. The young Austrian's name, he told me, was Florian Freund.

Two days later we picked up our car in *Munich* and drove to the Autobahn that would take us to *Salzburg, Bad Ischl* by way of *Wolfgangsee* and finally to *Ebensee* . It was glorious to speed along the Autobahn among forests and stunning landscapes on our way to the region's many lakes or "sees." Snow still covered the higher levels of the Austrian Alps. When we arrived in *Ebensee* we made a quick visit to *KZ Ebensee*, on a plateau overlooking the town. As a prisoner there I had not been able to appreciate its beauty as I did at this moment.

When we arrived at Schloss Roith we were all very tired but I had to do several things for the following day, Saturday, because everything would be closed after 1:00 P.M. I wanted to order a wreath to lay at the Main Memorial, there being as yet no Dutch Memorial, and I also wanted a Dutch flag to place on the wall. My hosts at the hotel suggested that the Trachten Store could help me with the flag. Although they had no Dutch flag, they had an Austrian flag with its two red stripes on either side of a white one. I pointed out that all they had to do was convert one red stripe into a blue stripe and I'd have a Dutch flag! They laughed, and said it would be ready for me to pick up early the next day.

On Saturday morning the three of us went to pick up the wreath and the Dutch flag before we drove on to *KZ Ebensee*. There we set up our display along the low stone wall of the memorial. First we hung the Stars and Stripes in the tree right above us. On the white stripes I had inscribed this message: "The prisoners of *KZ Ebensee* thank the men of the U.S. 3rd Cavalry for liberating us on May 6, 1945." Then we secured the Dutch flag, a very long one, to the stone wall and against it we placed the five blown-up pictures of *KZ Ebensee* I had brought along. The pictures showed various views of *KZ Ebensee* taken a few days after our liberation. I also placed the wreath against the wall. Needless to say a lot of visitors looked at our display. One Yugoslavian man, who spoke a little English and turned out to be a physician, asked me why I was there. When I explained to him that as a prisoner at *KZ Ebensee* I was invited onto the first tank of the American liberators, he gave me a big bear hug. He had been there, he said and seen it all. This was music to Pat's ears because she treasured every bit of first-hand verification beyond my own about that liberation day.

The ceremonies began when each of the various national groupings marched into the camp carrying their national and city flags and the wreaths they planned to place at their monuments. Chairs and benches had been set out for about 2,000 people, who had come from all over Europe to remember their fellow citizens who had been murdered there. Then the official program began: a welcome by the Mayor of *Ebensee*, speeches by the foreign delegates in their own languages (German translations provided by *Ebensee*), some musical arrangements and, finally, a speech by an invited guest. Before we left *KZ Ebensee* David and I gathered in the Dutch flag, the Stars and Stripes and the five enlarged photos in order to donate them to the local museum, which had just opened that very year.

David, Pat and I then dined at a restaurant next to the new *Ebensee* City Hall, with Florian Freund, Italo and Carla Tibaldi, Mrs. Thonet and her two sons and George Havas, a former inmate of *KZ Ebensee*, originally from Czechoslovakia. Except for the Tibaldis everyone at our table spoke English; Italo spoke Italian and French so there was some difficulty in conversing with him and I tried my best to act as an interpreter. George Havas lived near *Washington, D.C.* and worked in the U.S. Library of Congress on Capitol Hill. Florian was eager to hear what we three survivors, Italo, George, and myself, could remember of our experiences in *KZ Ebensee* as well as the other camps we had been in. The Thonets, of bent-wood furniture fame who lived in *Vienna*, were at *KZ Ebensee* because a Catholic priest they had known died in *KZ Ebensee* and had been honored during these memorial ceremonies. Mme. Thonet, originally from Italy, was also honored because she had been instrumental in helping the Italian underground.

During lunch I mentioned that Pat had written a book about my life and my experiences in the various camps I had survived. George Havas was interested to hear this because he had planned to write a book about *KZ Ebensee* and his experiences. George had arrived in the camps when only 16. When I told him that Pat and I had been unable to locate our liberators he responded, "I can help you. When you get back to the States call this person and he will be able to direct you." George Havas gave us the key to finding our liberators, one of our goals in making this trip. But we weren't quite ready to return to the States. Before we left the table Florian Freund requested that I come by his place in *Vienna* a few days later so he could interview me.

The next day Pat had a serious injury to her toe which kept her in the *Gmunden* hospital for a few days, but she insisted that despite her continuing pain she was ready to go on to *Vienna* so I could keep my scheduled appointment with Florian. His apartment was located in a workingmen's neighborhood quite a distance from the center of town. I spent several hours with him in this interview, all very enlightening. Only once did we discover conflicting information: I told him we had been liberated from *Ebensee* around noon, but he had learned from a diary by Drahomir Barta, a Czech Communist and scribe in *KZ Ebensee*, that we had been liberated at 14:50. Though I was adamant that it had been close to the noon hour, we parted on good terms. When I told Pat about the severity of his living conditions we decided to send him money on occasion, which he told us he appreciated very much. But the immediate question as to why there should be conflicting stories about the time of the liberation haunted us for the rest of our travels, and on our return to the States.

Pat, David and I enjoyed getting to know *Vienna*, its architecture, its history, its art. After a few days there we drove to *Venice* where David left us for Greece as planned. At this point Pat and I learned from our daughter Tania's phone call that we had our first grandchild, Nicholas. For many days we celebrated with champagne as we enjoyed *Ravenna's* mosaics and drove on along the Italian and French Rivieras to *Monte Carlo*. From there we drove to *Carcasonne*, a medieval town that still looks today as it had looked then, with its outer walls still intact. Next we had a nightmare ride through the Pyrenees in a downpour to *Barcelona*, Spanish city of Art Nouveau and Antonio Gaudi, which both of us knew well from our books, and here we were, right in the midst of Las Ramblas! We fell in love with *Barcelona* and vowed to return when we could spend more time. Our next stop was *Toulouse* where we visited the museum and workplace of Vasarely, one of our favorite contemporary artists. We bought one of his prints and I got Pat a beautiful shawl with one of his designs on it.

After all this traveling we were very eager to get home to start our inquiry about the men who had liberated *KZ Ebensee* on Sunday, May 6th, 1945, and among other details to get their version of what time they had arrived there. Pat and I were very pleased that we had followed my desire to return to *Ebensee* for the fortieth anniversary of its liberation, for we now knew, thanks to the guests we sat with at the anniversary luncheon, exactly whom to contact in the States so we could meet my liberators at last.

On our return to *San Francisco* I took over my responsibilities as head of my architectural firm and wrote a letter to Salvatore S. Pappalardo, Secretary of the Third Cavalry Veterans Association, the person whose name George Havas had given me at the *Ebensee* luncheon. After a few days he called me, wanting to know who I was and why it was so very important for me to find the men who liberated *KZ Ebensee*. I briefly told him my story and asked if he had a list of the men in his units. I added that I would of course pay any expenses related to that request. He was happy to comply once I put in writing all that I had told him by phone, and observed that he believed the men of "F" Company of the 3rd Reconnaissance Squadron were the men I was looking for.

When his book came, it was a heavy tome which held the names of all the men who had been members of both the 3rd and 43rd Reconnaissance Squadrons of the 3rd U.S. Cavalry Group (Mech). It included the names of those who had been KIA'S as well as those who had died since then. All the listings were in alphabetical order, mixing both the 3rd and 43rd squadrons together. Pat and I now had the task of separating out all the men in the 3rd unit of Company F and writing a letter to each of them.

Pat and I must have sent out over 100 letters and we got back about 20. All of them expressed surprise that someone had been looking for them. We learned that two tanks and a Jeep had found *KZ Ebensee* and that 1st Lt. George A. Garbowit had been in charge of that Platoon. The tank commanders were Sgts. Bob Persinger and Dick Pomante, both of whom had been a part of that unit since its inception in 1943. So began the next phase of my search for the men who liberated me from *Ebensee*.

A year later, in 1986, I retired from the business Pat and I had started in 1960, and because of the contacts I had made with the men of F Company, 3rd Squadron, Pat and I were invited to attend their reunion in *Chicago*.

Although we had to miss that one because of previous commitments, George Garbowit encouraged me to attend the next reunion in *El Paso*, Texas. In early summer 1987, he called to say he was attending a family affair down the *San Francisco* Peninsula. I immediately invited him and his wife to our home for luncheon, and picked them up at their hotel an hour later. Pat had whipped a beautiful luncheon together on very short notice. As we dined George asked me as many questions as I had asked him, and Pat was shouting from the kitchen to wait for her because she, too, had questions for him. Here was a second person who could verify the things I had told her about our liberation and my subsequent involvement with F Company of the 3rd Recon. Squadron. We talked at length about that famous day for me, when my life was handed back to me, to be reborn, and what it had meant to him to be in charge of the platoon that had liberated *KZ Ebensee*. Here we were, survivor and liberator, reliving the experience together. He exclaimed that it gave him a wonderful feeling. As we drove them back to their hotel we continued to bombard each other with questions that had no end. I told him that I would see him at *Fort Bliss*, in *El Paso*, Later that year and hoped to meet Sergeants Persinger and Pomante at that time. George and I stayed in touch with each other.

REUNIONS AND TRAVELS

Pat had made up her mind not to go with me to *El Paso*, feeling the moment should be mine alone as I met my liberators for the first time in 40 years. So I flew by myself, a little nervously, to Fort Bliss, Texas, where the 1987 Reunion of the 3rd U.S. Cavalry Group Veterans Association was being held. Luckily, the motel in which the reunion was to be convened was within walking distance of the airport so I walked there having only one suit bag with me.

I was anxious. The only person I knew was Lt. George Garbowit. *El Paso* is hot and humid. It was, incidentally, the place where the 3rd ACR (Armored Cavalry Regiment), successor to the 3rd U.S. Cavalry Group, was located. Every plane brought additional Troopers and their wives and some arrived by car. (Incidentally, they are still called Troopers, although they replaced the old Horse Cavalry long before World War II.) A few of us sat around the swimming pool and talked about our individual experiences during the war. Many introduced themselves and welcomed me, here and throughout the reunion. To my relief I was treated as one of them. Among the first to introduce themselves were Bob Persinger and Dick Pomante, the tank commanders who liberated me from *KZ Ebensee*, along with their wives Arlene and Anita. They were particularly genial that weekend, and in the course of the decades to follow became close friends. We had so much to talk about, so many memories to share.

While many of the original inductees, most of whom came from around the Great Lakes, had been wounded or killed in action, their replacements were just as ardent about the 3rd Cavalry as the men who liberated me. George Garbowit observed that their great "Esprit de Corps" came partly from serving during World War II under General George S. Patton, Jr., Commanding General of the 3rd U.S. Army, of which the 3rd U.S. Cavalry Group was a part. He was delighted when I told him that General Patton had been in *KZ Ebensee* in the days following my liberation. As noted in Part I, I had seen him in all his glory, and heard him tell his troops to bury the dead camp prisoners along the roads of *Ebensee*.

The Saturday night dinner in the Main Dining Room of Ft. Bliss was the reunion highlight. I was seated with the men (and their wives)of F Company who had liberated *KZ Ebensee*. We were all photographed many times as the official procedure unfolded. Never before had I seen such a display of old military traditions and patriotism. At the head table sat General James H. Polk, West Point graduate, who had led the Unit through Europe after the original colonel had been taken prisoner. He had been given command of the 3rd by Gen. George S. Patton, Jr. Also at the head table, along with several of the troopers and their wives, was the sixty-second Colonel of the Regiment, Colonel Jarrett J. Robertson and his wife. The dress uniforms of the officers, and even the enlisted men, were truly elegant. But more important was the animated conversation as we all shared memories of our experiences in 1945. After dinner I presented to Col. Robertson a copy of the U.S. Flag on which I had written the same text that I had hung at *KZ Ebensee* two years earlier. They were overcome!

After the official ceremonies were over there was dancing and more picture-taking. I was glad to be among them. I agreed that I would be at the next reunion and that we would remain in touch during the year ahead. When I told Pat on my return about my experiences in *El Paso* she was ready to make reservations for both of us to go to *Milwaukee* in 1988.

I kept in touch with George, Bob and Dick during the year, and Pat was eager to meet them and their wives at the 1988 reunion. We were all very comfortable together as we got to know each other better, and beyond that I found myself volunteering for an assignment that would occupy Pat's and my time for the next couple of years. During the Saturday dinner in *Milwaukee*, one of the fellows mentioned that the 3rd Cavalry Troopers had planned to return to *Ebensee* in 1973 but had to abandon that trip because gasoline shortages increased travel costs considerably. Suddenly it occurred to me that I might be able to arrange a trip for the 45th anniversary of the end of the war. When I suggested this to the group, they looked at me in wonder. With a few calculations I surmised that in order for it to become reality at least eight couples would have to sign on, in addition to Pat and me. After this announcement, twelve couples signed up by the end of the 1988 reunion.

By the time the 3rd Cavalry Group left for Europe in April 1990, 90 people, two busloads, were aboard. I had researched the battle route of the 3rd Cavalry through Europe and planned to follow it closely. We started our excursion on the Normandy Beaches where the 3rd had landed in early August 1944. I had seen to it that they would be feted in *Paris* by a group of fellow survivors. We were also honored in *Luxembourg* because the 3rd had been one of the liberators of that city. Since we had two buses, one bus held 3rd Recon. men and wives while the other bus was filled with 43rd Recon. men and their wives and I suggested that the men should talk about the things that happened to them during combat. The interesting thing that Pat and I learned on this trip, as it was related to Pat by the wives of these Troopers, was that their men never spoke at home about their battle experiences but here, on the bus, they all opened up and their wives were very pleased to find out what heroes their husbands had been when such very young lads. Another plus was that their commanding officer, Captain Timothy C. Brennan, Jr., who had never attended any of the F Company reunions, joined us, with his wife Vera, in *Salzburg*. This meant a great deal to all of us, and they were good company.

And then we came to *Ebensee*. I had ordered a plaque to be made by a local stone mason and it was to be unveiled during their anniversary visit to the Camp they had liberated. The U.S. Marines were there in full dress uniform, thanks to the efforts of the U.S. Embassy in *Vienna*. It was going to be wonderful except that it began to rain, then pour, and it did not stop. When I suggested curtailing the ceremonies, the Mayor and his contingent replied, "if you could live through the war and the liberation here we certainly can use our umbrellas for a couple of hours." After many speeches I unveiled my plaque commemorating the occasion, and it was well-received. The plaque is still there.

The next day we drove to *KZ Mauthausen* for the annual March of Nations, a tremendous gathering of survivors of every camp in the area. I had suggested that the Troopers and their wives should wear the yellow baseball hats and neck scarves with green patches that I had included in their travel packs, and any other clothing that emphasized the unit's colors. When the U.S. Ambassador saw nearly a hundred people sporting green and yellow and learned that they had liberated *KZ Ebensee* on Sunday, May 6, 1945, he announced that this was the largest U.S. contingent that had ever walked in the March of Nations. Our Troopers were impressed with the solemnities, the many different nationalities and flags that marched that day, and they tried to communicate with survivors from all over the globe.

From there we visited *Vienna* for several days and then left for our homes in the U.S.A. After that memorable experience with my liberators Pat and I attended every reunion. We were indeed part of the Unit and were treated as one of their own. We continued writing our Quarterly Newsletter during the years that followed, in which we printed or summarized stories of their war experiences which the Troopers sent me. This project brought us all closer together in knowledge and understanding of what we had been through.

In 1995, we returned without the large contingent from the 3rd Cavalry for the Fiftieth Anniversary of the end of World War II. The local people in *Ebensee* had organized a public assembly in which three survivors of *KZ Ebensee*, myself among them, were present, as were Sergeants Bob Persinger, Dick Pomonte and Captain Tim Brennan of the 3rd Cavalry as well as Florian Freund, the historian whose book *Zement* had been published in 1989 in *Vienna*. After each of the survivors had told their stories, Freund gave a brief summary of how *KZ Ebensee* had come into being. The audience then posed questions, one of which was very important to me. Captain Brennan was asked, "Did you know that other American troops had been here before you got here?" After the question was translated for Captain Brennan he gave a very curt "No." The person who posed the question then spoke at length, but after the translation Brennan did not respond. Here was a matter I wanted to pursue.

In the days that followed I asked Bob Persinger and Dick Pomante if they could shed some light on Captain Brennan's curtness. I also asked them specifically whether Lt. Garbowit had told them to "find"

KZ Ebensee or whether he had given them directions about how to get there. They both responded that they had been given directions. I suddenly recalled something that had occurred at *KZ Ebensee* five years earlier. After my memorial plaque had been unveiled, two men came up to me and told me they had found and opened this camp that Sunday morning, May 6, 1945. I asked them what Unit they belonged to and they answered "B Troop." I was stunned. I asked them if they would be at next year's reunion and they confirmed they would. I urged them to get other men from "B Troop" to attend so we could ask them further questions.

When we came back to *San Francisco* after this 1995 trip, Pat learned that she had colon cancer and our activities were very severely limited because of the chemotherapy she now had to undergo. We had to stop writing the Quarterly Newsletter, but we were both able to go to the 1996 reunion. The men of "B Troop" were there as promised, and now I learned that their Platoon had received orders to "find" concentration camp *Ebensee*, believed to be in this area. They reported that they left *Traunkirchen* at 1000 hours, drove very slowly, and found the camp by approximately 1045 hours. This they reported to their Captain Baldwin (now deceased, as are many of the men who were part of that Platoon). After the B Troopers were ordered by their Lieutenant to walk through the camp, one trooper had to remain with each of the nine vehicles that were part of the Platoon. In order to turn around and get back to *Traunkirchen* where they were billeted, they had to drive through the camp. They reported that they arrived back in *Traunkirchen* at about noon. At last I understood why we prisoners believed the Americans had entered the camp around noon, while Florian Freund believed we had been liberated at 1450 hours. In the 10 years since we first met Florian, the question of our liberation time was finally cleared up. "B Troop" came first on surveillance, and "F Company" followed a couple of hours later for the liberation described in the opening chapter.

In the years that followed many of the Troopers had died, including Dick Pomante. However, we continued to attend the reunions and many of the ladies, particularly those who were cancer survivors, took Pat under their wings. The last Reunion we attended was in *Ft. Carson*, Colorado, in 2001, at Pat's insistence, despite her failing health. The Troopers and their wives kept in touch by mail and telephone, all wanting to know how Pat was doing and if there was anything they could do for either of us.

She lived less than a year after that reunion. In the next chapter I have tried to convey what Pat omitted about herself in the original book, insisting that this was my story, not hers. But now I know that both our stories are one, intimately connected. Without sentimentality, I want to capture what Pat meant to me during our experiences together, and what a difference she made in my life. I hope the reader will remember the events she described in detail throughout this book, and add my personal emendations to those.

This photo of Pat and me, at a door in our hotel during Tania's wedding to Dan Fowler, is a simulation of the original wedding photo about 46 years earlier of Pat and me standing in front of the door to the Judge's Chamber. This photo was requested by Tania. Pat died three months later.

PART 8

Pat

PAT

In 1954, I thought I was reasonably well settled in my ground floor studio apartment on Nob Hill in *San Francisco*. The apartment, one medium-sized room with a Murphy bed, its window overlooking a parking lot to the east, had a small bathroom and an incredibly small kitchen in which one could hardly turn around. Basic as it was, I chose it because I could easily walk from there to most of the architectural offices downtown.

I furnished the apartment minimally. The south wall I had painted totally black and the others pure white. On the black wall were a number of 12" x 12" acoustical tiles each of which I painted in a basic color. On each I fastened an art print or notice of upcoming events in town. On the north wall, I put together a low bookshelf, with concrete blocks between planks, in order to store the art and architectural magazines and books I had gathered, some of which dated back to my younger years in *Amsterdam* and were written in Dutch. Between the window and the bookshelf stood a "Hardoy" chair with a black cloth seat. My clothes, the few I had just then, were hung or stacked between the Murphy bed and the black wall. This was my first American home, and I was pleased with it!

I had lived there since my discharge from the U.S. Army Language School at the Presidio of *Monterey* that summer. I had also become a regular usher at the *San Francisco* War Memorial Opera House, and soon was asked to usher in the Geary and Curran Theaters as well. Evenings, during the season, I saw all the operas that were put on by the *San Francisco* Opera Company as well as many musicals and theater productions. I could also see all the performances at the *San Francisco* Ballet Company and could listen to the *San Francisco* Symphony Orchestra. I was a busy guy and enjoying myself fully, always contrasting this life with the one in the camps. I had also acquired a Studebaker convertible, although the joys it gave me were offset by the difficulties of finding a parking space for it.

Now that I had become a draftsman in an architectural office and was assured a weekly paycheck, I was able to pay someone to come in on Saturday mornings to clean my little place. Nevertheless, since I nearly always wore woolen argyle socks that had to be washed by hand and then placed on metal stretchers, I thought it wise to do that chore myself and hang the socks to dry on the roof.

The view from the roof was glorious; one could look over the entire *San Francisco* Bay from the Golden Gate Bridge, past Alcatraz, to the *San Francisco-Oakland* Bay Bridge and when the sun was out, and warm, it was a marvelous place to sunbathe. One spring Saturday morning in 1956 I climbed the stairs to the roof of my building with my freshly-washed argyle socks on their metal stretchers. Until now I always had the roof to myself, but this morning when I opened the door there was a young woman lying on the roof, in a bathing suit, reading. She was as surprised to see me as I was to see her. I said "hello" to her and she responded in kind.

The next morning I went back to the roof to gather my socks and there again was the young woman in yet another bathing suit, reading. It was already warm, as it often is during the spring months. This time I spoke to her and as our conversation developed I learned she was a new arrival in our small apartment building and that she worked for the *San Francisco* Heart Association. I then asked her to join me that afternoon for a ride. When she asked me where I was planning to go, I told her that I wanted to drive into Marin County and look at some Eichler homes that had been built there, as I might be interested in buying one. She agreed to come along because she wanted to see those homes herself. At the appointed time she came out of our apartment house and exclaimed when she saw that I drove a green Studebaker convertible that she had owned a red one just like it. I empathized when she told me she sold it because she had too much trouble finding a parking place for it.

We drove across the Golden Gate Bridge and deep into Marin County. We looked at the homes, and she liked them but only for married people who had families. After we drove back to our building, and I found a parking place for the car, I invited her into my place.

She stood in the entryway looking up at what hung above her. "What is that?" she wanted to know.

I told her "A Buckminster Fuller Space Frame."

"A what?" I had to explain.

During our ride I had told her who I was, where I came from, what my ambitions were, what I had done. I had not told her about the space frame, not to mention the black wall, because I did not think it important. She stood there dumbfounded. She saw the "Hardoy" chair. It really was the only chair in the room, and she sat down in it. She perused the bookshelf and found Andre Malraux's book *The Voices of Silence* and started to read it. I sat on the bed. She read as did I and, at times, I looked at her. I could not figure her out, but she intrigued me.

We read for hours. Finally, I asked her if she wanted to go out and have some dinner. I mentioned going next door where there was a small, very small, restaurant, but she demurred. I then suggested that we join the items in each of our tiny refrigerators. She said with a smile that I would be very disappointed about what I would find in hers. She was right. I made a scrambled egg with ham dish, as I recall, and made some tea. She told me she didn't know how to cook, never having had to do so, and we enjoyed our little meal together. Then I placed the dishes in my kitchen, and we both continued reading as if we had known each other for years. I never had felt such calm in the presence of a young woman. Usually I would be busy planning a strategy of some sort, but not this time. I did not know what had afflicted me. Finally she told me she had to go upstairs and asked me if she could borrow the book she was reading. I consented, glad to have a reason to see her again, to know her better.

After she had left I called a friend of mine, Lucretia Scott, whom I had gotten to know ushering at the Opera House, and told her that I had met the girl I was going to marry. She, a little wary of this sudden development but as kind as ever, invited me and Pat to her place for dinner with her and her boyfriend George. Instead of cooking she had bought some crabs, sourdough bread, wine and a salad, and we sat on the floor, in her living room, talking enthusiastically as we enjoyed this delicious feast. After the meal, Luke, as we called her, took me aside and told me that she thought I was right. She liked Pat. She liked her simplicity and her forthrightness.

I was on cloud nine!

I now knew that my initial reactions had been right ones and this was love. The problem I now had was to make sure that she shared my feelings, but I knew that it would be difficult for me to win her over. She had many male friends. Most of them were tennis partners, some were suitors. I did not play tennis or golf. Over the noise of the motor and the wind as we drove together in my convertible I told her of my background, that I was Jewish, from a poor family in *Amsterdam*, lacking a full education, and that I had been in concentration camps. I told her my parents and younger sister had been gassed, that I was also an immigrant, alone, who needed help from psychiatrists both within the Army and without. All these things would turn most girls off. But she understood, and what's more, she was not afraid. She was not afraid to get to know someone who was outside her milieu, way outside!

Then when I listened to her tell me about her life and her schooling at Middlebury College in Vermont, I realized that our lives were so different that it would be difficult, indeed, to win her over. Pat, as everyone called her, taking the first letters of each of her names, Priscilla Alden Thwaits, was the middle daughter of Edmond and Helen Thwaits. Pat was a descendant of both the Aldens and the Putnams who came over on the Mayflower in 1620. She had an older sister, Helen, and a younger sister Lucia. All of them grew up on the north shore of Long Island in *Plandome*, near *Manhasset*, where Pat had been a champion sailor and tennis player. Pat had been going steady for almost a decade with a fellow student from *Middlebury* who was an outstanding golfer. Pat realized she did not love the young man who had been squiring her for nine years and she decided to break from her family and return to her roots in the west where she was born. In doing so Pat gave up a blossoming career as an editor for *Newsweek* magazine.

She invited Lucia to join her and they moved to *Albuquerque*, New Mexico, found a place to live and jobs, in that order, and enjoyed a new life with many friends. They lived together for about a year, until Lucia met Peter Church, became engaged to him and Pat moved west once again in October 1955. Pat had no trouble finding an initial job in *San Francisco*, but she was biding her time until she would come across something she'd like better.

I became very serious about courting her and often I would visit her top floor apartment and look out at the view that, as I've said before, was almost painfully beautiful. We talked and read, read and talked for hours on end. I enjoyed her company and found her very interesting. Other times we just sat, and read for hours, hardly speaking to each other. A quietness had settled in over us. I invited her on excursions to art museums and art galleries, and to view Bay Area architecture. She divided her free time between me and her tennis playing friends, nearly all of whom were men. By now I was very smitten and one evening went up to see her. Pat was lying on the couch and, as usual, was reading. She took one look at me and asked if something was the matter with me because I looked awful.

"Yes," I told her, "there is."

"Well what is it, Max. Let's have it."

"Pat," I responded, "I love you and want to marry you. I want you to marry me."

"Are you crazy?" she asked.

"Pat," I replied, "I'm not leaving here until I have an answer."

"You mean I will not get a night's sleep until I give you an answer?"

"Yes," I said fearfully.

There was a long silence. Finally she said "You are dead serious, aren't you?"

"Yes," I replied.

"I'm not going to get any sleep, is that right?"

"You are not getting any sleep until I have your answer," I replied.

Another long silence.

"If I give you an answer you will let me sleep?" she asked.

"Yes," I replied.

After another extended silence she looked at me and said "Yes, I'll marry you."

I kissed her and left her place to let her get the sleep I had promised her. I danced down the stairs! My happiness, at that very moment, knew no bounds.

The next day I called her, not believing I had heard right. She kidded me and wondered if I wanted out already. That day I did not produce much at the office where I worked.

That evening we got together to set a date for our wedding, and she introduced me, by telephone, to the rest of her immediate family. They had had no inkling and were really astounded. Who was I? Where had I come from? How did we meet? Why are we in such a rush? What do I do? "The wedding should be at home in *Plandome*," said her mother. "No," answered Pat, "that's precisely what I do not want. Max and I will be married here in *San Francisco*, in Judge's Chambers." So spoke the future Mrs. Max R. Garcia, and so it would be. I now got a little idea of what my future wife could, would, be like when push came to shove.

All of what I have described took place in little less than three weeks. It was about the end of May, 1956. Our plans were to be married in August, 1956, which would give me ample time to pay back the money I owed which was about $200.00. We also had to buy our rings. She then confessed that she had about $800.00 in the bank. "If we are going to be married and will spend the rest of our lives together you can use my money," she said firmly. I paid back the money I owed and we bought specially made rings we both liked.

We spent many hours talking, and she questioned me, not comprehending at first, about my history. She was pleased to hear me tell of finding my way back to Judaism, but, later, when we had committed ourselves to getting married I broached the idea of her converting to Judaism; she refused the idea of conversion in order to marry. She knew little about Judaism, she reminded me, and she believed that sharing a common religion was insufficient reason for marriage. Recalling my broken engagement, I did not push that point.

I had continued my ushering job at the War Memorial Opera House and the local theatres on Geary Street, and now introduced Pat to this new adventure. She then met some of my opera and symphony friends and joined me in those duties.

We had planned to marry in August, 1956, but since Lucia and Peter still lived in *Albuquerque* and planned to visit the Thwaits family in *Plandome* in June, Pat and I decided to get married ahead of our scheduled plans so I could meet the rest of the family, and they could look me over as well. Pat and I got married on June 29th, 1956, in Judges' Chambers, as she desired.

During the time I was getting to know Pat, I had never physically imposed on her nor had I even kissed her until she agreed to marry me, and that kiss was a fleeting one at that. The evening before our wedding I suggested to Pat that we should consummate our marriage this very night, since we would be on an airplane flying to New York City the next night, right after the ceremony, the celebratory luncheon and grand dinner with friends on our wedding day. She agreed and told me to stand by while she went upstairs and changed into her pajamas. Soon thereafter she returned in her PJ's wearing a coat over them, not taking any chances of running into someone on the stairs. To my delight, she wore an anticipatory, conspiratorial smile.

She was an eager learner, I soon found out, not having known anything at all about making love except for what she had read in novels. She enjoyed it very much as did I, having such an enthusiastic student. We had an encore the following morning. Soon thereafter our pajamas hung in the closet. She was twenty-nine years old, and I had turned thirty-two the day before.

We spent our first married night together on that flight from *San Francisco* to *New York City*, a nightmare red-eye trip. We had the last two seats in the airplane and after we left *San Francisco* I spent the first 20 minutes in the toilet due to my excessive drinking after our wedding. When I finally returned to my seat the stewardess gave me an ice-pack. Earlier she had removed the corsage I had given Pat and pinned it to the overhead luggage compartment. She then wanted to know when we had gotten married and when we told her that very morning she really took pity on us. I have lost track of the number of cities we stopped at to take on new passengers and let others off during the night, but I do know that from the moment we took off until we got to *New York City* 14 sleepless hours had gone by! Needless to say I was not in the best of spirits after the endless champagne toasts on our wedding day. When we walked down the stairs from the airplane, the heat and humidity hit me hard in the face.

A welcoming delegation was waiting for us at the airport. I was exhausted, dehydrated and hungry all at once from that very long flight, but everyone was happy and full of smiles. I met Helen and Ed, Pat's mom and dad, and Greg, Pat's boxer dog, who was so happy to see her that he jumped all over her, and me as well, and all I could think of were those dogs that had snapped at us and guarded us in the various concentration camps. After collecting our luggage, we drove to Helen and Ed's *New York* apartment where now I met young Helen, her husband Bob, and their two boys, Jeff and Steve. A few days later I would meet Lucia and Pete who were coming in from *Albuquerque.*

Ed had put champagne on ice for his middle daughter and her husband, and we were all seated on the rear balcony of the apartment when Ed came in with an open bottle and wanted to start drinking. I said, "No, I can't drink now I must eat first." In that family, at that time, that was blasphemy! And I hadn't yet recovered from my wedding day excesses. Helen, Pat's mom, immediately told Ed she could understand how her new son-in-law-felt, told Ed to wait, and brought the lunch she had prepared. After enjoying her delicious meal I was almost ready for a glass of champagne and many rounds of toasts, though wilting in *New York City's* late June heat and humidity. Ed, who had become accustomed to Pat's former boyfriend of nine years, always a dependable drinking companion, could not understand what Pat had brought home. It took him a number of years to accept me and consider me his equal.

Ed and Helen had given us their apartment while we were in town, and they moved back to their home in *Plandome.* There they held a great reception for us and for Lucia and Peter so we could meet all their friends and neighbors as well as several of Pat's *Middlebury* classmates. As I knew no one there I had to learn a lot of names and faces in the shortest possible time, but it was a real celebration, with an extravagance of food and champagne, and guests spilling from the house into the garden.

What I remember about our honeymoon, aside from the usual

things one remembers most, were the theater tickets we received as wedding gifts. We saw "My Fair Lady", which had hit Broadway in March, and we saw it from aisle seats way up front. This gift came from Amy Quinn, Pat's *Middlebury* College classmate and close friend. The other, from Helen and Ed, was the play about Anne Frank, "Het Achterhuis." I cried almost the entire performance because it hit home so very hard. Then there was the formal dinner at Mama Leone's, a favorite *New York* restaurant of Ed's and Helen's, where the cuisine was top-notch and they were well known. What an incredible feast they served us! The next day we enjoyed a farewell dinner with the family at their *Plandome* home. Pat and I, her two sisters and their husbands as well, and Helen and Ed had learned quite a bit about each other in those few days. Everything had gone very well and everyone had a very good time. As it turned out, that was the only time we all gathered in the family home before Ed retired and they moved to Colorado in 1962.

The next day we climbed aboard the 20th Century Express train to introduce Pat to Arthur and Jean Clark, my sponsors to the United States. We had reserved a bedroom—what luxury, compared to the first time I traveled to *Buffalo*, New York to meet them on September 30th, 1946, almost a decade earlier! Arriving at 2 A.M., we took a taxi to the hotel where I had reserved a room. During the summer months it was common for them to move to the other side of Lake Erie, in Canada, where they owned a large summer home. There were trees all about, and the lake's shore was not far away. When they met Pat the next morning they liked her immediately. At that point the thought might have crossed their minds that I held promise after all. Their three daughters, one of whom hadn't even been born when I arrived at the Clarks' residence in 1946, looked upon me as a total stranger as well they might because now they were teenagers, and I had known them as small children. We continued by train to *Milwaukee* where I introduced Pat to Floortje, my mother's sister, as well as to Joep and Anneke. We spent many hours reminiscing before they took us to the airport for our long flight home.

Although Pat wanted to keep our separate apartments on our return to *San Francisco*, Pat's to sleep in and mine to eat in, I was of the strong opinion that we should start our married life together in a new place. We found a comfortable apartment in the outer Sunset District of *San Francisco*. Neither she nor I had any inkling of what we were to face when the foggy season hit us, but we learned all too quickly in the next few months.

Pat had gone back to the *San Francisco* Heart Association on Sutter Street, and I had gone back to the office where I worked on Montgomery Street, and within 10 days of our marriage vows Pat was pregnant. Of course, for all newlyweds this was good news, but not so for Pat who thought it all was happening too fast, too fast. We would meet every lunch period in Union Square, sit down on the grass and have lunch. On one such day, when Pat was in full bloom and oh, so pretty, I told her that I thought the time was near for her to give notice and prepare herself for the coming event. She would not hear of it, and we had our first real spat. I insisted that where I came from it was the custom that the husband is responsible for his wife, and child, and that henceforth she'd be staying home. Her response was brief and to the point: "You're in the United States now!" I agreed but would not waver. Pat did give notice but was not very happy about it since she had wanted to continue working until she had to go to the Delivery Room at Stanford University Hospital in *San Francisco*.

David Alden Rodrigues Garcia was born on April 24th, 1957, after having been shaken up, inside the womb, when Pat was shopping at Safeway during one of the Bay Area's worst earthquakes. The family was duly notified of his birth and one could hear a nationwide sigh of relief when all of them realized that David had been born more than 10 months after our wedding. Fears that Pat and I had a shotgun wedding, faded away quickly. Pat and David came home and Pat looked radiant. I was very proud of our joint accomplishment. Grandma Helen, Pat's mother, was there to help out, I being no help at all, and Pat having to learn very fast. Pat had learned to cook a little, but her mother was a great help teaching her, and me, how to do things in the kitchen. Once again it became very obvious to me that Pat was a very quick learner in anything and everything she undertook. I was a very fortunate man indeed!

David needed a lot of attention from Pat and me. At times we had to pace each other. Sleeping was a difficult problem, especially as I had begun to study seriously, spending long evening hours hunched over my books, or in classes, preparing for my state boards in architecture. I had made up my mind that I was going to get my California license to be a practicing architect.

However, things were not going so well for Pat, who was "locked-up" in our apartment and although it was summer for everyone else, those of us who lived in the Sunset District had to concern ourselves with the condensation that covered the windows of our apartment when fog was in. It looked as if we were constantly being rained upon. After a while Pat could no longer take it, nor could I, and soon after we had spent our first Christmas and New Year in this soggy place, her cries of "get me out of here" became louder and more frequent. Soon thereafter we moved to Telegraph Hill. It was a considerable improvement, and Pat was much happier to be on her favorite hill again. We remained on Telegraph Hill for the next two years until our second child was due, and then we moved to Jackson Street, in Pacific Heights. Shortly after Tania Sippora Alden Rodrigues Garcia was born, on March 7th, 1960, I received notice that I had passed all my exams and I would soon receive my California Architectural License. As my practice developed and grew after that, our flat was looking more like a nursery than an architect's office. By the time our third child, Michelle Rozetta Helen Alden Rodrigues Garcia arrived on May 2, 1961, I knew it was time for me to rent office space downtown, on Mission Street at Second.

But these were difficult times for Pat and me. While I was pleased with the quality of the projects I completed, we were never sure whether new ones would come up as quickly as we needed them. We took turns being anxious about my practice, But we liked what we were doing and felt good about life. At the same time there were still many nights when Pat cuddled up to me or cradled me in her arms when my severe grinding of teeth awakened her, or I was having nightmares from my camp experiences. She'd awaken me, caress me, stroke me, calm me down and tell me in her soft voice, not wanting to waken the children, "you're OK now! It's all behind you! You're safe now! You're free now!" and she'd continue doing this until I calmed down and fell asleep again.

I realize now that she was my Pygmalion and I her Galatea. She had improved my English and softened the typical American Army language I had learned after my liberation. She made sure I would be able to socialize with people by changing my speech and my manners.

What I am now is all due to her. She was my social instructor, a nurse when needed, a caretaker when warranted, a lover when inspired, a mother who adored her children, and a secretary who typed my letters and my specifications and remained a part of my business throughout my life although I did not want her to come to my office to work. And she would not permit me to put her on my payroll. One of her greatest thrills, business wise, was the day I had to hire two young women to do the work Pat had been doing at home for me.

Whenever I went to services during the High Holidays Pat accompanied me and began to familiarize herself with Judaism through reading, observing, and asking questions. She had also met my Jewish friends. After Tania and Michelle had arrived Pat decided to study with a rabbi at Temple Emanu-El, a reform congregation in *San Francisco* we had joined, and then she converted to Judaism all on her own volition. In fact, I had not known about her study sessions at all until I was called at my office by the rabbi on the day of her conversion, asking me if I was going to be there. As I said earlier, even if by heritage she could not be Jewish, or, by nature reject her own heritage, she hoped that by this act she could make sure that our children, her children, the children of our family would want to live as Jews and stand in the places of those Jews lost to Nazism's "final solution." From the time David was born, Pat wanted him to be raised a Jew. David celebrated his Bar Mitzvah at the age of 13, as is the custom. One by one, all three children were confirmed at Temple Emanu-El.

In 1975, Pat had the idea that she wanted to write down for our children what had happened to me during WWII and why our children never knew my parents or their aunt Sienie. This idea had been growing in her mind, as she told me, and she now realized that it was no longer going to be an essay but would become a book instead. As described in the final pages of Part 6, I told her if she really wanted to take on such a huge project she'd best go to Poland with me to see *KZ Auschwitz* for herself. That summer we flew to *Amsterdam*, had a car waiting for us, and as soon as we had retrieved our luggage we drove from *Amsterdam* to *West Berlin*. Though it was late we managed to find barely acceptable lodgings with the help of the *West Berlin* Tourist Office, and crashed after a long day's drive. We had to go to *West Berlin* because it had the only point of entry – Check Point Charlie – into *East Berlin*. From there we could drive through East Germany into Poland.

The next afternoon we shopped for sandwiches and drinks at KDW, the major *Berlin* department store. An entire floor was completely devoted to food and we had such a good time looking at the array of delicacies that we stayed for a fine dinner right there in one of their eateries. We left *Berlin* very early on Monday morning and arrived in *Krakow*, Poland, at about 1:00 A.M. Tuesday. All those 4-lane Autobahn became 2-lane roads and when in the countryside, most of the time, we nearly always got stuck behind a horse drawn farm cart or wagon. It was a long, hard day.

Throughout all of this Pat kept wondering if this trip was really necessary but after we arrived in *KZ Auschwitz* the next morning, during a mix of rain and heavy drizzle and I led her through the camp, she began to see the value of it all. As noted earlier in Part 6, *KZ Auschwitz* had been made into a museum and also into a political educational institution with lots of students and military personnel. Visitors like us as well as Poles and other Eastern Block nationals were led about and shown how we lived within those brick Blocks.

Some of the Blocks had been turned into memorials to their murdered compatriots by citizens of various European countries. Some, though not many in 1975, were imaginative exhibits; others were crude. Since *KZ Auschwitz* was in Poland, the Polish memorials outnumbered those from other countries, but their tiny pictures and miniscule texts could not begin to tell the stories of each of those individuals, or what kinds of lives they had lived until the day of their capture and incarceration. What was most interesting to me, however,and I mentioned it to Pat, was that they included not a single Jewish prisoner. By the time *KZ Auschwitz* was evacuated in January 1945, thousands upon thousands of us had suffered and died there.

The steady drizzle put a damper on all we were allowed to see and our plans were to get to *Vienna* late in the afternoon. So after about three hours in *KZ Auschwitz*, described in detail at the end of Part 6, we left. For a number of hours we drove silently together, totally absorbed in the things we had seen and could not bring ourselves to talk about it. At last, after several hours of silence, Pat spoke and began to ask all sorts of questions. What was life like in the camp? What was the daily routine? We stopped in a small Czechoslovakian town to get something to eat and drink but we found the things available to us meager and tasteless. We couldn't wait to get to Austria. By now I was in a more conversational mood and Pat continued to bombard me with questions that she had started some time ago. My responses made their way into the first edition of this book.

We were delighted when the Austrian border appeared at last, but two hurdles remained: the Czechoslovakian border guards carefully went through our rented car, and we had to declare how much of their money we were carrying. As we still had some Polish money as well as Czech we were compelled to spend it at their dingy little store. We bought some Polish Vodka and some North African slippers and left the rest of the money on the counter. At last we were free to leave Czechoslovakia and enter Austria. The comparison between Communist Czechoslovakia and Democratic Austria was dramatic. From "Darkness at noon" to the brightness of Austria even in the early evening hours was a most welcome change.

Although this trip had little of the pleasure of our family trip in 1971, Pat agreed that this one had given her real insight as to what my life had been as a prisoner in *KZ Auschwitz*. Seeing it again after thirty years also helped to sharpen my memory of my time there. When we returned to *San Francisco* and I began in earnest to recall for her my life in this and other camps she was able to envision and write about *Auschwitz* as well as *Ebensee* from the feeling of being there. This book began with *Ebensee* and *Auschwitz* and my experiences in the camps. After seeing the actual place well before most Americans traveled there, her words joined with mine as she relived my story.

In our 46 years together, Pat and I had raised three fine children, enjoyed a rich life of art and music, a shared Jewish Holocaust experience, and the shared writing of this book. We had worked together developing my architectural practice which had grown into a business that by the time I retired had 25 employees, including myself. Thanks to her intelligent ways of handling money we had a considerable nest egg with which to retire and our own house that was almost paid for. We were able to enjoy our retirement years in financial comfort. How very cruel that as our children grew up and I turned my business over to my young partner David Wagner, and as we got to know my liberators and to travel many times to Europe together, she succumbed to that relentless cancer. She died on our wedding day, June 29, 2002. I shall always miss her.

Essays about Max

written by
Max's and Pat's children
and grandchildren,
listed in order of
birthdate.

David

After we visited Europe for the first time as a family in 1971 the book idea began to take off, and it was an intense time around the house. The Vietnam War had been going on for years, Watergate was about to happen along with Nixon's resignation; the ongoing civil rights and women's movements as well as the Beatles were all center stage. But at our house it was World War II and concentration camps every night, like reruns for dinner, over and over and over again.

These were my teenage years and my first taste of marijuana; for the first time in my life I felt some relaxation. It was the escape I was looking for but I still could not understand how I could have the only set of right wing parents in all of *San Francisco*. I needed to get away from the house, the war and my parents, for Dad's "Holocaustness" had become stifling. For me and possibly my sisters it was used to place him and his achievements above everyone else's. Knowing that no matter what I did, it would pale in the face of what my Dad had been through, that was and is hard to get over.

With my years in college came some confidence and strength and I could allow myself to visit aspects of the Holocaust and my father's past. Visiting what family remained in *Amsterdam* and numerous trips with Dad to his liberation ceremonies in Austria over the years helped me to put together pieces of the puzzle and to understand the magnitude of the event, not just my father's story. Just recently he told me that his father was not really on good terms with his own Dad before the war ever broke out. At one time in my twenties, like my two nephews who actually did this recently, I considered having Dad's *Auschwitz* number tattooed on my arm as a proud way to keep his and his family's memory alive. But I chose not to, and I now know it was because it had always been so hard to find my own identity in a family where Dad was bigger than life itself, where he wanted and needed all of the identity and Mom was willing to give it to him at the expense of herself.

As my mother took her last breaths my sister Tania, Mom's sister Helen and I held her. Dad was reading the newspaper with his back to all of us. It was another stark reminder that Dad had not, as he so often told us, "learned everything I needed to know at the University of *Auschwitz*." There he had learned how to turn his back on death, to keep it away and not let it get close to him. It was a very understandable and a necessary reaction to the horrific realities of life in the camps. But after almost 60 years Dad has not been able to accept death in some natural way. He has never learned how to deal with his emotional side on a level that would help himself or his family. Since Mom's passing I have realized that participating in your parent's death is their last lesson to you in life, one that my father missed through no fault of his own. But he never thought or realized that he needed to grow, that for his children and family, life was not the Holocaust or ever would be.

Now at the age of 51, six years after Mom's death, I am beginning to accept grief as a part of the deal. To be there with Mom at the end was the most moving moment of my life and as friends and pets die it helps me to understand that most death is not at the hands of murderous people and that the dreams I had at the age of 5, of my grandparents being cremated in giant brick ovens, of dead bodies stacked like cordwood was something that I never should have been exposed to at such a young age. Our parents should have been protecting us from this knowledge, these images, until we were older and stronger. But through the course of my therapy and having met so many other survivors I see this need to be heard and for the story to not die – and how the hell would I have handled it? There it is that question again but now it pertains to the next generation, my sisters and me. Maybe that is part of why I never wanted to have children.

The bottom line is that although Dad was a very tiny pawn in one of the 20th century's many horrific moments he suffered hugely. His is a story of intuition, smarts, a strong will to live, and lots of luck. Mom's book will be there to record Dad's incredible story and to place it within the context of history, a history that includes my father's family in the Spanish Inquisition in the 15th Century when they were forced to leave or die for their religion, a history that we as a family know nothing about. And that is history, it just gets older.

In this moment of time, September 2008, I would prefer to talk about why we – the United States of America, the shining star that delivered the world from evil more than 60 years ago, the country that my father believes is the paragon of good and whose military is there to free the world – why is it that we have a Guantanamo Bay and secret torture prisons in other countries? Why do we go to war with a country that has not attacked us or anyone American? How is it that in my travels last year I found we have become the most feared country in the world?

Darfur, Zimbabwe, Iraq, Palestine – how can we "never forget" if we're not paying attention?

David Garcia

If I Had a Voice. . .

I remember being about 5 years old and worrying about Nazis; my young years were filled with nightmares of hunting Nazis and Hitler, doing awful things to them; of screaming and clutching their knees while my parents readied themselves to go out for an evening, sure that Nazis would hunt them down and finish the business they had started. I remember waking to hear my father screaming from the nightmares that relentlessly had him reliving his camp experiences over and over again while I lay frozen in my bed crafting hideous visions in my minds eye and hearing him swallow sleeping pills so he could forget for a little while and just sleep. I kept praying his family was magically still alive and we would run in to them on our first trip to Europe in 1971. I remember crying, lots of crying.

By the time I was a teenager, I was sick of hearing about the Holocaust as a nightly topic of discussion at the dinner table. My parents were engaged in writing this book and opening up the *San Francisco* Holocaust Library and so the dialogues were frequent and terrifyingly vivid. I would beg them to please let us get through a meal without discussing the now dreaded subject as it just ate away at me as I tried to eat. I loved being invited and often negotiated invitations to other people's houses for dinner – my escape.

With age, I was able to see how this monumental event in history had transformed a potentially normal childhood into a childhood wary and fearful of what people were capable of, wary of trust. These seeds planted deep inside of me will no doubt haunt me forever; I had too close a view into the dark side.

I can't remember a time in my life when I was not conscious of the horrors of the Holocaust and its dark cast upon our family. My parents strongly believed that it was in their kids' best interest to know, from an early age, the history of our father's life and all the wreckage that lay within. I have had strong differences with my parents about letting us in on this nightmare way too young, yet I also know they did what they thought would be best for us so that we would always have one eye open to the world. The problem was I learned to keep two eyes wide open and my innocent childhood wasn't so innocent in the end. I once told my father that despite his horrific experiences, experiences I could never begin to comprehend, he still enjoyed a childhood free of Nazis and the Holocaust for about 15 years in *Amsterdam*, while his own children had never had a childhood free of the Holocaust. We had been tormented, one generation removed.

The benefits of this immediate family history have been great as well. I am not naïve or ignorant and have never been a follower. I am strong, have a powerful voice and am not easily intimidated. I value these things as I go about my relatively happy life knowing they were born from much suffering of those who came before me and paid a staggering price. I take so much away from my dad's life and his story. I deeply understand what prejudice is about and how cruel and insidious it is. I get the palpable anger that many people of color feel. I have had the nasty Jewish insults hurled at me and of course I grew up missing half a family because of their beliefs and the accidents of their births.

Life is full of contradictions. While I longed for a normal childhood and wasn't thrilled with the way my parents dealt with the overwhelming presence of the Holocaust in our lives, I was always enormously proud and deeply moved by all that my dad had been through; that he made it and had done so well with his life. As a mother of three beautiful boys of my own, I think about my dad's parents often and have always wished that they knew, somehow, that he lived.

But, with the benefit of hindsight, if people were to ask me if it would be good or helpful to share such horrors with young children, I would ask them, how well do you know your children? How do you think they might take your story and work it into a young brain that has no context for such horror? How might it impact them for the duration of their lives? What is your reason for wanting to share such grave information with people so young? If I had a voice in how I was raised, I would have asked them to have waited until I was old enough to be able to put all the gory details into some manageable context. Years ago the singer, Jewel, wrote a song that still resonates loudly with me. Part of it goes like this:

"...Why's it gotta be so complicated?
Why you gotta tell me if I'm hated?
So please be careful with me, I'm sensitive
And I'd like to stay that way..."

Tania Garcia Fowler

Michelle

A person recently asked me if I "was a Holocaust survivor's daughter every day of my life." Without having to think deeply about this, I responded with something like, "Yep, every day I live is defined in part by the Holocaust." As a survivor's daughter, I have always seen the world through the filter of my father's Holocaust experience. Talk to me about the benefits of religious or political groups and I will quickly respond that it is dangerous to believe in "mass thinking." Pass by free pre-packaged granola bars at a conference and I will be the one to grab three or four of them to squirrel away in my bag to make sure I am never at risk for being hungry. See a penny on a street and I will be the one to bend over and pick it up, knowing that you have to start somewhere to make sure you have enough later in case someone tries to take it all away from you. I was the kid who cried on the city bus thinking I was going to get arrested when my mom tore off a tag from a pillow we had just bought that said on it "do not remove under penalty of the law." Through my child's eyes, I thought people were easily arrested and thrown into the camps or the American equivalent, jail. As a child I remember thinking that Nazis were hiding around every corner as well as in the closets in my house. Well into my adulthood I believed that no matter how hard I worked to build a career, some crazy power monger would come in and take it away from me, forcing me to be a servant to someone else. From all my experiences growing up with the insanity of trying to understand the Holocaust, what I got from it was that bad things happen, not to other people but to my family. I was a nervous kid with a big mouth.

You don't "grow out" of being a Holocaust survivor's daughter, you grow into it. When I was young I saw my dad as happy, optimistic, fun to be with, energetic, and successful. A virtual holocaust super hero! And yet I knew his heroism came from a dark place. The Vietnam war was in full swing; I equated it to the Holocaust and panicked, fearing my brother would be drafted. I hated watching the TV show "Laugh In" when they did skits on the war since I was so worried my brother would be killed (he wasn't even drafted!) It was all really confusing and scary. The world outside of our house was not as safe as inside the house.

In adolescence, I saw my dad as demanding, insistent he was always right, causing me to become frustrated, deeply at times, by his behavior. He would not let us girls sleep in, we had to "get up and be productive!" I wanted to have him acknowledge I could be right about things, but he would not allow for that. He could not acquiesce to my teenaged needs and desires: I lusted for salami, bologna and Monterey Jack cheese but the refrigerator was always crowded with Bloodwurst, Gouda and Pig's Knuckles. Only later did I realize he was still being raised himself by my mom to bring him out of the Holocaust. Mom had more kids to deal with than she had bargained for!

I felt my dad would barely acknowledge me if I didn't accomplish something exceptional. We had great pressure on us to succeed. He told us we had to do well to make up for the loss of his sister and parents in the Holocaust. There were times when that message was just too heavy. However, as much as my dad could drive teenaged and young-adult me crazy, I didn't think I could rebel because he had already "been through too much." My mom reinforced that message. I watched what made him upset and avoided those things to prevent him from becoming really angry. I protected him; my sister and I discussed our need to protect him. None of that was helpful in my adult years; it took me a long time to learn to develop my own emotional vocabulary and to stand up for myself even if it wasn't what people wanted to hear.

At the same time, as a teen I was incredibly proud of my dad. Not only did he survive, but he had a good sense of humor and on most of his days he was charming, funny, clever, even if he was (still is) incredibly opinionated and stubborn. When I had him come speak about the Holocaust to my classes in high school I would sit in the audience and cry. At home we would joke about his experiences. That is something I have always appreciated; even the worst things were things we could joke about, which helped to relieve some of the stress: "Hey dad, you didn't have it so bad; you got to go to camp for two years!"

In my late twenties and thirties, I got angry with his absoluteness. I got tired of trying to "do it all" to make up for those who died. I struck back. I was angry. I focused on his mistakes.

Now in my late forties, I am better able to see him as a real person who has lived through an experience that has never ended. He is out of the camps but not truly "free." Now I see my dad as much more vulnerable and human, and often times needing assurance that we are there for him. He rarely calls us; he wants us to call him. He wants us to reach out and keep proving to him we love him and will not leave him. He doesn't tell us this with words but it is there for us to see. Throughout our lives, he has let us know that we are the only ones he can truly depend on. Without us he would be an adult orphan. He has emotional pains he will never find words to describe. Activity keeps him away from introspection.

In some aspects it is hard to see my dad in less than the Super-Holocaust-Survivor-Super-Hero image I had painted of him in my youth, but at the same time it is good to see now he is just a man with a very moving story. Just as my hairdresser is a woman from Vietnam with an equally compelling story.

Humans are remarkable in their persistence to try making their lives better, in spite of their painful memories and stories. Even though societies at times allow outrageous groups to do outrageous things, people as individuals are fundamentally good and can make positive contributions, one person at a time. The lessons I have learned from my father that sustain me are not about how he survived during the holocaust; they are about how he survived all these years since. Clearly humor and resilience are keys.

Michelle Garcia Winner

Max with all of his grandchildren. L to R: Nick Lush, Heidi Garcia Winner, Max R. Garcia, Caleb Lush, Robyn Garcia Winner and Max Lush. Photo taken November 27, 2008.

Nick

In many ways, growing up as the grandchild of a Holocaust survivor has been a much more rewarding experience than it had been for the children of those survivors. The sheer magnitude and horror of that event is so terrifying that I think it needs to be diluted some in order for the true morals and messages of it to shine through. For the second generation, the memory of the event seems to have been too ubiquitous, too all consuming and too sharp a contrast to the relative ease of their daily lives in America. For my part, at least, hearing and reading my grandfather's story has provided me with a necessary contrast to my own life.

I have grown up reaping all of the benefits of a middle class upbringing in the U.S. and my knowledge of what has happened in my family's past has done much to keep me more grounded, more attuned to the suffering of others than many of my peers. It has instilled in me a deep sense of charity and responsibility, one that has defined the way that I approach my club affiliations and jobs. I feel lucky because I have been allowed to come to terms with the story in my own way, unencumbered by the weight of seeing my parent deal with still open wounds. Instead, I have been able to appreciate the full weight of the story, and having the book on my shelf has allowed me to share that experience with friends and colleagues in ways that extend far beyond a simple story told in passing. In some ways they make that story their own because they are moved not only by the story itself but also by its physical manifestation in their friend and co-worker, the next chapter in what has come from the depths of human tragedy to an uplifting (if not ironic) triumph of the will.

Nick Lush

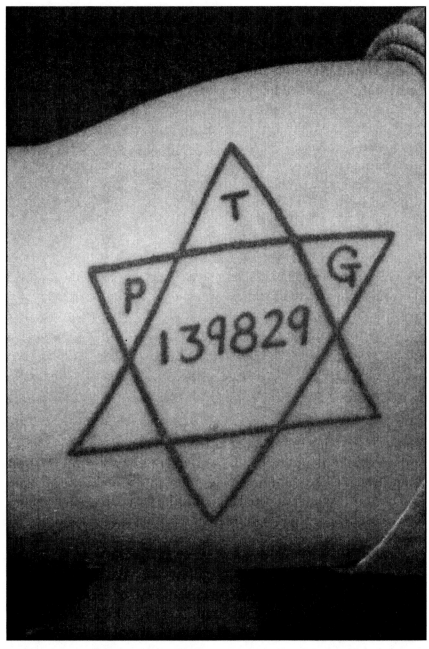

"Hearing and reading my grandfather's story has provided me with a necessary contrast to my own life." – Nick Lush

Heidi

The Holocaust to me, the grandchild of a Holocaust survivor, has always seemed like a horror story out of the movies. When I was younger I would try to understand it, to make it personal, but the only physical indicators of it lay in the number on my grandpa's arm and the absence of his family. It was very present though, in other means; through history lessons, television specials and the stories of my grandpa. When I was in second grade my grandpa came to give a lecture to the fifth grade class at my elementary school about his Holocaust experience. Though I tried to make the words meaningful, what excited me the most was seeing the 5th graders listen to my grandpa.

Then there would be those moments of clarity. I remember awaking from a nightmare in which I was hiding on a rooftop behind a post from uniformed men with guns, only to realize that once that had been my grandpa's reality. And there were the times when reading my grandparents' book about his life that I just couldn't stop crying. But feeling the Holocaust is elusive - it's so detached from daily life that you first have to convince your emotions that it actually happened.

Art became a way for me to connect to the Holocaust, and to my family's past. I dug through books trying to understand the politics of the Holocaust, and the emotions. Descriptions of concentration camps became like running movies in my head, and like someone who had mistakenly wandered onto the film set I tried to understand the atmosphere. I came to know well meaning people transformed into beasts under the symbol of the swastika. I saw Hitler and his political officials and I attempted to comprehend their motivation. I shared bunks with the prisoners and I worked along side them. I witnessed the rows of people before the gas chambers, waiting for a miracle while waiting for death. I felt my skin growing tight around my bones. I was captivated by their stories, person by person, page by page, story by story. In my painting, "Arbeit Macht Frei," I attempt to construe the sequence and sentiment of the Holocaust into something that will catch someone's eye, to make him pause and provoke a thought, perhaps even to cause emotion.

In "Arbeit Macht Frei" the little boy has been branded. He, who will soon be having power over so many others, has no power over himself. He has been brainwashed; a Hitler machine. The skeleton arm bears my Grandpa's number from Auschwitz, 139829. The barbed wire represents Hitler's control, and though it is bound it is not secured around the arm. The row in the back symbolizes the succession of the victims of the Holocaust. Above their heads lay the ironic "Arbeit Macht Frei", which in English translates to "Work Makes You Free." During liberation the survivors stood for all of the Holocaust victims as they walked past the barbed wire and out of the camps, breaking the Nazi regime.

Through my art I have been able to connect with the past of my family, if only through seeing the experiences as they went through in my head. Though I'll never be able to understand what the Holocaust was like first hand, I can imagine enough to realize that it should never happen again. The best we can do now is to learn, and to teach. Though each next generation is one removed, the stories are no less powerful. Let yourself feel it. Find that place where all the accounts of the Holocaust come together and wash over you for a moment; that is the closest you will get to it - and thank God it's so. When we feel, what we learn becomes personal; and the better we can teach it. And we must teach it – to avoid a reoccurrence – we must teach it.

Heidi Garcia Winner

"Art became a way for me to connect to the Holocaust, and to my family's past." – Heidi Garcia Winner

Caleb

Every day, someone asks me about the significance of the tattoo on my right bicep. On most of these occasions, the question is immediately followed by a sarcastic prediction. For example, I constantly hear, "What is that on you arm? Is that your license plate?" Or, "Why do you have your zip code tattooed on your arm?" Even though these presumptions are not malicious by any means, my response always inspires a complete change in approach. Since the subject is so overpoweringly serious, this is to be expected. Unfortunately, it is an unintended side effect of the message I try to convey with my tattoo. In fact I decided to get my tattoo for two reasons: to constantly remind myself that I can overcome anything that lies in my path; and, to show respect for my grandfather, his character, and his unbelievable story.

Life is a complex process for anyone. It consists of glorious moments of triumph, dark times filled with seemingly insurmountable misery, and everything inbetween. With a permanent mark on my right arm, my stronger arm, I am forever branded by something horrific, yet inspiring, in my family's past. Therefore, when I succeed I can look at my arm with gratitude for my grandfather's struggle; when my outlook is grim, my tattoo discourages the desire to resort to self-pity, and motivates optimism. Tattoos have a reputation of dereliction and destruction, but my tattoo has enriched my life in addition to my perspective.

I realize that Judaism is not fond of tattoos; however, I am not a practicing Jew. My grandfather's story is not about Judaism's survival of oppression, it is a miraculous journey of an individual man against all odds, with the help of other prisoners, the Allied Forces, luck, and most importantly, himself. And I thank him with every second my body exists, because without his heroic efforts to survive certain death, I would never have taken a breath.

Thanks Grandpa.

Caleb Lush

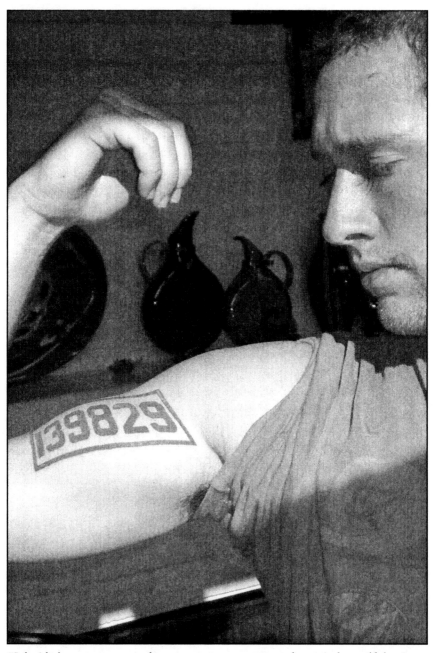

"I decided to get my tattoo for two reasons: to constantly remind myself that I can overcome anything that lies in my path; and, to show respect for my grandfather, his character, and his unbelievable story." – Caleb Lush

Robyn

As far as I can remember, I have always known the story of my grandfather's survival of the Holocaust. However, throughout my life, the significance of his ordeal has changed in meaning as I have matured. When I was a child, I was not able to fully grasp the reality of the horrific events that befell him; it was merely a really 'cool story' I could tell my friends. And when I began to learn about World War II in school, I felt more mentally connected to what we were learning because it was literally a part of my family's history, but emotionally I was not affected. It seemed that even the teachers did not completely understand the weight of the curriculum they were teaching. I was being taught the information as facts; like times, dates, amounts of people killed, places, etc., without any emotional connection. There was no real importance to the information except to know it to pass a test.

However, my emotional disconnection to my grandfather's story changed at the age of nine when my grandparents took my entire family and me on a trip to Europe. While in Europe my grandpa took us on a tour of his life both before and during the Holocaust. We got to see where he was raised, and all of the beautiful cities that surrounded the area. Then, we were taken to *Mauthausen* and *Ebensee*, two of the four concentration camps that my grandfather survived. In these camps we saw the sleeping barracks and the small stacked beds, where the prisoners struggled to survive. Then we walked through the gas chambers where millions were murdered, including almost all of my grandfather's family and relatives. Lastly we saw the furnaces where all who died were burnt out of existence. Being at the camps firsthand, it finally hit me; what my grandfather went through was so much more that just facts on a paper or a 'cool story' to tell my friends, it was a reality. Words cannot express the hell he survived; however, finally I emotionally understood. While in the camps, at that time about half a century later, I stood alive where countless innocent people had died.

Now as an adult, I too am faced with challenges of my own,

ranging from school to friends to family. Usually when I am faced with these challenges I can take them head on, and overcome them. However, as in any young adult's life, there are always those times when it seems there is no escape from whatever challenge is getting you down. Times like this I feel so helpless; but then I remember my trip to Europe, and recall the emotions I felt when I realized the truth behind what my grandfather went through, and I realize what I am facing does not even compare to his ordeal. If he could survive for two years in four concentration camps, knowing that every day he lived thousands more died, then I could overcome my challenge. His blood runs through my veins, and because of this I know if I put my mind to it, I can do anything.

Robyn Garcia Winner

My Grandpa Once Told Me

My Grandpa once told me "Forgive, but don't forget." Those simple words have stuck with me for some time now. I am amazed that someone who has had so much wrong done to him in such a horrific event as the Holocaust could even think of forgiving the ones who did it to him. That saying told me that there truly is good in every human, and we need to hold every human accountable for their actions.

My Grandpa's story has given me such a great sense of pride in my everyday life. It helps me stay grounded. While I do live a much better life than most people, his story has taught me to stay within myself and that I will achieve nothing unless I fight for it. In the concentration camps my Grandpa could have easily given up, but he kept fighting and showing the Nazi guards that he was still alive inside, and that is the main reason why he was able to survive. Growing up knowing about what happened gave me the sense of self awareness and need for friendship at a young age. My Grandpa's story shows, in his friendship with Lex, that good friends are one of the most important things to have, and that if you build strong relationships it will lead to a much better life.

It is an honor to be part of such an extraordinary story as my Grandpa's. Not everyone hears all the shocking survivor stories that need to be told and the time for these stories to be told is running out.

This book is important because it documents a truly amazing story about an event that most people shy away from talking about. In my senior year of high school my Grandpa came and talked to all of the senior history classes, about 100 students, and I have never seen a room so full of teenagers so quiet and attentive as they were listening to my Grandpa's talk. It was surprising how many classmates came up to me and said how amazed they were by his experiences and seemed extremely touched by his time with them.

To me the knowledge I have gained from reading and hearing

this story helps me understand better the kind of person I want to be and to apply my Grandpa's lessons to my everyday life.

Max Lush

Max Rodrigues Garcia was born in Amsterdam, Holland. He now resides in San Francisco, California.